THE LITTLE BOOK
OF REVELATION

THE LITTLE BOOK
OF REVELATION

The First Coming of Jesus
at the End of Days

To Robert —
Believe!

5-19-2014

Tasos

Eli of Kittim

Library of Congress Control Number: 2012921048
ISBN: Hardcover   978-1-4797-4707-8
                   Softcover   978-1-4797-4706-1
                   Ebook   978-1-4797-4708-5

This book was printed in the United States of America.

To order additional copies of this book, contact:
www.TheLittleBookofRevelation.com
Xlibris Corporation
1-888-795-4274
www.Xlibris.com
Orders@Xlibris.com
124566

To the Achaean teacher
who bestowed on me the Ionian blessing
and encouraged me to set my passion to words
this little book is cordially dedicated.

"for those who search"

FOREWORD

Anonymous

A study of biblical eschatology, prophecy and hermeneutics always runs the risk of being called an eisegesis, a reading into the text of one's own personal agenda. A valid approach out of the complexities of this dilemma entails that the scriptural interpreter establishes criteria, which appropriate meaning directly from the text per se with the unvarying precision and specificity that the context intended.

Eli of Kittim has accomplished that, and what at first glance appears to be a radical and unique exegesis, on his part, turns out to be a demonstration of the very words of scripture. Few scriptural interpreters have painted such an apocalyptic and controversial portrait of Jesus as has Eli of Kittim. He suggests that a postbiblical cover-up has forced upon us an alternative history of the man and his teachings. His perspective on Christ is unprecedented, completely disrupting the fabric of traditional religious ideology.

The author's treatment of the biblical sources is a first-of-its-kind endeavor; it is without question an innovative and pioneering work. The conclusions are as startling as they are thought provoking. His numerous epoch-making discoveries will most certainly change the course of history. In the final analysis, the author radically redefines and accentuates the essential nature of Christian thought.

CONTENTS

TO BIBLARIDION: THE LITTLE BOOK

And I saw another strong angel coming down out of heaven, clothed with a cloud; and the rainbow was upon his head, and his face was like the sun, and his feet like pillars of fire; and he had in his hand a little book which was open. . . . And the voice which I heard from heaven, I heard again speaking with me, and saying, "Go, take the book which is open in the hand of the angel." . . . And I went to the angel, telling him to give me the little book. And he said to me, "Take it, and eat it; and it will make your stomach bitter, but in your mouth it will be sweet as honey"

(Rev. 10:1-9).

My heart overflows with a good theme; I address my verses to the King; my tongue is the pen of a ready writer

(Ps. 45:1).

Among them was a certain man clothed in linen with a writing case at his loins

(Ezek. 9:2).

Then behold, the man clothed in linen at whose loins was the writing case reported, saying, "I have done just as Thou hast commanded me"

(Ezek. 9:11).

Oh that my words were written! Oh that they were inscribed in a book!

(Job 19:23).

And beginning with Moses and with all the prophets, He explained to them the things concerning Himself in all the Scriptures

(Luke 24:27).

PREFACE

The central argument of this study attempts to substantiate two main points: that Christ's visitation has not yet occurred in the world of time since it is a future event, and that his origin will be derived from the Greeks, not the Jews, when he does appear. We solve this paradox by employing a simple decoding process that essentially allows scripture to interpret itself. The evidence pointing to these conclusions is predicated on sound biblical scholarship and research. These two premises reflect the results drawn from an extensive comparative analysis of the scriptural material. Where nonbiblical sources are concerned, such as the prophecies of the famed seer Nostradamus or the Dead Sea Scrolls, these will be employed for the purpose of conveying a consensus of the uniformity of thought among all of the discussed figures and spiritual traditions.

Many years ago, the author received an *inspired* revelation. Given that it contradicted the conventional Jesus account, he refused to believe it. After some time, however, he set out to find whether it would be possible to reconcile it with the Bible. This study is the outcome of that inquiry. Therefore, the author empathizes with the reader's plight since he found himself in the same predicament not too long ago. So let this work teach you as it taught him; for "the time is short" (1 Cor. 7:29, *New King James*). His message is more needed today than ever before in history.

Yet history is not without its consequences. For it has given rise to the greatest postbiblical conspiracy of all time. The original account of Christ has been thoroughly altered, and in its place, a false gospel has been devised. Although the text may have been deliberately disguised by the deity for reasons to be discussed later, and despite the obvious literary confusion that surrounds it, religious authorities have taken full advantage of this situation to serve their own ends. Our main focus will be on exploring the scriptural legitimacy of their claims, not on any particular religious institution per se.

Scripture firmly states that "a different gospel" will be preached in an effort to pervert and "distort the [exclusivist] gospel of Christ" (Gal. 1:6-7). This will be an adulterated version of scripture, saturated with half-truths and *"TEACHING AS DOCTRINES THE PRECEPTS OF MEN"* (Mark 7:7). It is not so much that another gospel is preached, but that a different interpretation is produced and reworked to make Christ's story more palatable to the masses (Gal. 1:7). Scripture says, "For this reason God will send upon them a deluding influence so that they might believe what is false" (2 Thess. 2:11). In fact, we have been the recipients of this false gospel down through the ages:

> But even though we, or an angel from heaven, should preach to you a gospel contrary to that which we have preached to you, let him be accursed. . . . For I would have you know, brethren, that the gospel which was preached by me is not according to man. For I neither received it from man, nor was I taught it, but I received it through a revelation of Jesus Christ

(Gal. 1:8-12).

We have all heard the story of the suffering Messiah who took his last gasp of air on that fateful afternoon of 33 AD. Shortly thereafter the earth quivered and the ground shook. And just as mysteriously as the son of God had appeared, he quickly evanesced without a trace while his silence covered the earth for the next two thousand years. But what conclusion can we draw from these events? Some argue that his mission on earth was a total failure. Actually, nothing so clearly indicates Christ's unsuccessful earthly mission to restore God's kingdom as his much anticipated return to set things right. What about the presumption that he was rejected by the Jews? This scenario seems highly unlikely given that traditional Judaism has always fervently believed in a coming Messiah. What is more, we simply do not have any reliable historical records of these events. In light of these contradictions and ambiguities, how much of the epic narrative is based on fact? Was it perhaps a cruel hoax? Did this story end at the tomb of Jesus? Or is there a part of the story yet untold?

We must enter a world of uncharted territory and trace the mystery back to the sacred text itself. This book is based on a fascinating detective story in search of the real Jesus. Our analysis involves a *biblical exegesis*, the hermeneutical process of drawing out the meaning from the text itself. The conclusions cannot be regarded as speculative imputations of scripture because they are grounded on a discursive inquiry. In fact, this work is the product of twenty years of research.

It is the author's hope that readers should endeavor to search and verify for themselves prior to passing premature judgment upon these views. Not only is this our message, it is also the biblical message as it encourages us to examine "the Scriptures" in order to ascertain whether current teachings, such as ours, are consistent with them (Acts 17:11). We have already done all the work for you by organizing and combining the appropriate scriptural passages that provide the necessary evidence for the particular topics under discussion. To verify the results, all you need to do is to consult our *documentation* (the supporting references). The reader will be satisfied with the conclusions of this study only after the entire volume is consumed. In fact, we are more than convinced that if one were to apply the central two-part premise of this book, everything in the Bible would start to make sense!

The postmodern world no longer cares for the Bible and considers it as irrelevant to the issues of the times. It has been thoroughly supplanted by a mysterious discipline whose subject matter is equally inaccessible to direct observation: the human mind. We are, of course, referring to modern psychology. What we have to realize, however, is that this period of transition came with a price: we have lost touch with the ancient wisdom that once guided us as life itself has been stripped of its meaning. The result is that mankind will be ill-equipped to understand the coming events that will soon be upon them. In this sense, this book is long overdue.

There can only be three possible reactions to this work. The first potential response involves *atheism*. From this position, all of the reported findings are considered completely fictional, incapable of eliciting any legitimate credibility. This view exhibits all of the nihilistic features of postmodernism. Another likely reception of this text intimates *theism*, the doctrine that affirms faith in the existence of a monotheistic God who is capable of instilling revelation upon the natural world. This is the flip side of the spiritual coin and proponents of this standpoint will weigh and consider the evidence with great care and sincerity given that they believe that the Bible is the authentic and inspired word of God. Lastly, there may be a third type of reaction to this volume involving what some view as the skeptical approach to metaphysical questions: *agnosticism*. The advocates of this position hold that the *truth value* of the theistic premise concerning the existence of a divine being is essentially unknown and unverifiable, incapable of being tested by empirical means. These "logical positivists," so to speak, represent the middle ground between the other two extremes.[1] Needless to say, this group maintains only a questioning attitude toward these mysteries, not total disbelief. Our argument is primarily addressed to these last two classes of people who are at least receptive to the subject of this book. Atheists can participate in reading this text out of mere curiosity, but they must consider the premises (for argument's sake) in order to fully understand the conclusions of the topics under discussion. After all, is it not true that all knowledge is based on some form of faith? Plato once defined knowledge as "justified true belief"!

All scriptural quotes, unless otherwise noted, will be derived from the New American Standard Bible of 1977. This is the version that most scholars use because it is more of a literal translation rather than an interpretation of the original text. To a lesser extent, the New Jerusalem Bible, the New King James, and the Authorized King James versions will be applied for purposes of comparison and contrast. This assemblage should produce a dimension of depth that enriches and elucidates the meaning of the text. Since "all scripture is given by inspiration of God" (2 Tim. 3:16), the inspired translations are uncompromising expansions of *meaning* that make the text more transparent. The more versions placed at our disposal, the less likely we are to overlook the semantic import of scripture. Christ says, "The words that I have spoken to you are spirit and are life" (John 6:63). In other words, they are to be understood as proceeding from the *spirit* ("pneuma" in Greek) of God.

It should be pointed out that many religious traditions are represented symbolically to conceal their identity as the oracles concerning them are invariably unfavorable: scripture is casting an aspersion on them. Readers should also be keenly aware that certain dates, names, and places pertaining to key prophetic revelations are not always openly disclosed in this volume but are disseminated instead through cryptic means. This is done for several reasons. The author does not wish to be portrayed in the role of a fortune teller who nails down specific dates similar to what certain biblical scholars are doing today. On the other hand, enough information is furnished so that readers can participate in the search process and figure out the answers for themselves. Last but not least, the reason for this cryptic dissemination of dates, names, and places is for the purpose of allowing the reader to judge for his—or herself without the need to trust the author's findings. It is also worth noting that symbols of prophecy may require more than one type of interpretation depending on the particular context in question. In an attempt to accommodate for this complexity, we have strived to offer diverse explanations wherever possible.

Another point of interest concerns the term "Jew" and its specific application. This word can mean one of two things: either a "Jew" by religion, irrespective of one's race or a "Jew" by race, irrespective of one's religion. For example, the former term may also include non-Hebrew converts to the Judaic religion while the latter term can involve Jews who might either not belong to the Judaic religion or who may be atheists altogether. In this study, we use the word *Jew* to refer to the latter meaning: a *Jew* by race, irrespective of one's religion. Actually, the word *Jew* is an abbreviation of the term *Judah* ("Ioudaios" in Greek), and in this sense, it implies a descendant from the tribe of Judah.

The message of this work is intended to all. It comprises our conviction that the current tenets of *Christianity* with regard to the origin and advent of Jesus are based on fundamental misconceptions.[2] Our findings are of paramount importance for believers because they point out that Jesus has not yet died, much less lived on earth. Multiple lines of evidence put Christ's act of *salvation* (his death) at a time when the world would come to an end (cf. 1 Tim. 2:6). As for the rest of the world, it is no small thing to have a firsthand experience of the forthcoming miracles of Jesus by witnessing his resurrection and ascension in their lifetime. Strange as this may sound, both theists and atheists alike will face the prospect of a divine encounter for the first time in human history!

But ours is no ordinary book. Tapping into these mysterious prophecies empowers us to be better prepared for what is about to come: events of epic proportions that will soon shake the world to its very core. This is why the progression of events leading up to the end of days has occupied students of the Bible throughout the centuries. Its oracles have mystified us. They have stood the test of time and continue to intrigue us, to console us, and at times, to horrify us.

The Bible is no less fascinating than myths or dreams. *Joseph Campbell* once said that "myths are public dreams, [while] dreams are private myths." The biblical language works in much the same way as the process of a dream in that it rigorously disguises and conceals its secret contents to prevent them from being discovered by the profane populace. Its meaning is often half-submerged in a sea of extraneous linguistic forms. And just as the characters in a dream frequently represent the dreamer, many biblical characters often represent the Messiah. These scriptural myths may actually lie on the confines of alchemy and science. Nevertheless, because of their celestial origins, there may be more truth to them than there is in any fact of science. Ultimately, scripture is a mystery book that outlines God's plan for the universe. It is based on prophecy, which is inspired by divine revelation (communication with a divine source). Sir *Isaac Newton*—the father of modern physics and an astute biblical scholar—once said that "the authority of the Prophets is divine" (Wojcik and Frontain, 98). It is with these views in mind that we present our volume in the hope that it will contribute to the understanding of Christian eschatology (the study of the end-times), most notably with respect to the origin and advent of Jesus.

But the question is, are these stories true or false? For the most part, these scriptural narratives are not true in the literal sense of the word. On the other hand, they are not false either since they depict, albeit metaphorically, the more salient features pertaining to key portentous figures, places, and events. It would be far more precise to refer to them as myths that are capable of imparting prophetic meaning. Yet not all of the biblical content is metaphorical since it also represents a series of actual figures and events that "will surely come" to pass (Hab. 2:3), such as the birth of *Christ* (Rev. 12:1-5), the arrival of the *antichrist* (Dan. 7:8, 24-25; 2 Thess. 2:3-4; Rev. 13), the *rapture* (Luke 17:34-36; 1 Cor. 15:51-52; 1 Thess. 4:15-17), and the like. Therefore, these prophecies should not be taken lightly as they are of the utmost importance.

Traditionally, the search for the *historical Jesus* represents a scholarly attempt to reconstruct the said figure using the *historical method* and its associated investigative techniques. However, those who subscribe to this paradigm have not found a single piece of conclusive evidence to prove the existence of the historical Christ, other than the Bible itself, which indicates that their argument carries little weight. Another approach comprises a *critical analysis* of the biblical text per se. Inasmuch as we propose that the *gospel* narratives are oracular, it is incumbent upon us to dismiss the historical method of inquiry and accept only the guidelines prescribed by critical analysis. This is due to the results of our findings; they are not indicative of a *historical Jesus*, but of a *Christ of Faith*: an *apocalyptic* Messiah as prophesied by scripture.[3] Our conclusions are given renewed impetus as there are no reliable extant records of the historical Christ found outside the sacred writings.

The author is well aware that he is running against the grain. Thousands of years have elapsed. Since then, churches were founded, books were written, and stories have been dispersed among the communities of Christians and Jews. It seems that our message is up against insurmountable odds with little if any chance of success. The stories given us in the Bible have become so engrained in our minds that one could even describe them as primordial in the Jungian sense.

It is the author's position that the two-thousand-year-old story of Jesus can be compared with similar views that the ancients held about the heavens. The accounts they transmitted were intrinsically correct, in the broadest sense, that there was a sun accompanied by planets in motion within the observable universe. Even so, their specific intricacies were not revealed until *Copernicus* established their true relationships; for instance, that the earth revolved around the sun, and so on.[4] Such a statement was so radical for that time that the mere mention of it involved the risk of imprisonment and even death. Equally, to question the specifics of the accepted Jesus account today risks nothing less than the contempt of the faithful and the anathema of the church. But for all our differences, there is one thing that every Christian can agree on: that we must never abandon our quest for the authentic Jesus. Our inspiration stems directly from Christ's own words which are never fully understood by anyone as they are invariably dressed in metaphorical garb:

> *And with many such parables He was speaking the word to them as they were able to hear it; and He did not speak to them without a parable; but He was explaining everything privately to His own disciples*

> *(Mark 4:33-34).*

The above quote indicates that there seems to be a dichotomy involved in the story of Jesus concerning those who comprehend his message and those who have to resort to guesswork in an attempt to interpret it. By implication, the general public is left only with the outer vestige of the *parable* (a story that exemplifies an ethical principle) whereas his inner circle is furnished with all the necessary details to aid their understanding (cf. Mark 4:11). This suggests that there is more to the external story of Jesus than the Bible would have us believe. In fact, these are scriptural intimations that denote the existence of a secret and forbidden knowledge. We must admit, then, that unless we are part of his inner circle, we lack the requisite means to grasp the messianic message in its entirety. This is precisely why Jesus declares,

> *These things I have spoken to you in figurative language; an hour is coming when I will speak no more to you in figurative language, but will tell you plainly*

> *(John 16:25).*

With the advent of *critical theory*—be it Adornian, Marxist, or Freudian—modern scholarship has called into question the older model of interpretation which held that the stories of the Bible should be taken literally and historically. A growing number of studies have argued that the biblical narratives are meant to be understood in a figurative rather than a literal sense. But this does not begin to describe the kinds of modifications that scriptural interpretation has undergone. At present, the function of biblical interpretation is a fairly contested issue, often baffling scholars and provoking much debate. Even the *church of Peter* had to succumb to the criteria of literary criticism as its teachings were met with considerable opposition. As matters stand now, the church's *Pontifical Biblical Commission* explains the apparent discrepancies of the historical gospel accounts as follows:

> *The truth of the Gospel account is not compromised because the evangelists report the Lord's words and deeds in different order. Nor is it hurt because they report his words, not literally but in a variety of ways, while retaining the same meaning*

(Historical Truth of the Gospels, *21 April 1964*).

Father *John Parks*, a member of the church of Peter, was once quoted as saying, "Yet many scholars doubt the reliability of the gospel narratives because the four gospels differ in historical detail, sometimes widely." He went on to say, "There is considerable disagreement about historical detail; . . . the exact time the empty tomb was discovered, for instance, changes from gospel to gospel." Thus the historical approach to the biblical narratives lends itself to serious doubts from both within, and outside the *visible church* (the community of the Christian faithful on earth).

If we apply critical thinking to the story of Jesus, we will notice that it appears to be an arcane and ambiguous mystery of sorts. If Jesus has not told us *plainly* and openly, we must concede that his message is incomprehensible. We may repeat the Christian saga verbatim over and over again, albeit without profit or insight, much like a child apes adult sounds without understanding their meaning or intent. In that respect, if the NT (New Testament) is a riddle that is not revealed to the undeserving public, except to the inner few, we must assume that the same principle must hold true for the OT (Old Testament) as well. Here is an example of such a riddle:

> *Where is He who has been born King of the Jews?*

(Mt. 2:2)

Although most people know that the Jews "were entrusted with the oracles of God" (Rom. 3:1-2), very few understand that the above verse is actually founded upon these OT prophecies concerning the advent of the Messiah. The ultimate question is not whether this verse is setting forth the pedigree of Jesus, but whether it presents him as the fulfillment of the Hebrew scriptures? And if so, does this allusion necessarily make him Jewish? This book attempts to answer this very question as well as the deeper mysteries pertaining to Christ's origin and advent.

Our most sincere gratitude goes out to the Achaean teacher! Without his inspiration and support, this project would not have materialized. We are deeply indebted to our friend with whom we had lengthy discussions and whose useful suggestions were assimilated into the text.

We are deeply grateful to our writing muse as well for her stimulating suggestions and criticism. She shall remain nameless but ever present in the text.

Many thanks are also extended to the person responsible for writing the foreword who participated in the process of reading the manuscript while providing a number of helpful recommendations. We have deemed it appropriate to withhold the name of this person. We made this decision based on the dangerous times we live in, when the expression of one's views can provoke reprisals from various fanatical groups.

Twenty years have elapsed since we first began to research and decipher the Bible. Many long hours of diligent study have finally paid off. This work is the culmination of what we know about scripture; it is a lifetime's work.

Eli of Kittim

2012

Behold, I am against those who have . . . led My people astray by their falsehoods; . . . you have perverted the words of the living God

(Jer. 23:32-36).

A General Introduction to the Exclusively Prophetic Biblical Text

Blessed is he who heeds the words of the prophecy of this book

(Rev. 22:7).

Einstein said that space and time are not absolute. Time is finite. And if we could travel at the rate known as the *speed of light*, we would experience the deceleration of this chronological phenomenon as its temporal components would vanish altogether. To a presumed immaterial demiurge that is considered by theologians to be "unoriginate" origin, beyond space and time and beyond being, the lifespan of the universe must be known even prior to its inception. The creator's prescience is not unlike Hegel's *Now* moment wherein all aspects of time—past, present, and future—seem to be simultaneously juxtaposed in a single point of the *space-time* continuum: an infinite interval into which all of space and time converge. Accordingly, it may be theoretically possible for the Creator of the universe to disclose future events before their actual occurrence.

The acclaimed biblical scholar known as *St. Augustine* articulates the eternal process through which the Deity addresses scriptural prophecy. It is wholly devoid of the concept of time:

> *Thou callest us then to understand the Word . . . which is spoken eternally. . . . For what was spoken was not spoken successively, one thing concluded that the next might be spoken, but all things together and eternally. . . . For in the Eternal, speaking properly, there is neither anything*

> past, as though it had passed away, nor anything future, as though it were
> not as yet, but whatsoever is, only is

> *(Augustinus 167).*

Augustine's statement reflects on how the Deity is capable of "declaring the end from the beginning" (Isa. 46:10). The sublime Spanish mystic of the sixteenth century, *John of the Cross*, affirms that prophetic literature is too often misunderstood until its appointed time of revelation:

> [God may] promise many things, not that they may be understood
> or possessed at that time, but that they may be understood at a later time,
> when it is fitting . . . or when their effect is attained

> *(150).*

The Bible ascribes these timeless promises and prophetic disclosures to the Supreme Being called *"the Ancient of Days"* (Dan. 7:9). We can then speak of a foreknowledge illuminated by the origin of existence—the source of all life forms which we call "God"—assuming we accept the premise that such an entity exists. This foresight permeates the entire oeuvre of the *Old* and *New Testaments*, collectively known as the Bible; it goes by the name of *prophecy*, which can best be defined as a foreknowledge of future events that is disclosed by human beings under the guidance of divine inspiration. It represents one of the many gifts bestowed upon man by the Spirit of God:

> Now concerning spiritual gifts, brethren, I do not want you to be
> unaware. . . . Now there are varieties of gifts, but the same Spirit. . . . For
> to one is given the word of wisdom through the Spirit, and to another the
> word of knowledge according to the same Spirit; to another faith by the same
> Spirit, and to another gifts of healing by the one Spirit, and to another the
> effecting of miracles, and to another prophecy; . . . but one and the same
> Spirit works all these things, distributing to each one individually just as
> He wills

> *(1 Cor. 12:1-10).*

In decoding the remote past, we are not rewriting the Bible; we are rewriting the two-thousand-year-old story of Christ. And this is done with good reason. Although the essence of the story is true, its ancient setting is completely fictional. In many ways, history is a myth-making process. The American historian *Roy P. Basler* once said, "To know the truth of history is to realize its ultimate myth and its inevitable ambiguity." The biblical narratives distill information in much the same way: they do not pretend to represent an accurate archival record of past ages except insofar as they facilitate the study of prophetic history leading up to the end of time. That is why biblical events are assumed to have taken place—since the authors often use past tense to describe them—even though these events contain prophetic import concerning the future.

We must come to realize that a large portion of scripture is written in the *historical past*: a dramatic technique of using past tense to recount events set in the present. In linguistics, it would be considered as the opposite of the rhetorical term known as the *historical present*, which employs the present tense in describing past events. The definition of the term *historical past*, however, entails a slight modification if it is to be applied to the Bible. In this case, it must reflect a narrative mode, written in the past tense, which specifically refers to events set in the future, not in the present. And this is exactly what we find, namely, that the use of past tense within the scriptural accounts does not refer to the approximate time in which the biblical books were written but rather to the future time when God's promises would be fulfilled. Thus, when the author of the *Epistle to the Corinthians* states "that Christ died for our sins" (1 Cor. 15:3), this comment is written in the *historical past*. The presence of this literary technique is then reinforced when the author adds the idiomatic phrase "according to the Scriptures" (1 Cor. 15:3). He is at pains to show that Christ's death is not based on the historical record but on the foreknowledge of the prophetic writings. The phrase "according to the scriptures" is something like a gestalt configuration: it could mean either *according to the historical records* or *according to these prophecies*. Given that the former view is open to criticism because of its incompatibility with what the New Testament scriptures have to say and since it is not in the least surprising, we vigorously denounce it and support only the latter view which, as we will see, enlightens the dynamics of the text.

It is not the intention of this work to dismiss the common teachings of the Christian tradition, which hold that Jesus is the Son of God, whose death and resurrection restores and elevates humanity to the divine realm. That is, we do not reject the divine authority to which scripture appeals for Christ's words and actions. Moreover, we do not deny that there is one Godhead emanating through three *hypostases* (persons). *Maximos the Confessor* (580-662 AD), a mystical monk and astute theologian, claims to have grasped the triune essence of the Deity through *theoria*, a contemplative vision of absolute being which instills *Noesis*: a keen sense of insight into the concepts of being and becoming (*The Philokalia* 2:126). He writes,

> *The Divinity is not partially in the Father, nor is the Father part of*
> *God. . . . For the Divinity is not divisible; nor is the Father, or the Son, or*
> *the Holy Spirit incomplete God. On the contrary, the whole and complete*
> *Divinity is completely in the complete Father; the whole and complete*
> *Divinity is completely in the complete Son. . . . For the whole Father is*

completely in the whole Son and Spirit; and the whole Son is completely in the whole Father and Spirit. . . . Therefore, the Father, the Son and the Holy Spirit are one God. The essence, power and energy of the Father, the Son and the Holy Spirit are one, for none of the hypostases or persons either exists or is intelligible without the others

(The Philokalia, *2:137-138*).

In the selfsame text, Maximos takes up this subject again in order to articulate how the *Son* and *Spirit* are not sequent to the Father in terms of the origin of their existence or subordinate to him insofar as their power or scope is concerned. This is the reason why Christ declares in the *gospels* that "I and the Father are one" (John 10:30):

Philip said to Him, "Lord, show us the Father, and it is enough for us." Jesus said to Him, "Have I been so long with you, and yet you have not come to know Me, Philip? He who has seen Me has seen the Father"

(John 14:8-9).

Similarly, the prophet *Isaiah* pronounces an oracle about the future Messiah in which he describes him as the father of all creation:

For a child will be born to us, a son will be given to us; and the government will rest on His shoulders; and His name will be called Wonderful Counselor, Mighty God, Eternal Father

(9:6).

In mystical theology, Jesus is more accurately described as one of the three reflections in the proverbial mirror of God. The New Testament defines the second person of the trinity as follows:

He is the image of the invisible God, the first-born of all creation. For by Him all things were created, both in the heavens and on earth, visible and invisible, whether thrones or dominions or rulers or authorities—all things have been created by Him and for Him. And He is before all things, and in Him all things hold together [subsist]

(Col. 1:15-17).

What is more, the tripartite essence or the paradoxical plurality of the singular Deity can be ascertained from scriptural sources as well: "God said, 'Let Us make man in Our image, according to Our likeness'" (Gen. 1:26). To this end, Maximos—who, similar to Plato and Heidegger, has envisioned the *noetic realities* (*The Philokalia* 2:122) beyond the physical plane of existence—delineates the triune nature of the Universal Mind:

> *One without confusion and three without division: The Father is unoriginate intellect, the unique essential Begetter of the unique Logos [Word], also unoriginate, and the fount of the unique everlasting life, the Holy Spirit*

> (The Philokalia, *2:165*).

It could be argued that Maximos's phenomenology attests to this mystical notion not out of sheer philosophical inquiry, but out of a transcendent existential experience. This involves a deep meditation in which the mind leaves all knowledge behind and passes over into a state of transcendent *unknowing* where the "intuition of naked truths" is "conveyed to the understanding" (John of the Cross, 182). Therefore, Maximos sets the theological standard against which all other theories are measured:

> *There is one God, because there is one Divinity, a Unity unoriginate, simple, beyond being, without parts and undivided*

> (The Philokalia, *2:165*).

The paradoxical nature of the Deity—being a unity in diversity—is further expounded by the NT:

> *There are three that bear record in heaven, the Father, the Word, and the Holy Ghost: and these three are one*

> (1 John 5:7, King James).

Most importantly, we do not intend to discredit any theological beliefs, such as the iteration of the *Nicene Creed*—God from God, Light from Light, and so on—which refers to Christ's divine origin. Nor do we wish to dismiss the essential tenets of the Old and New Testaments; rather, we would like to qualify them.

A pertinent question might be, how can we differentiate between the essential and the artificial elements in the text? Allow us to use an example to address this issue. God refers to the prophet *Ezekiel* (Ezek. 6:2) using "the phrase 'son of man' [which] is [an] Aramaic idiom (*bar enash*) [sic] for 'man'" (Harrington, 164). On the other hand, given that Christ is scripture's promised Messiah, he takes precedence with respect to this title as he ascribes it to himself (Matt. 24:27). Yet no one is exactly sure what the idiomatic phrase *Son of man* really means. One can only guess that it must be a particular reference to Jesus's human embodiment: born of man (cf. Num. 23:19). Thus when Christ uses this idiom as a sign of his coming, he is at once prophesying the end of the world and the startling revelation that bears no resemblance to anything we have ever heard before: his future incarnation! (Luke 11:30). The undermentioned prophecy exemplifies our argument:

> *They will see THE SON OF MAN COMING IN [the] CLOUDS with great power and glory*

> *(Mark 13:26).*

Therefore, there is good reason to believe that God calls Ezekiel *"Son of man"* (Ezek. 2:1) in an effort to draw an analogy between this great prophet and Christ. Interpreters are not forced to assume that Ezekiel is a real historical figure, at least as far as the story is concerned, a view that would fail to address the true identity of the *Son of man*. This does not mean that the prophet Ezekiel never existed. But we can hardly expect the scriptural narratives to give us a historical account of the said figure. Taking the Ezekiel narrative at face value, we neglect to extract the deeper prophetic message from the allegorical theme: Ezekiel seems to represent the future Messiah (cf. Matt. 13:35).

Ezekiel complains to God that his message received but little favor because he only speaks through the medium of parables (Ezek. 20:49); something comparable happens to Christ in the *gospels*:

> *The disciples came and said to Him, "Why do You speak to them in parables?" And He answered and said to them, "To you it has been granted to know the mysteries . . . but to them it has not been granted"*

> *(Matt. 13:10-11).*

We also want to parenthetically state that the word *gospel* comes from the Greek term *eu-agellio*, which means "good tidings" or "good news." Now with regard to our discussion, it is not inappropriate to say that the Christian tradition has distorted *the mysteries* of Jesus due to his constant use of figurative language (John 16:25); they have failed to comprehend *the mysteries* vis-à-vis the external story. Not only have they been misled about Jesus, but they have misunderstood other biblical personages as well. *Plotinus* (ca. CE 205-270), the celebrated Neoplatonist mystic philosopher of Alexandria, once wrote,

This is the purport of that rule of our mysteries: Nothing divulged
to the uninitiated: The supreme [God] is not to be made a common story,
the holy things may not be uncovered to the stranger, to any that has not
himself attained to see [the vision]

(VI, 9 [11]).

Pascal, the famous French physicist and philosopher, confides in us that the Bible is *figurative*, speaking with *hidden meaning*, which is not meant to be comprehended before the proper time (204). The alleged disciple credited with being the author of the *Epistles of Peter* scripturally confirms this assertion:

In the foresight of God the Father . . . who in his great mercy has given
us a new birth into a living hope . . . through faith until the salvation
which has been prepared is revealed at the final point of time

(1 Pet. 1:2-5, New Jerusalem Bible).

The aforementioned passage declares categorically and unequivocally that Christ's salvation—his soteriological sacrifice, which delivers mankind from eternal death and divine deprivation—will be revealed at the end of days. It is no accident, then, that this salvation is described as *a living hope*. Like so, Pascal's explanation that the hidden meaning of the Bible is not meant to be understood prior to the appointed time is substantiated by scripture as it clearly indicates that Christ's salvation will be "revealed at the final point of time."

We must come to terms with the notion that a figurative veil has covered the essential and intended meaning of scripture until the appointed time:

But as the ancient Prophets, borne aloft in Vision . . . their dread
vibration to this hour prolonged?

(Wordsworth, 381).

As we have seen, the overt allegorical account of Jesus appears to contradict the hidden truths pertaining to him, just as the parables seem to be diametrically opposed to *"the mysteries."* It is a semantic war between those to whom "it has not been granted," and those to whom "it has been granted to know the mysteries." Most people belong to the former category of the uninitiated and are therefore unaware that they know little, if anything, about the mystery of Jesus the *Christ* (*Khristos* means "anointed" in Greek). This is why scripture indicates that the "gospel is veiled . . . to those who are perishing" (2 Cor. 4:3). It is as if a curtain has been pulled over the gospel to prohibit outsiders from corrupting its sacred knowledge. As the text reminds us,

> *All these things Jesus spoke to the multitudes in parables, and He did not speak to them without a parable, so that what was spoken through the prophet might be fulfilled, saying, "I WILL OPEN MY MOUTH IN PARABLES"*

(Matt. 13:34-35).

The church of Peter is mainly responsible for this confusion not only because it handed down the faith in distorted form and forbade any private interpretations but also because it had ample time over the centuries to investigate the mysteries of scripture and inform the public. The church did not disclose its findings, so it is without excuse. The secret archives in its dusty old library remain locked in a sealed vault to this very day. Though the church of Peter was largely responsible for transmitting the writings of the New Testament, which were at first preserved in oral form by the early fathers, it also engaged in interpretative manipulations by imposing its own meaning on the text for reasons which we will briefly touch on at a more appropriate time.

It is also conceivable that the composition of the NT may not have taken place in ancient Palestine, as is commonly believed. Such a scenario is certainly possible because the original NT manuscripts were not written in Hebrew. Equally, no one can argue that the Hebrew scriptures were written by anyone other than the Jews. And who is to say where these NT authors are from? So even though they wrote the NT texts in the Greek language, these authors employed a unique *apocalyptic* style of writing, analogous to the literature of Judaism, to suggest that they were Jews residing in Jerusalem.

From the outset, and during a time when social norms and standards required the worship of multiple gods, the Deity revealed himself to the ancient Israelites as one God. On the whole, it is obvious that the biblical *story*—the Old Testament narrative of God and his people—would take on a unique Hebraic form since the worshippers were exclusively Hebrews. The OT books attest to that fact as they are written in the ancient Hebrew and Aramaic languages of the Semites. But the biblical story does not end there. Just as there is plot and character development in literary writing, there is also a biblical evolution that takes place over the next several hundred years, after which the OT undergoes a marked transformation that will expand it to include the NT's more mature and spiritual approach: the concepts of *Spirit* and *love* replacing the older laws of *Moses*.

And so the OT finds its way into the NT, set in the land of Israel. The Hebraic underpinnings of the texts are maintained, even though the NT is written exclusively in the Greek language and revolves to a large extent around newly developed

Christian Greek communities. In fact, there are more *Epistles* (letters) written to Greek communities than any other: 1 Corinthians, 2 Corinthians, Philippians, 1 Thessalonians, 2 Thessalonians! The purpose behind the setting of the NT *story* in Palestine is to make the connection that Christianity is not a new cult but a direct descendent and continuation of the Judaic tradition of the OT. That is to say, the NT *tale* now becomes the fulfillment of the earlier messianic promises of Jewish scripture. That is why the genealogy of Christ is inserted in the Gospel texts: to ensure that this connection is established. The result is a divinely transcribed allegory of a *Jewish* Jesus, set in ancient Palestine, with a vast array of literary characters from biblical times: Romans, Jews, high priests, and the like. But this narrative is only half the story.

The purpose behind the so-called *Jewish* Jesus account is to convey that he comes to fulfill all that was foretold about him in the OT. Does that mean that he must of necessity be Jewish? Under these circumstances, the answer, of course, is no. The apparent historicity or the specific time of when these events take place, in the life of Christ, is not fully disclosed in the *synoptic gospels* except insofar as these accounts contain esoteric truths beyond the literary vehicle of narration. By contrast, the authentic "prophetic history" of Jesus is revealed to a large extent by the *NT Epistles*. Isaac Newton referred to the prophecies of the Bible as "histories of things to come" (*Portsmouth Papers*). *Stephen Snobelen,* a prominent historian of science and religion, explains what Newton meant by this: "Biblical prophecy . . . shows history in advance. It's as if history was written centuries before it happened." It could be argued that this comment sums up the NT story of Jesus!

The apparent historical timeline of the gospels is itself also part of the biblical setting—the time and place in which the figurative story takes place—and thus it should not be interpreted literally as an exact historical reenactment of the Messiah. To that extent, we must differentiate between the *historic* and the *historical* Christ. The term *historic* refers to the significant or seminal events in history, such as a historic expedition, whereas the word *historical* denotes the authentic events that have de facto occurred in the past. For the most part, the gospels only convey the *historic* Jesus, whereas the NT epistles chiefly prophesy of the *historical* Christ. On the other hand, if we were to take the figurative gospels in the literal sense, including their apparent chronology, immense contradictions would follow when compared with other passages that clearly indicate the actual time of Christ's advent and sacrifice on the cross, as we shall see in part 1 of this book. For that reason, both the literary origin of Jesus as well as the figurative *pseudohistorical* account of his life, set in Palestine two millennia ago, seem to be entrenched in the gospel narratives in an attempt to portray *a contemporary Jew*—one of the Hebrew people; a son of Abraham, Isaac and Jacob—one whose scriptural bloodlines go back to the OT, the *Torah* and the Judaic Tradition. By contrast, notice how in the genealogy of *Luke's gospel* Christ is not an actual Jewish descendant per se but *supposedly* so and for argument's sake:

> *And when he began His ministry, Jesus Himself was about thirty years of age, being* supposedly *the son of Joseph, the son of Eli, the son of Matthat, the son of Levi, . . . the son of Enosh, the son of Seth, the son of Adam, the son of God*

(3:23-38, emphasis added).

To prove that Christ is the fulfillment of the Hebrew scriptures, it is imperative to construct a detailed exposition of a *Jewish* character that fills this role within the allegorical biblical genre. This process is analogous to the methods used in the formation of myths. Additionally, this person must live during a time when Israel existed as a nation. Otherwise, no one would view Jesus as the messianic fulfillment of the Jewish prophecies or grasp the connection between the OT and the NT, between Judaism and Christianity; it is that important! Along these lines, the authors of the NT conveniently set the purported account of the Messiah's epoch as if it existed just prior to the dissolution of the Israeli nation, which was known at that time as the *Kingdom of Judah.* This nation came to an end in 70 AD when the Romans burned down the Jewish temple in Jerusalem and displaced the Jews from their homeland. The latter were subsequently scattered among the nations; they would not return to Palestine until roughly two thousand years later. In any event, insofar as the NT setting is concerned, the literary effect is achieved: it establishes the notion that Christ is the fulfillment of the Jewish Bible because he is allegedly a Jew living among the Jews of ancient Israel. The end result establishes a metaphorical and literary connection between the Old and New Testaments. However, the problem that plagued successive generations is that they became infatuated with "the Jesus myth," thus being unable to reach the prophetic truths hidden under the apparent meaning. Jesus himself encourages us to go beyond the figurative language of scripture so as to unearth the opaque and hidden mysteries that define him (John 16:25).

Make no mistake; the NT account of Christ is essentially true. It discloses a superhuman figure whose miracles and teachings transform the world. This character's existence must be taken literally since it represents an actual, albeit prospective, historical person. But as to the deeper questions that pertain to the *specifics* of the story, we must go beyond the device of story telling, much like deciphering a Greek myth where the truth lies beneath the surface. In other words, Christ's *being* can be taken in a literal sense, but there are dangers when we do the same with the text. As you will see in the following sections, scripture has a hidden message to reveal: a *secret knowledge* previously undisclosed to earlier generations (Eph. 3:3-5).

A plethora of authors have contributed to the writings of the prophetic literature known as the *New Testament.* It turns out that the NT itself is the culmination of countless oracles gathered from the ancient Hebrew scriptures. Since all these books, spanning many centuries, were supposedly written for the religious purpose of worship, the implication is that their contents must be taken seriously insofar as spirituality is concerned; for they are still held as sacred. And much more than that, these works are filled with messianic fervor dating back to the time of antiquity. As has already been said, the veracity of their substance can only be revealed by the deity to those to whom "it has been granted to know the mysteries." Under these circumstances, we must penetrate the veil of scriptural secrecy so as to uncover the mysteries which lie beyond our common understanding:

> *"When the Messianic era comes, God will unveil the white (letters) [sic] in the Torah in which the letters are now invisible to us, and this is what the term 'new Torah' implies"*
>
> (Rabbi Levi Isaac de Berditschew, qtd. in Derrida 345).

This brings us to another decisive dilemma: is the Bible a book on history or a collection of prophecies? Scholars have long wrestled with this question and seem to be divided over this issue. The debate rages on. Scripture is primarily a collection of myths, not of recorded history, but of prophetic signs and disclosures about the approaching messianic age. Although conventional Christianity is increasingly sure of itself, one cannot but be startled by the recurrent cryptic references to the end-time Messiah found from *Genesis* to *Revelation*. From the mythical story of creation, in which God prophesies the coming of Christ (Gen. 3:15), to the tale of Abraham's sacrifice of Isaac (Gen. 22) right through to the last book of the Bible where a mythic seven-headed dragon attempts to devour God's son (Rev. 12), we encounter manifold oracles pertaining to a forthcoming Messiah. The scriptural narratives cast these prophecies in the form of stories, even though these collections of tales have no basis in fact, let alone history.

In rare cases, however, the Bible does present a synthesis of actual history and prophecy in order to provide us with a tool by means of which we can increase our precision in foretelling the future. For instance, it may depict famous historical figures and empires but only for the direct purpose of facilitating an accurate calculation of end-time events. Nevertheless, if one mistakenly takes the overall *historic* account of scripture literally, confusion will inevitably set in. A perfect example is *King Nebuchadnezzar* who is called "king of kings" (Daniel 2:37). This scriptural title is reserved exclusively for Jesus Christ (Rev. 19:16). Hence, the Bible is simply drawing a parallel between the aforesaid figures. In retrospect, Nebuchadnezzar—just like Ezekiel who is called *Son of man*—seems to prefigure Christ, which leads us to believe that the literary Nebuchadnezzar is not an accurate portrayal of the actual historical king of the neo-Babylonian Empire who reigned between 634-562 BC.

Our work does not represent any specialized code that only a few distinct biblical theoreticians can decipher and understand. Quite the contrary, it is predicated on a simple comprehension of consistent biblical terminology that is scattered throughout the text. This type of inquiry is based on a process called *biblical concordance.*[1] Once we have grasped the scriptural jargon, comparative studies of passages and biblical versions become the litmus test of verifying the findings. For instance, the terms *caught up* or *taken,* which are used consistently in the Bible, are most often associated with flying in the air or through the clouds. We learn that *Enoch,* an upright ancestor of Noah, was *taken* (Genesis 5:24). The messianic child, as described in the *book of Revelation* (or simply *Revelation*), was *caught up* and flew away into the heavens (Rev. 12:5).

Other terms found within the biblical story, such as the words *rise* or to *arise,* are not meant to be taken always in the literal sense. Decoded within a specific context, they usually imply resurrection from the dead (Isa. 26:19; Luke 18:33) as when we encounter one of these terms within the undermentioned messianic oracle:

The sun of righteousness will rise with healing in its wings

(Mal. 4:2).

In the context of the aforesaid verse, and other comparable verses like it, the New American Standard Bible typically denotes the word *rise,* whereas the New King James version often renders it as *arise.* It is fair to assume that they are interchangeable terms and are used as such, depending upon which version of scripture is being read. We are beginning to realize that the Bible has a unique and consistent terminology, and readers are encouraged to familiarize themselves with it so as to enable them to go beyond the mythic prose. As a matter of fact, you cannot read the Bible, as you would any other text, prior to mastering its unique terminology. Interpretation, to be effective, requires that we peer at each and every word of scripture as if with a telescope. For each word is a world unto itself. Even common words that appear to be insignificant may hold the key to understanding the sacred text. Thus, we must pay incredible attention to detail. Unless one is familiar with the use and application of scriptural terms, the hidden meaning will remain elusive. Most biblical passages are not easy to read, let alone understand. This is because scripture is a rather large coded message that cannot be laid open by a perfunctory or uncritical reading approach.

The Bible contains God's blueprint concerning the transformation of the universe: a series of events that culminate in a unique final crescendo at the end of time. During this high point, signs are revealed as we get closer to the final showdown of the approaching *Armageddon*: the final great battle between good and evil that has been known since the time of Zoroaster. Many biblical stories, from the book of Genesis to the book of Revelation, point to this final age of world history because of the significance imputed to these apocalyptic end-time events. A case in point is Moses's symbolic miracle, the parting of the Red Sea that seems to prefigure the so-called *rapture* of the faithful (1 Thess. 4:15-17) who will depart this world and fly away to the farthest stretches of the universe at the end of days. Concerning this end-time phenomenon, *Paul*, a prolific NT writer, says,

> *We who are alive . . . shall be caught up . . . in the clouds to meet the Lord in the air*

> *(1 Thess. 4:17).*

To illustrate this point, consider the following cryptic terms being used by scripture to describe the second day of God's creation: "the Spirit of God" parted *"and divided the waters"* of the heavens (Gen. 1:2-8, *New King James*, emphasis added). Upon closer examination, we find that the exact same terms are being used to describe Moses's miracle pertaining to the parting of the Red Sea: *"and the waters were divided"* (Exod. 14:21, *New King James*, emphasis added). Involved in the phraseology of "the divided waters" are identical terms that are featured in two distinct passages of the OT wherefore the Bible suggests that their hidden meaning may be prophetic rather than historical. And this would explain why Moses's miracle was later duplicated by other prophets (2 Kings 2:8, 14).

For those of us who are unconvinced that OT allegories may be precursors of future events, examine and compare the series of judgments that Moses inflicted upon Egypt to the final judgments in the book of revelation, and sure enough, you will notice that both descriptions appear to exhibit identical events taking place: water turned to blood (Exod. 7:17; Rev. 8:8; 16:3-4), frogs come forth (Exod. 8:2; Rev. 16:13), animals die (Exod. 9; Rev. 6:8), abhorrent sores appear on men (Exod. 9:9; Rev. 16:2), and finally, there is the manifestation of the locusts upon the earth (Exod. 10; Rev. 9:3). Therefore, we can draw parallels between the judgments of Moses and Jesus since they are strikingly similar. Could it be mere coincidence? We think not. Since all of the previous passages are derived from the Bible, and given the consistency of the jargon found in the text, it is difficult to argue that the affinity between Moses's and Christ's judgments is accidental. In that case, we are beginning to see how the allegorical account of Moses—which is not unlike other dramatic tales of the OT—may be a prophetic forecast of an end-time apocalyptic scenario that takes place upon the earth.

While we are on this subject, it is a matter of common knowledge that *Modern Literary Theory* thoroughly rejects the notion that Moses was the author of the *Pentateuch* (variously known as the Torah), the first five books of the OT (Larue Ch. 3). This modern orientation has triumphed over former theories of scriptural authorship. As a consequence, *literary criticism* confirms our findings that there is little evidence to suggest that the legend of Moses is founded upon any historical chronicles. That Moses's name (*Mosheh* in Hebrew) may be an allusion to the Messiah (*Moshiah* in Hebrew) is borne out by a verse from the *book of Exodus* in which

Moses is depicted as God himself: "Then the LORD said to Moses, 'See, I make you as God to Pharaoh'" (7:1). It appears, then, that beyond the metaphorical figure of Moses—who is often depicted in exalted terms so as to heighten the dramatic effect of the text (cf. Exod. 34:29)—we become cognizant of a deeper mystery with prophetic import: the arrival of a divine Judge at the end of time! (cf. Acts 7:37).

Within the text itself, it is not uncommon for divine beings to disclose pivotal moments in human history. An angel imparts the following words to *Daniel* the prophet:

> *I have come to give you an understanding of what will happen to your people in the latter days, for the vision pertains to the days yet future*

(10:14).

Elsewhere, a celestial being proclaims an impending message which suggests that our current age may represent the appointed time of the apocalypse:

> *But as for you, Daniel, conceal these words and seal up the book until the end of time; many will go back and forth, and knowledge will increase*

(Dan. 12:4).

In the book of Revelation—a mysterious text teeming with strange visions and mystical predictions—Jesus says,

> *And behold, I am coming quickly. Blessed is he who heeds the words of the prophecy of this book*

(22:7).

Despite those for whom prophecy is not easy to accept, one cannot help but notice that the Bible, at its core, is a collection of oracles culminating toward that final cadence "at the consummation of the ages" (Heb. 9:26). *Vincent Bridges*, a scholar and historian, is quoted as saying, "Prophecy, particularly in the Greek and Roman sense, is a precursor to everything we think of as science." Secular humanists may attack the concept of mystical *vision*, but little do they realize that the humanistic disciplines could not have evolved without it. *Vision*—the penetrating, spiritual perception of the metaphysical essence of being—is the foundation of western philosophical thought. The ancient Greek philosophers appreciated its value and coined it *Theoria*: the contemplative vision of the Platonic *Forms* (the realities hidden beyond our apparent world). Ironically, without *theoria*, there would have been no philosophy to speak of. The same concept of *theoria* gave rise to the collection of prophecies known as the *Bible*.

Biblical conclusions, however, must not be based on isolated passages or private interpretations but on a multitude of verses that support specific themes, thus adding more clarity to the overall picture in hand. For instance, there is a passage that sheds light not only on the mysterious origins of Christ but also on the new economy of God's messianic promises:

> There is neither Jew nor Greek, . . . for you are all one in Christ Jesus. And if you belong to Christ, then you are Abraham's offspring, heirs according to promise
>
> (Gal. 3:28-29).

Although the term *offspring* has a variety of uses, it is oftentimes associated with a special and unique biblical meaning. In particular, it refers to the precise lineage through which the Messiah will come to earth (Gal. 3:16, Heb. 2:16, Rev. 22:16). Having said that, it is most peculiar how Christian interpreters have neglected to read the aforesaid passage in relation to this messianic promise. Instead, they have hitherto ascribed this extract to the concept of *salvation*, as if the Gentiles (non-Jews) simply represent additional converts to the original flock of Jewish believers. In other words, they interpret this passage to mean that God has allowed the Gentiles to become part of this Jewish family of early Christians.

The previous quote (Gal. 3:28-29), however, does not speak to that in toto. On the contrary, it actually incorporates traditional *Jewish messianism* into a global context. For example, who "are Abraham's offspring, heirs according to" the promises of God? The passage clearly negates the old view that the Jews are the exclusive heirs to the messianic covenant by suggesting that the Greeks are equal partakers of that promise (Gal. 3:28-29). The first verse (3:28) makes much the same point by means of an equation: Jews have no precedence over the Greeks as far as the messianic lineage is concerned, for "there is neither Jew nor Greek" in the spiritual sense of scripture. The implication is that the terms *Jew* and *Greek* may be synonymous within the metaphorical nomenclature of the Bible. If Jews and Greeks are spiritual equals, then this excerpt opens the door to the possibility of a Greek Messiah because "Abraham's offspring," known as the *heirs* of the promise, represent the lineage through which the Messiah is born (Gal. 3:16, Gen. 22:18). Because of this, Paul, the apostle who never saw Christ in person, confides in us the following secrets:

> There was made known to me the mystery . . . and by referring to this, when you read you can understand my insight into the mystery of Christ, which in other generations was not made known to the sons of men, as it has now been revealed to His holy apostles and prophets in the Spirit; to be

> *specific, that the Gentiles are . . . partakers of the promise in Christ Jesus*
> *through the gospel*

> *(Eph. 3:3-6).*

If this passage is referring to the popular concept of salvation, then why was this mystery (*mysterion* means "hidden or secret" in Greek) kept concealed for so long and from all previous generations? This is the major drawback of this view to which our main objection is directed. That is to say, why would it be considered as an incredible secret to proclaim that non-Jews could be saved by Christ? Moreover, what is the purpose of withholding this information from all previous ages? And what is the great insight that Paul gained "into the mystery of Christ"? That the Jews are not the only race on the planet to be saved? This is the great mystery Paul is talking about? No, the issue is clearly not about mankind's deliverance. Rather, Jesus's human origin is at issue. For to this end, Paul emphatically says that the "knowledge of God's mystery . . . is Christ Himself" (Col. 2:2). Therefore, this postulate fails to give a satisfactory explanation of Paul's surpassingly great revelation "into the mystery of Christ."

We cannot presume to understand Christ's *mystery* any more than we can quietly brush it aside for lack of knowledge. For any hermeneutical position to hold sway it must correspond to the dictates of scripture. We must therefore take exception to the traditional view concerning the concept of salvation because it does not meet the criteria for an "insight into the mystery of Christ" (Eph. 3:4). The only other possible explanation that remains is also the one that Paul himself necessitates, namely, that the long-kept secret, "which in other generations was not made known," is the revelation "that the Gentiles are partakers [heirs] of the promise in Christ Jesus." The Gentiles are called "partakers" in that they have supplanted the Jews as heirs of the OT promises, just as the Greek NT has replaced the Hebrew Scriptures (Gal. 2:16, Heb. 8:13).[2] And since these promises pertain to Christ (Eph. 3:6), it means that the Messiah himself will no longer figure in any Jewish genealogy as previously suspected. Now this is worthy of being labeled as an amazing insight that turns our world inside out; which is why it was hidden for so long! (cf. Gal. 2:2). It makes perfect sense, and therein lies its strength.

In another passage, Paul confirms our interpretation and adds an explanation of his own:

> *For they are not all Israel who are descended from Israel; neither are*
> *they all children because they are Abraham's descendants [Jews]. . . . That*
> *is, it is not the children of the flesh [by birth] who are children of God, but*
> *the children of the promise are regarded as descendants*

> *(Rom. 9:6-8).*

Paul's secret and radical message reveals that the numerous scriptural references to *Israel* do not indicate the Jewish heritage per se, nor do the promises in Christ materialize through the Jewish lineage simply "because they are Abraham's descendants." Paul qualifies his elaborative statement by making a peculiar and unorthodox articulation. He states, in effect, that the promised messianic race, which will give birth to Christ, is not the Jewish by birth, but a spiritual *Davidic line,* which represents the children of the promise. We explore this theme at length within the body of this work. As you can see, the attempt to comprehend the biblical material is a daunting task:

> *None . . . will understand, but those who have insight will understand*

> *(Dan. 12:10).*

In determining the issue of Christ's origin, a cryptic equation reveals his apparent connection to the Gentiles. Paul is addressing the people of Ephesus when he says,

> *Therefore remember, that formerly you, the Gentiles in the flesh, who are called "Uncircumcision" by the so-called "Circumcision" [Jews], which is performed in the flesh by human hands— . . . you who formerly were far off have been brought near by the blood of Christ. For He Himself is our peace, who made both groups into one, and broke down the barrier of the dividing wall, by abolishing in His flesh the enmity, which is the Law of commandments contained in ordinances, that in Himself He might make the two into one new man, thus establishing peace*

> *(Eph. 2:11-15).*

A simplified version of this excerpt runs thus: *the Gentiles in the flesh* are equal (=) to the people of *"Uncircumcision."* By contrast, the Jews *in the flesh* (*performed . . . by human hands*) are equal (=) to the people of *"Circumcision."* But to which of the two groups does Christ belong *in his flesh?* The secret is to be found in Paul's mysterious articulation. If we are told that Christ annulled the Jewish covenant of the Mosaic law *in His flesh,* then this would mean that he is not a Jew by birth. In other words, "by abolishing in His flesh the enmity, which is the [Mosaic] Law of commandments contained in [Judaic] ordinances," scripture concedes cryptically that Christ is a Gentile. Nevertheless, the hostility (*enmity*) of Judaism towards a Gentile Messiah will be resolved when Christ's sacrifice (Eph. 2:16) will unite the two religions, making "both groups into one, . . . thus establishing peace" between Judaism and Christianity!

This is why Jesus tells Paul in a vision to *"get out of Jerusalem quickly, because they [the Jews] will not accept your testimony about Me"* (Acts 22:17-18). Scripture's *"testimony about"* the Messiah is epitomized in Christ's own words to Paul: *"Go! For I will send you far away to the Gentiles"* (Acts 22:21). Paul was recounting these visions to an adamant crowd of Jews (Acts 21:28-22:2), pleading his case after being beaten and arrested (21:32-33). He was accused of bringing "Greeks into the temple," thus having "defiled this holy place" (21:28). Anyhow, everything was going well until Paul mentioned what appeared to be an allusion to the Messiah being sent *"far away to the Gentiles,"* because it is precisely during this statement when a riot broke out and an angry mob tried to kill him:

> And they listened to him up to this statement, and then they raised their voices and said, "Away with such a fellow from the earth, for he should not be allowed to live!"

> *(Acts 22:22)*

But here is the key question. How can the *enmity* of the Jews be explained in any other way? Are they infuriated simply because Paul's mission includes proselytizing the Gentiles? Or is it because of a deeper message that Christ himself knows *"they will not accept"* about him? (Acts 22:18). Paul's type of Christianity was certainly not based on any Mosaic laws and "legalistic" practices to begin with (Acts 21:21), so it is difficult to see how converting non-Jews to Jesus could have affected traditional Jews, let alone inciting them to murder! On the other hand, they most certainly would have wanted to kill Paul if he had blasphemed by claiming that the Messiah *"will [be sent] . . . far away to the Gentiles"* (Acts 22:21). According to *Acts* (variously called the "Acts of the Apostles") 21-22, the latter idea reinforces the likelihood that the concept of a Gentile Messiah must have been the cause which exacerbated the Christian-Jewish tension.

The last point we would like to stress is that the overall conclusions of our study are by no means fictitious. All the claims are substantiated, leaving no room for theoretical invention or speculation. Furthermore, our methodology is not aimed at disproving the Bible but rather at exposing false interpretations and beliefs concerning it. The concepts presented herein may seem radical at first to the uninitiated reader—even extreme, at times—but rest assured that they are based on sound biblical scholarship and should not present many difficulties to the learned scriptural experts other than the fact that they represent an alternative view. Actually, the ideas put forth in this work stem directly from the Bible. By the same token, readers are encouraged to search the scriptural sources so as to make up their own minds without the stipulation that they must trust the conclusions of our book.

We deemed it incumbent upon us to report a historical cover-up pertaining to the postbiblical interpretation of Jesus. These falsehoods have historically shaped our underlying assumptions about Christ, and our study attempts to expose them. If our exposition seems controversial, this is because it is simply reflecting off the genuine mirror of scripture, not because it is founded upon any personal conjecture. Our task has been to remain truthful to the contents of the text so that nothing is taken out of context. Another point worthy of mention is that we cannot take credit for these ideas as they are not our own; they are the property of the Bible. In fact, we are not the only ones who are cognizant of this message; we are simply the first to write about it. The author allows the Bible to interpret itself. Trust is not necessary. You should judge for yourselves.

Paul, according to the wisdom given him, wrote to you, as also in all his letters, speaking in them of these things, in which are some things hard to understand, which the untaught and unstable distort, as they do also the rest of the Scriptures

(2 Pet. 3:15-16).

PART I

The Future Incarnation of Christ

CHAPTER 1

THE FIRST COMING OF JESUS AT THE END OF TIME

Christianity, if false, is of no importance, and if true, of infinite importance. The only thing it cannot be is moderately important.

—*C.S. Lewis*

We will now explore what the scriptural sources have to say in regard to the authentic visitation of Christ. We will present a compilation of evidence that speaks volumes insofar as this advent is concerned. The mysteries which surround it will be fully disclosed. Apparently, the NT authors were strongly influenced by *mysticism*—a personal communion with the Divine Being—and relied heavily on their own visions, and those of others, to write their successive accounts. This may come as a surprise, but the sacred writings confide in us that our salvation in Jesus has been preached *beforehand*. Contrary to popular opinion, the so-called *witnesses* of Christ testified in the *spirit* and in advance:

> *God raised Him up on the third day, and granted that He should become visible, not to all the people, but to witnesses who were chosen beforehand by God*

> *(Acts 10:40-41).*

In stark contrast to what we have been taught, this astonishing passage conveys the explicit idea that Jesus was never seen in public; rather, he was spiritually discerned only by certain prophets who were already handpicked by God. *Paul*, the author of numerous NT letters, explains how Jesus "appeared to Cephas [Peter], then to the twelve" and finally "to more than five hundred brethren [believers] at one time" (1 Cor. 15:5-6). But then he says, "And last of all, as it were to one untimely born, He appeared to me also" (1 Cor. 15:8). In other words, Paul is stating

45

that Christ "was seen by me also, as by one born out of due time" (1 Cor. 15:8, *New King James*). Similar to other eyewitnesses whom he cites earlier, Paul did not behold Christ in the flesh (Gal. 1:15-16) but in a vision (Acts 9:3-7) that delivered him prematurely, so to speak, before the appointed time of salvation. Due to this fact, he refers to himself as "an apostle (not sent from men, nor through the agency of man, but through Jesus Christ, and God the Father) [sic]" (Gal. 1:1).

Quite honestly, if Jesus existed prior to the NT writings, then how could he possibly be "the hope of the gospel that you have heard"? (Col. 1:23). Moreover, there would be no need for the epistles to refer to a "promise in Christ Jesus" (Eph. 3:6). When we take into account what the following NT *Epistle to the Romans* has to say about hope, we realize that it is a yearning for an expected Messiah whose salvation has not been actualized but is rather potentially intertwined with "the hope laid up for you . . . in the word of truth, the gospel" (Col. 1:5):

> For in hope we have been saved, *but hope that is seen is not hope. . . . But if we hope for what we do not see, with perseverance we wait eagerly for it*
>
> (Rom. 8:24-25, emphasis added).

This unseen hope for Christ's redemption is clarified by the selfsame scriptures:

> *Blessed are they who did not see, and yet believed*
>
> (John 20:29).

As Paul so poignantly put it, "Do not grieve the Holy Spirit of God, by whom you were sealed [sanctified] for the day of redemption" (Eph. 4:30).

In the book known as the *Acts of the Apostles*, we encounter another unadulterated confession:

> *Men of Israel, listen to these words: Jesus the Nazarene, a man attested to you by God with miracles and wonders and signs which God performed through Him in your midst, just as you yourselves know—this Man, delivered up by the predetermined plan and foreknowledge of God, you nailed to a cross by the hands of godless men and put Him to death*
>
> (2:22-23).

According to this excerpt, how was Christ "delivered up" and "nailed to a cross by the hands of godless men" who "put Him to death"? The answer is "by the foreknowledge of God"; through a knowledge that existed prior to the actual occurrence of the event! *"Foreknowledge"* presupposes knowing in advance. Undeniably, this is exactly what the text firmly reveals:

> *The gospel of God, which He promised* beforehand *through His prophets in the holy Scriptures, concerning His Son, who was born . . . according to the flesh, who was declared the Son of God with power by the resurrection from the dead, . . . Jesus Christ our Lord*
>
> *(Rom. 1:1-4, emphasis added).*

If we paraphrase the essence of the foregoing quote, it would read as follows: "This is the gospel which God promised in advance through the prophets, and recorded in these scriptures, about his son who would be incarnated and later acknowledged as the powerful son of the Supreme Being owing to his resurrection from the dead, namely, Jesus Christ our Lord." As *Paul*, the author of the foregoing epistle to the Romans, says in another letter, this was "the proclamation with which I was entrusted" to reveal the divine secrets (Tit. 1:3). It seems, then, that the oracles of Christ's forthcoming advent that were promised two millennia ago were committed to the custody of Paul for the purpose of dissemination. It certainly was not Paul's *proclamation* per se but one that had been *entrusted* to him (1 Cor. 15:3-4). The fact that he discloses this information makes this scriptural transmission all the more curious. Most historians believe that some of the Pauline letters predate the writings of the gospels. But we have to underline again that, according to Paul, much of the content in his letters does not represent his own personal message even though he himself later received various revelations (Eph. 3:3, 7). So how did God transmit his as yet unwritten *word* to mankind during those early formative years of Christianity? He most certainly relied on *gifted* men (prophets) through whom he communicated his message (Rom. 12:6, 1 Cor. 12, Eph. 4:11). The gospel of Luke produces a similar theme:

> *Inasmuch as many have taken in hand to set in order a narrative of those things which are most surely believed among us, just as those who from the beginning were eyewitnesses and ministers of the word delivered them to us, it seemed good to me also, having had perfect understanding of all things from the very first, to write to you an orderly account*
>
> *(1:1-3, New King James).*

The reference to "those who from the beginning were eyewitnesses" is tantamount to saying the "witnesses who were chosen beforehand [in advance]" (Acts 10:40-41), namely, the prophets of God. It appears that after having received this prophetic knowledge—"foreknown before the foundation of the world" that Christ would appear at the end of days (1 Pet. 1:20)—each NT author subsequently wrote an "orderly account" for the sake of posterity. Furthermore, the allusion to the "ministers of the word" signifies those invisible angelic beings (Zech. 12:8) who initially transmitted God's plan to the chosen prophets:

> For if the word spoken through angels proved steadfast, . . . how shall
> we escape if we neglect so great a salvation, which at the first began to be
> spoken by the Lord, and was confirmed to us by those who heard Him, God
> also bearing witness both with signs and wonders, with various miracles,
> and gifts [visions] of the Holy Spirit, according to His own will?

> (Heb. 2:2-4, New King James).

That this salvation was first announced by angels is further demonstrated in the words: "Are they not all ministering spirits, sent out to render service for the sake of those who will inherit salvation?" (Heb. 1:14). And this makes perfect sense, for how else would the prophets gain this *inspired knowledge* if it were not for these divine messengers? (cf. 2 Sam. 14:20, Heb. 12:22). The entire book of Revelation is based on just such a divine transmission (Rev. 1:1). These celestial beings were also instrumental in communicating the oracle of Christ's birth to mankind (Luke 1:26-31). Scholars concede that "angels were often used in biblical revelation, especially in the revelation of prophecy" (Fruchtenbaum, 10). In fact, the word *angel* is derived from the Greek term *angelos,* which means "messenger." According to Luke, it was these *ministering spirits* who first "delivered them [these oracles] to us" (Luke 1:2).

Therefore, the scriptural events that testify to Christ's manifestation are devoid of any actual historical significance. These oracles are not bound by the constructs of space and time but by the direct transmission of the divine matrix. Alternately stated, scripture is not portraying the NT authors as if they were contemporary witnesses to the Messiah but rather witnesses to the visions thereof. The criterion for the biblical term *witness* is defined as follows:

> The one who believes in the Son of God has the witness [Holy Spirit]
> in himself; the one who does not believe God has made Him a liar, because
> he has not believed in the witness that God has borne concerning His Son.
> And the witness is this, that God has given us eternal life, and this life is
> in His Son. He who has the Son has the life [Holy Spirit]; he who does not
> have the Son of God does not have the life

> (1 John 5:10-12).

In Christian theology, the Holy Spirit is designated as the *Spirit of the Lord* (Isa. 61:1); the prophet Isaiah insists that this is *the spirit of knowledge* (Isa. 11:2). On these grounds, it appears that the indwelling spirit (Holy Spirit) was the so-called *witness* in the gospel narratives about the life and death of Jesus who then, together with the ministering spirits, imparted this knowledge to Christ's followers: the prophets who would become known as the apostles. Infused with the spirit of prophecy, they set out to document it. The result was the New Testament. Jesus affirms this point when he tells of a divine spirit who transmits the thoughts of God to mankind:

> *But when He, the Spirit of truth, comes, He will guide you into all the truth; for He will not speak on His own initiative, but whatever He hears [from the Father], He will speak; He will disclose to you what is to come [future events].*

> *(John 16:13)*

Thus, having *heard* of the plan of God "from the very first" and having "most surely believed" in the certainty of God's "word," Luke *understood* and set out to write a narrative concerning it. This detailed account implies that he *foreknew* and *believed* all things about Jesus long before Christ's *Advent* (*Parousia* means "presence" or "arrival" in Greek; cf. Matt. 24:3) ever took place. And it is at this point that he undertakes to recount the prophetic story of Jesus, as he understood it, in the gospel of Luke. There is clear indication that Luke gained this *foreknowledge* of Christ through the *ministering spirits* (angels) of God. Evidence of this *foreknowledge*, derived from the *spirit* of prophecy, abounds in the scriptures. One such passage affirms,

> *The Lamb [Jesus] slain from the foundation of the world*

> *(Rev. 13:8, New King James).*

During a discourse on the Lord's Day, Jesus makes a peculiar comment concerning his earthly visitation:

> *But of that day or hour no one knows, not even the angels in heaven, nor the Son, but the Father alone.*

> *(Mark 13:32)*

Some have mistakenly used this verse to argue that we can never know the times and epochs appointed by God. Yet the Bible reminds us that "God does nothing unless He [first] reveals His secret counsel to His servants the prophets" (Amos 3:7). And although many falsely claim that Jesus's advent has already occurred, in view of

Mark 13:32, *"No one [really] knows"* the actual time or *"day"* of his visitation. Observe that even the *"Son"* is not privy to this information. But how can that be? If Jesus is God, how can he not know the day of his manifestation? It certainly sounds like an oxymoron. The reason why this time period is unknown even to Christ himself is that he is on the earth, not in heaven during this momentous event!

We have some remnants of ancient prophecy, which give us a clear sense of how early Christians understood Jesus's incarnation. There is an OT pseudepigraphical text which was once part of a wide tradition that may have held sway over Christianity for the better part of four centuries. The story probably dates back to the fifth century AD, while its author remains unknown. The work is called the *Testament of Solomon*. In one of the most prophetic passages in the book, the future incarnation of Christ is clearly revealed:

> *[And the demon said] we shall lead astray the inhabited world for a long season, until the Son of God is stretched upon the cross.*

> (65)

CHRIST'S SACRIFICE ON THE DAY OF THE LORD

Behind every word of scripture lies a mystery. According to most biblical researchers, the idiom known as *the day of the Lord* (Isa. 13:6-13, Mal. 4:5) invariably refers to the end of the world (Fruchtenbaum, 51). *Zephaniah*, an OT prophet, substantiates this conclusion by means of a profound oracle:

> *The day of the LORD is near, for the LORD has prepared a sacrifice.*

> (*Zeph. 1:7*)

You will come to realize that there is something groundbreaking in this verse. Zephaniah adds that "on the day of the LORD'S sacrifice," God "will punish the princes" and the kings (1:8). The foregoing verse constitutes sufficient proof to indicate that Zephaniah equates *the day of the Lord* with the Lord's sacrifice. It has long been known that Christians associate the Lord's sacrifice with Jesus's crucifixion (Isa. 53:3-5, Luke 23:33). In fact, Zephaniah goes on to exclaim emphatically and unequivocally that *the day of the Lord* refers to the *Day of Judgment*:

> *A day of wrath . . . , a day of trouble and distress, a day of destruction and desolation . . . , darkness and gloom . . . , indeed a terrifying one, of all the inhabitants of the earth.*

> (*1:15-18*)

To our shock and amazement, Zephaniah's impressive oracle clearly indicates that the *Day of Atonement*—representing Christ's *sacrifice* (Zech. 12:10, John 19:34, Rev. 1:7)—and *Judgment Day* are one and the same! In a similar vein, Paul exhorts his inner circle about the approaching *day of the Lord*:

> *For you yourselves know full well that* the day of the Lord *will come just like a thief in the night. While they are saying, "Peace and safety!" then destruction will come upon them suddenly like birth pangs upon a woman with child; and they shall not escape.*

> *(1 Thess. 5:2-3, emphasis added)*

Thus, the explicit language of the Bible substantiates the premise that *the day of the Lord* represents *Judgment Day* (cf. Matt. 24). There's a lot to be said for this terminological connection because it explains why Christian theologians have always referred to the "Last Judgment" as the "Day of the Lord"!

But let us not lose sight of Zephaniah's assertion (1:7) that *"the day of the Lord"* also means the appointed time of God's visitation upon the earth. Here, we are using the word *visitation* loosely, the definition of which includes, but is not limited to, the resurrection and the rapture. So the concept of *"the day of the Lord"* acts as a common denominator between the themes of Christ's forthcoming *"sacrifice"* and *Judgment Day*. Of the thirteen NT epistles attributed to Paul, only one contains some of the most mysterious prophetic verses ever written. Nothing so clearly indicates that "the day of Christ" (Phil. 2:16) is equivalent to "the day of the Lord" (1 Cor. 5:5) as Paul's second letter to the Macedonian Greeks (cf. 1 Cor. 1:8, 2 Cor. 1:14). There he sets about bringing these seemingly disparate ideas together so that "the coming of our Lord" (1 Thess. 5:23) or "the day of Christ" (Phil. 1:10) and "the day of the Lord" (2 Pet. 3:10) become more or less synonymous terms. In this epistle, called *2 Thessalonians*, Paul resoundingly corroborates Zephaniah's message while repudiating claims that *the day of the Lord*, and by implication that "the day of Christ" has come:

> *Now we request you, brethren, with regard to* the coming of our Lord *Jesus Christ, and our gathering together to Him, that you may not be quickly shaken from your composure or be disturbed either by a spirit or a message or a letter as if from us, to the effect that* the day of the Lord *has come. Let no one in any way deceive you, for it will not come unless the apostasy comes first, and the man of lawlessness [antichrist] is revealed, the son of destruction, who opposes and exalts himself above every so-called god or object of worship, so that he takes his seat in the temple of God, displaying himself as being God.*

> *(2:1-4, emphasis added)*

Much to our surprise, Paul admonishes us not to follow any Christian tradition, which claims that *the day of the Lord* has come to pass! Paul adds, "Let no one in any way deceive you," for *the day of the Lord* will not come until the epoch of the antichrist finally arrives. Every biblical expert on the planet knows that the era of the antichrist will approach at the end of all the ages (1 John 2:18, Rev. 20:7-10). According to Paul's message (2 Thess. 2:1-4), we have been deceived into thinking that *the day of the Lord* is a thing of the past. Oddly enough, we are asked to believe that this event occurred approximately two thousand years ago. Could this be the authentic biblical message? You be the judge. The author of the NT epistles of Peter writes,

> *He was marked out [known] before the world was made, and was revealed at the final point of time for your sake.*

> *(1 Pet. 1:20, New Jerusalem Bible)*

Beginning with this verse, we start to get our fair share of explicit revelations about Christ that will soon alter our preconceived mindsets. In the New American Standard Version of the Bible (NASV), which is the primary scriptural source that will be used in this book, we are told that Jesus "has appeared in these last times for the sake of you" (1 Pet. 1:20). In other words, Christ will come to rectify the human condition on our behalf since man's disposition has been tainted by *sin* (cf. John 8:44-47). Scripture defines sin not simply as a particular action but as a state of being (Ps. 51:5). The latter exists in what can accurately be described as the "old self," whom we must dismantle through a new birth (Col. 3:9-11, Rom. 6:5-6). It is akin to what *Karen Horney*, a prominent psychoanalyst, calls the *False Self* (Eph. 4:22-24). Paul writes,

> *For our struggle is not against flesh and blood, but against the rulers, against the powers, against the world forces of this darkness, against the spiritual forces of wickedness in the heavenly places.*

> *(Eph. 6:12).*

Under these circumstances, it is befitting to call sin spiritual.

In any event, the specific era of Christ's manifestation is clearly emphasized by denoting that he "has appeared in these last times" or "at the final point of time" (1 Pet. 1:20, *New Jerusalem Bible*). But this raises another lingering question: if that is true, then why is the author employing past tense to refer to a forthcoming event? As mentioned earlier, in the introduction to this work, the NT authors are using a narrative technique of applying the past tense to events set in the future; we call it the *historical past*. Logic tells us that "the final point of time" represents the end of the world. Yet this event is clearly described in the past tense: "He . . . was revealed at the final point of time" (1 Pet. 1:20, *New Jerusalem Bible*). Only if the sentence conveys the future-in-the-past will the specific time frame for Christ's appearance make any sense. In a passage that deals exclusively with the *great tribulation* of the end-times, we find another future event that is described in the past tense; it reads, "From the tribe of Judah, twelve thousand had been sealed" (Rev. 7:5, *New Jerusalem Bible*).[1]

This is the tense storytellers often use for dramatic effect. Perhaps the biblical authors are using the *historical past* in order to keep this *secret knowledge* hidden until the appointed time of the apocalypse (cf. Pascal 204; John of the Cross 150). The word *apocalypse,* which is synonymous with the term "revelation," is a transliteration of the Greek word *apokalypsis,* meaning to "unveil" or "disclose" secrets and represents "the things [or events] which must shortly take place" (Rev. 1:1) at the end of the last age (1 Cor. 10:11, Rev. 10:7). This helps to explain why the last book of the New Testament is actually called "the Revelation of Jesus Christ" (Rev. 1:1). Because it reveals the previously undisclosed timing of his incarnation during the end of days!

But it is equally feasible that these oracles were often written in the past tense to denote that the narratives themselves represent the inspired utterances of the Deity. To God, who dwells in eternity, all that takes place on earth up until the end of the world is considered to be a past event (cf. Isa. 46:10). This explains why it can be *seen* by God and foretold by his prophets. In essence, it is God who is writing the script, not the scribes. Otherwise, the authors would contradict themselves by using the past tense to refer to the final days of the world. Conversely, if we accept the current theory that Christ appeared two millennia ago, it follows that those were the *last days* coinciding with *the day of the Lord.* But then where was Zephaniah's prophetic *Judgment Day* that was supposed to ensue immediately afterwards? By contrast, all the biblical authors categorically repudiate the notion that *the day of the Lord* has already arrived (Zeph. 1:7, 2 Thess. 2:1-3). They claim that both *the resurrection* (2 Tim. 2:17-18, 1 Cor. 15) and *the Lord's Day* will usher in the end of days "at the final point of time" (1 Pet. 1:20, *New Jerusalem Bible*), during a time period, which is said to be concurrent with the advent of the antichrist (2 Thess. 2:1-4).

In order to pinpoint the exact era of the *Messianic Age,* we must identify both the biblical terms concerning the end of days and the precise events to which they refer. For instance, the idiom known as "the end-times" refers to the specific time period that is associated with "the day of the Lord" (the Final Judgment) when the earth will be in great turmoil (Joel 2:10-11, Mal. 3:1-5). The connection between the so-called *"LAST DAYS"* and the *"DAY OF THE LORD"* is given in Acts 2:17-20; both terms represent a particular age in which *"THE SUN SHALL BE TURNED INTO DARKNESS, AND THE MOON INTO BLOOD."* Obviously, this *"end of the age"* (Matt. 28:20) scenario cannot possibly include pre-Pauline times, or two thousand years of history because (1) it represents a prophecy, (2) it specifically refers to Judgment Day, and (3) these unprecedented earthly events have yet to happen (Fruchtenbaum,

67-68). For example, there are specific verses in the book of Revelation that perfectly describe the sudden impact of a nuclear detonation: "There was a great earthquake; and the sun became black . . . , and the whole moon became like blood; and the stars of the sky fell to the earth," and so on and so forth (6:12-13; cf. Zech. 14:12-13). The next verses tell us that "the sky was split apart . . . ; and every mountain and island were moved out of their places. And the kings of the earth . . . hid themselves in the caves and among the rocks of the mountains," willing to die rather than face "the wrath [judgment] of the Lamb [Jesus]" (Rev. 6:14-16). In other words, *Revelation* conveys that Christ's appearance is concurrent with a nuclear holocaust. And how does this apocalyptic passage end? By showing us how terrible it will be when this "great day" finally arrives: "for the great day . . . has come; and who is able to stand [who can endure it]?" (6:17; cf. Joel 2:11; Mal. 3:2, 4:5).

The *epistle to the Hebrews* describes the exact time of Christ's appearance with unsurpassed clarity and precision:

> But now once at the consummation of the ages He [Christ] has been manifested to put away sin by the sacrifice of Himself. . . . And after this comes judgment

(9:26-27).

What an unbelievable statement; truly unique and extraordinary! It could be considered as an extension of Zephaniah's thought, namely, the idea that the messianic sacrifice will be accomplished on *"the day of the Lord"* (Zeph. 1:7). If we compare both of these passages, we will find that they are not only similar in substance, but also utterly transparent: they leave no room for idle speculation. Specifically, Zephaniah's statement (1:7) is not dissimilar to its counterpart from the epistle to the Hebrews, which exhibits the notion that Christ appears "once," for the first time, to put away sin by sacrificing himself. That much is clear.

The only remaining question pertains to the precise timing of this event. Similar to Zephaniah's proclamation, the answer from the epistle to the Hebrews is both unequivocal and categorical: "at the consummation of the ages"! This exciting passage discloses that the Messiah will be manifested and subsequently slain during the completion of all the ages, which is otherwise known as the end of time. Make no mistake; these verses constitute an important new find not only because they play an integral part in helping us understand the proximate time of his one and only visitation, but also because they undermine everything we thought we knew about Jesus. Insofar as scriptural prophecy is concerned, there is much more unmistakable evidence indicating that Christ has not yet arrived upon the earth:

But now once in the end of the world hath he appeared to put away
sin by the sacrifice [death] of himself

(Heb. 9:26, King James).

This is graphic language! It emphatically spells out not only the precise time frame of Christ's coming, but also the reason for his appearance: "to put away sin by the sacrifice of himself." In fact, the text describes Christ's "end of the world" visitation with such utter clarity and precision that it spawns an eerie resemblance to what is now known as the first coming of Jesus. As various passages begin to converge and coalesce, their clear and unified message begins to emerge. As a result, we can neither ignore nor deny these findings.

In the following verse (Heb. 9:27), we are told that the execution of *judgment* commences immediately after Christ's sacrifice. It is, in effect, an echo of Zephaniah's message which also connects *"the Lord's sacrifice"* with judgment day (Zeph. 1:7-18). They appear to be two facets of one continuous event. According to these prophecies, the first coming, which occurs "once in the end of the world," is then followed by Christ's resurrection; the latter event in and of itself implies the so-called *second coming* or the subsequent implementation of Judgment from above. Evidently, the aforesaid quote from the epistle to the Hebrews (9:26-27) firmly establishes that the two occasions—namely, Christ's death and judgment day—coincide chronologically; it is tantamount to saying that they are sequential and contemporaneous events.

There is compelling evidence to show that "at the consummation of the ages"—during the time period known as *the day of the Lord*—Christ will be manifested to atone for humanity's sins by laying down his own life (Heb. 9:26, Zeph. 1:7). The text also informs us that Jesus's visitation occurs "once and for all" (Heb. 9:26, *New Jerusalem Bible*). The ultimate question that remains to be asked is the following: if conventional wisdom holds that Christ's resurrection has already occurred, then why is it that these prophetic events did not ensue at that time? For instance, where was the "fear and trembling" of God's *judgment?* (Ps. 55:5). For that matter, where was the general resurrection of the dead? (Dan. 12:2; 1 Cor. 15:22-24; Matt. 27:52-53). Perhaps it would be more fruitful to ask whether the people who handed us the faith wittingly or unwittingly indoctrinated us into a misconstrued belief system. In a verse that is as startling as it is shocking, Paul affirms that this is precisely what has happened! Let us see how he describes the religious authorities responsible for the transmission of the articles of faith:

[These] men . . . have gone astray from the truth saying that the
resurrection has already taken place.

(2 Tim. 2:18)

Isaiah, one of the preeminent prophets of the OT, supports the premise regarding the short chronological sequence that exists between the *resurrection* and *judgment day*:

> *Now it will come about that* in the last days . . . *He [the Messiah] will judge between the nations, and will render decisions for many peoples; and they will hammer their swords into plowshares, and their spears into pruning hooks. Nation will not lift up sword against nation, and never again will they learn war. . . . For the LORD of hosts will have a day of reckoning . . . and men will go into caves of the rocks, and into holes of the ground before the terror of the LORD, and before the splendor of His majesty, when He* arises *[from the dead] to make the earth tremble.*

> *(Isa. 2:2-19, emphasis added)*

As can be seen readily, Isaiah's disturbing end-times message is similar to Zephaniah's (1:7, 14-18) and comparable to the theme from the epistle to the Hebrews (9:26-27) in that he insists that God's resurrection is closely followed by *the day of judgment*. The above illustration depicts "men . . . go[ing] into caves," fleeing the all-engulfing terror of God's wrath that is exemplified by *the LORD* who "arises" from the dead "to make the earth tremble." If paraphrased, an abridged version of this passage would read, "In the *last days*, after the resurrection, *Judgment day* ensues." In addition, a more accurate description of this punitive figure is the specter of the fierce son of God (Ps. 2:7-9):

> *Do homage to the Son, lest He become angry, and you perish in the way, for His wrath may soon be kindled. How blessed are all who take refuge in Him!*

> *(Ps. 2:12)*

Therefore, we must come to terms with the notion that a *secret knowledge* exists in the Bible: an untold conundrum, which has not been solved. It constitutes "the mystery which has been hidden from the past ages and generations" (Col. 1:26). Indeed, this is a theme to which Paul constantly reverts. In one passage, he explicates this idea with utter prophetic clarity:

> *We speak God's wisdom in a mystery, the hidden wisdom, which God predestined before the ages to our glory; the wisdom which none of the rulers of this age has understood.*

> *(1 Cor. 2:7-8)*

To put it another way, Paul is saying that the Bible is basically a book of secrets whose prophetic content has been consequently misinterpreted and distorted! As noted earlier in the book of Acts, mention was made of Jesus who was "nailed to a cross" "by the predetermined plan and foreknowledge of God" (2:22-23). Hence, these concurring passages reveal that scripture is essentially a collection of prophecies, not a record of past events. That Christ's first coming is still prophesied across vast expanses of biblical literature is a common theme that runs across the entire NT. A prime example is found in the book of Acts. Using the technique known as the *historical past*, the author of this document writes,

> *I know that you acted in ignorance, just as your rulers did also. But . . . God announced* beforehand *by the mouth of all the prophets, that His Christ should suffer.*

> *(3:17-18, emphasis added)*

Most people assume that this passage is exclusively referring to the OT prophecies. But—much to the dismay of the staunch, old-line Christians—it includes the NT oracles as well. To be sure, there were disciples who alleged to have *witnessed* the resurrection of Jesus (Acts 2:32). But this incident was supposedly linked to other notable simultaneous occurrences. For instance, an immense and "severe earthquake had occurred" during the resurrection (Matt. 28:2, cf. Rev. 6:12-17). The same can also be said for other events: "the tombs were opened; and many bodies of the saints who had fallen asleep were raised" from the dead (Matt. 27:52). This is not the kind of thing that happens every day. And yet, surprisingly, there is no conclusive historical record of these events ever taking place, nor do we expect to find one. In fact, according to the text, there were no eyewitnesses to Christ's resurrection: "For as yet they [the disciples] did not understand the Scripture" (John 20:9). In other words, they did not realize that these events would not occur until thousands of years later.

Subsequent generations had a tendency to take this story literally, as if these events actually took place. But what they failed to understand is that the alleged *witness reports* surrounding these events were not founded upon any strict empirical grounds, but were rather the result of prophetic visions. This brings us to another question. How can we accept a literal interpretation of these so-called *witness reports* if scripture itself attests to Christ's *Passion* (his suffering and death) as being "announced beforehand"? As a result, we can apply the following maxim: first came the gospel, and then came Jesus; not the other way around. Otherwise, scripture would not be involved in prediction proper, but in *postdiction*, predicting after the fact. This explains why Christ was proclaimed to large segments of society "by the predetermined plan and foreknowledge of God" (Acts 2:23). It constitutes the "mystery, the hidden wisdom, which God predestined before the ages" (1 Cor. 2:7).

Therefore, the sacred writings convey the message that all the promises about Christ, as foretold in the gospels, will inevitably be fulfilled at some future time period: *"For the testimony of Jesus is the spirit of prophecy"* (Rev. 19:10).

CHRIST IS REVEALED IN THE LAST DAYS

> *God, after He spoke long ago to the fathers in the prophets in many portions and in many ways, in these last days has spoken to us in His Son, whom He appointed heir of all things, through whom also He made the world.*

> *(Heb. 1:1-2).*

According to this spellbinding oracle, it is fundamentally groundless to attribute this event to ancient times, for God's son speaks to us in the *last days*! In contrast to the perennial teaching of the church, this noteworthy extract makes a conspicuous distinction between past ages and the *last days* of the world. Similarly, there is a mysterious scene in which *Daniel*, an OT seer, is visited by an angel who imparts a profound omen about the former's resurrection during the *last days* of creation. The angel proclaims to him the under mentioned prophecy:

> *You will enter into rest [death] and rise again for your allotted portion at the end of the age.*

> *(Dan. 12:13)*

Whether we refer to this specific time frame as the *last days* or as "the end of the age," these terms always represent the end of the world throughout the Bible (Isa. 2:2; Hos. 3:5; Mic. 4:1; Acts 2:17; Jas. 5:3; 2 Pet. 3:3; Matt. 13:39-40, 49; 24:3; 28:20). In answer to the question regarding the events that will take place during the end of days, Daniel foretells, among other things, the time of Christ's resurrection, but he ascribes to him the allegorical name *Michael*:

> *Now at that time Michael, the great prince who stands guard over the sons of your people, will arise [from the dead]. And there will be a time of distress such as never occurred since there was a nation until that time; . . . and many of those who sleep in the dust of the ground will awake, . . . and those who have insight will shine brightly . . . and knowledge will increase.*

> *(12:1-4, emphasis added).*

Having received this revelation, Daniel is subsequently told by the heavenly angel that "these words are concealed and sealed up [withheld] until the end-time" (Dan. 12:9). Notice also that the time period of Christ's resurrection coincides with *"a time of distress"*; that is, with the approaching Judgment Day. In reiteration of previously stated prophecies, it is during this end-time, "in these last days," that God "has spoken to us in His Son" (Heb. 1:1-2). Another passage continues to restate the same astonishing theme:

> But when the fulness of the time came, God sent forth His Son, born of a woman.

> (Gal. 4:4)

Two critical concepts are simultaneously incorporated and juxtaposed in the foregoing quote: the "Son, born of a woman," and "the fulness of the time." The former idiomatic clause is an integral part of the above passage because it explicitly refers to Christ's incarnation (as *"the Son of Man"*; cf. Matt. 24:27, 44) so that this event is not confused with a Messiah who suddenly appears out of the sky through supernatural means. The latter idiom is equally important in that it refers to the specific timing of Jesus's visitation upon the earth: "the fulness [or completeness] of the time" represents the last age of human existence when all things will come to an end (Eph. 1:10, Acts 3:20-21). A modified version of this idiom can be found in Romans 11:25-27 wherein the mystery of redemption is accomplished in the latter days, during the period called "the fulness of the Gentiles." Therefore the aforesaid quote (Gal. 4:4) offers an undeniable conclusion that Christ will be incarnated at the completion of time, variously known as "the end of the world" (Heb. 9:26, *King James*). This point is symbolically furnished in the gospels:

> Now on the last day, . . . Jesus stood and cried out.

> (John 7:37)

To sum up our findings, we notice that a series of diverse scriptural terms turn out to share a common and consistent theme: the Messiah's sacrifice during the *last days* of human existence. The unique but different terms being used to denote this time period are interchangeable: *the day of the Lord,* which signifies the day of the Lord's sacrifice (Zeph. 1:7), Christ appears in the *last times* (1 Pet. 1:20), *once at the consummation of the ages He has been manifested to put away sin by the sacrifice of Himself* (Heb. 9:26), and finally, Jesus speaks to the world in the *last days* (Heb. 1:2), as he is *born of a woman* at the *fulness* of time or at the completion of the ages (Gal. 4:4, Matt. 13:39). These amazing and clear-cut prophetic signposts about the future incarnation of Christ point to the final days of creation while forming a strong and valid argument that will be most difficult to refute.

Another telling prophecy is brought to bear on the issue of Jesus's visitation that may well force us to rethink our current assumptions. It openly falsifies the theory of Christ's *second coming* from above. After his purported ascension into heaven, two angels make their appearance and instruct humanity not to look to the sky but to the earth in order to find Jesus. The angels proclaim,

> *Men of Galilee [Galilee means circle or earth], why do you stand looking into the sky? This Jesus, who has been taken up from you into heaven, will come in just the same way as you have watched Him go into Heaven.*

> *(Acts 1:11)*

What did the multitude see according to this allegory? First and foremost, they saw Jesus standing on the earth prior to his ascension. Therefore, the angels ask, *"Why do you stand looking into the sky?"* That is to say, why do you anticipate Christ's coming from the heavens? Contrary to all expectations, he *"will come in just the same way as you have watched Him go"*; in other words, as a man! This eye-opening verse illustrates the prophecy that will occur at the end of time: Jesus's resurrection and ascension into heaven.

TWO SIGNS OF CHRIST'S INCARNATION AT THE END OF DAYS

We will now explore the subject of *symbolism* within the Bible. Here are some examples. In an important verse containing the quintessential scriptural mode of messianic representation, Paul references *Adam*, the first human being, and writes that he was "a type of Him [Christ] who was to come" (Rom. 5:14). In other words, Paul cites the creation story of Genesis to justify that Adam was not the Messiah per se (cf. 2 Cor. 5:21), as some mistakenly believe, but a figurative precursor of the one to come. Another interesting analogy to reflect upon is the portable sanctuary that the Israelites carried in the wilderness prior to building their own temple. According to scripture, the "tabernacle . . . is a symbol for the present time" (Heb. 9:8-9); in fact, it is described as "a mere copy of the true one," which is Christ (Heb. 9:24). In like manner, there are strong scriptural indications that *Elijah* prophetically signifies the forthcoming Messiah. In the last book of the Jewish scriptures, virtually the last words of the entire OT are as follows:

> *Behold, I am going to send you Elijah the prophet before the coming of the great and terrible day of the Lord.*

> *(Mal. 4:5)*

This is probably the single most perplexing oracle in the Bible because the only figure who is expected to arrive on earth during *the day of the Lord* is Jesus Christ himself. And he is not only known as a prophet, he is also known as the *Lord* (Rom. 13:14, 1 Cor. 15:57). Let us try to piece together the unfolding prophetic puzzle that eludes us. According to the biblical story of Elijah, we know that this prophet certainly did not exist in the end-times. Legend has it that he lived thousands of years ago. Having said that, you might rightly ask: how can we reconcile the end-times figure named Elijah with the earlier Elijah of the OT who, according to other portions of scripture, flew away into the heavens? (2 Kings 2:1, 11). Could it be that the earlier Elijah narratives, from the *books of Kings*, were prophesying about the time of the end? Since no ordinary human is either qualified or prophesied to accomplish such extraordinary feats, we are left with only one conclusion: the last days' *"Elijah"* can be none other than the foretold God-Messiah! In that event, this oracle regarding Elijah can be viewed as a subtle allegorical sign of Christ's incarnation *"before the coming of the great and terrible day of the Lord."* When recombined with the earlier proof pertaining to Jesus's future incarnation, Elijah's association to the Messiah seems inescapable. Consider how Christ exposes the complex set of metaphors used by scripture:

> *Jesus began to speak to the multitudes about John [the Baptist], . . . [saying,] "For all the prophets and the Law prophesied until John. And if you care to accept it, he himself is Elijah, who was to come. He who has ears to hear, let him hear."*

> *(Matt. 11:7-15)*

A dramatic turn of events takes place when Jesus suddenly announces that John is the fulfillment of the Law and the prophets: *"For all the prophets . . . prophesied until"* the time of *"John."* The implication is that the period of time concerning *John the Baptist* corresponds to the end of the world since that is when all the prophecies will cease and the time of the apocalypse will begin (Dan. 9:24, 12:4, 9). However, according to Matthew 5:17, Jesus alone is the fulfillment of the law and the prophets. So we begin to see prophetic parallels between John and Jesus. At any rate, in Matthew 11:14, Jesus throws another bombshell: John is really Elijah, *"who was to come."* He is, no doubt, citing the aforementioned OT prophecy concerning the arrival of Elijah before Judgment Day (Mal. 4:5).

But what does all this mean? According to scripture itself, who is said to be the true fulfillment of all prophecy? (cf. Matt. 5:17, Luke 4:17-21). And who is expected to arrive *"before the coming of the great and terrible day of the Lord"*? Answer: the Messiah! Thus we receive a lesson in logic. The equation runs as follows: (a) if we know that Elijah represents Christ (Elijah = Christ), and moreover, (b) if we are told that John *"himself is Elijah"* (John = Elijah), then it follows that (c) John signifies Christ (John = Christ). The Bible itself answers this question by declaring that "the people were in a state of expectation and all were wondering in their hearts about John as to whether he might be the Christ" (Luke 3:15). Hence why we find so many biblical similarities between the birth stories of John the Baptist (Luke 1:5-25, 57-80) and Jesus (Luke 1:26-56); even their respective families are presented as if they were relatives (Luke 1:36).

But because of the literal and historical interpretations, which however ill-founded assume a veneer of legitimacy, we are unable to receive this apocalyptic message. This is why prior to disclosing this revelation, Jesus precedes it with a cautious warning: *"If you care to accept it."* It explains why Christ rebukes both Jews and Christians alike, by saying to them, *"[You are] invalidating the word of God by your tradition [religion] which you have handed down"* (Mark 7:13). The only logical conclusion we can draw from this discussion is that Jesus is conveying to us the notion that John, who *"is Elijah,"* is also a symbolic representation of himself (cf. Mark 6:14-16). In fact, according to one account, it appears as though the twelve disciples (practitioners) of Jesus were at one time following John the Baptist (Acts 19:1-7) as the text is arguably suggesting the close affinity between the two figures (cf. Luke 1:13-17, 26-33). It is not a matter of coincidence that Jesus asks his disciples, "Who do people say that I am?" (Mark 8:27). Notice the emphatic scriptural response:

And they told Him, saying, "John the Baptist; and others say Elijah."

(Mark 8:28)

As a rule, scriptural questions and comments typically provide the truth of the matter in hand. In this particular case, the text is indicating that Jesus is indeed prefigured in the aforementioned characters! (See Acts 1:6-7 in which a single question reveals that the epoch of Christ is concurrent with the restoration of Israel).

This type of symbolism is then carried forward into the book of Revelation where we find two "last days" witnesses who prophesy for 1,260 days (Rev. 11:2-13). In the text, God declares, "I will grant *authority* to my two witnesses" (Rev. 11:3, emphasis added). But let us back up for a moment. Was it not Jesus who once said, *"All* authority *has been given to Me in heaven and on earth"*? (Matt. 28:18, cf. Rev. 18:1, emphasis added). Thus, the biblical jargon is suggesting an intimate relationship between these figures and Christ. Returning to our vignette, the two witnesses are also capable of performing astonishing miracles, and just like Moses and Jesus, they even "have power over the waters to turn them into blood, and to smite the earth with every plague, as often as they desire" (Rev. 11:6, 14:19-20, 19:15, Exod. 7:20). At the end of their ministry, they are killed in a "city which mystically is called Sodom and Egypt, where also their Lord was crucified" (Rev. 11:8). So they prophesy in the same place where Jesus lived, and they die in the same city where he died. We think you can guess the rest of the script: "And after . . . three . . . days the breath of life from God came into them, and they stood on their feet [they were resurrected]" (Rev. 11:11). Once again, we find a symbolic prophecy of Christ's visitation in the Bible. The fact that there are two witnesses says more about the timeline of these events than about the number of people involved. This symbolic clue can be found by doubling their allotted time of prophecy (Rev. 11:3). That is to say, the two witnesses represent the twenty-five-hundred-year interim between the rebuilding of the temple and the coming of Christ! (Rev. 11:1-3).

We raise concerns about the traditional tale of Jesus because it has diluted the authentic message of his coming. It is a case where we can apply Marshall McLuhan's iconic expression: *The medium is the message.* In other words, the conventional story of Christ (*the medium*) has actually supplanted the authentic mystery by becoming itself the alleged *message* of the Messiah. But in doing so, it has compromised the scriptural insights, which shed light into the apocalyptic Messiah. For instance, one such gross distortion is that the Bible reveals history, not prophecy (cf. Rev. 1:3). Yet in the book of Revelation, Jesus himself claims that his coming is a matter of scriptural prophecy:

> Behold, I am coming quickly. Blessed is he who heeds the words of the prophecy of this book
>
> (22:7).

The *"book"* reference pertains to the Bible, which has a large collection of prophecies, more so than scholars are willing to acknowledge (Rev. 22:10, 18, 19). In particular, the book of Revelation compiles the highest degree of prophetic end-time events. Here is a case in point:

> And a great sign appeared in heaven: a woman clothed with the sun, and the moon under her feet, and on her head a crown of twelve stars; and she was with child; and she cried out, being in labor and in pain to give birth. . . . And she gave birth to a son [Jesus], a male child, who is to rule all the nations with a rod of iron; and her child was caught up [ascended] to God and to His throne.
>
> (Rev. 12:1-5).

Given that the entire book of Revelation exclusively forecasts prophetic content, there is no reason to assume that the aforesaid oracle is any different. Biblical scholars have not fully appreciated the foregoing prophecy due to the confusion stemming from the two-thousand-year-old Jesus church lore, which has become even more popular of late. Their reasoning is based on the following assumption: if Christ already came, then who is this child in the book of Revelation? Thus they speculate that the aforementioned quote must be referring to the past coming of Jesus. This conclusion, however, is both unsatisfactory and incomplete.

The reference to the first *great sign* (*semeion* in Greek) "seems to refer to a significant person rather than to a significant happening," and "the action John is describing seems to take place on earth" (Morris, 152). In other words, the sign of "a woman clothed with the sun" represents the incarnation of Christ. The "great sign" of this child is then paired with "another sign" of a red dragon (Rev. 12:3-4) to show that they are contemporaneous events. In fact, *the dragon* is later presented as a symbol of the final earthly empire during the *last days* (cf. Rev. 17). If the two occurrences are simultaneous, then the child must of necessity also appear during the end of days. The prophetic imagery embedded in the earlier quote (Rev. 12:1-5) can be deconstructed as follows. The "woman clothed with the sun" signifies Mary, the mother of God (cf. Luke 1:27). The child, of course, is Jesus, prophesied to be incarnated at the time of the end. The "crown of twelve stars" denotes the precise time period in which the Messiah will be born, predicted to occur after the completion of twelve centuries. By the same token, the sign of "the moon under her feet" indicates Christ's victory over the anticipated military forces of the *Moon religion*. This topic will be dealt with in the forthcoming chapters. For the time being, all that is required of us is to understand the chronological connection between the first "great sign" of the messianic incarnation and the "sign" of the red dragon, both of which refer to events that will culminate at the end of days.

On the whole, this prophetic event is set for an appointed time in the future. We can also determine this fact by decoding the biblical terminology which states that the child was "caught up"; that is, ascended to the divine realm. The concept of ascension unquestionably presupposes the prerequisite death and resurrection of Christ. Scripture confides in us that Jesus must first descend into death before he can ascend into heaven (Eph. 4:9-10). Jesus, then, is the modern *Orpheus* who enters the underworld in order to seek the beloved souls of God and retrieve them back to heaven (1 Pet. 3:18-20):

> *WHEN HE ASCENDED ON HIGH, HE LED CAPTIVE A HOST OF CAPTIVES, AND HE GAVE GIFTS TO MEN. (Now this expression, "He ascended," what does it mean except that He also had descended into the lower parts of the earth?) [sic]*
>
> (Eph. 4:8-9)

Our earlier studies certainly validate the content of these omens that portend a messianic visitation in the last days. Insofar as the aforementioned oracle (Rev. 12:1-5) pertains to the future incarnation of Christ, it is inexcusable for scriptural experts not to give it credence or the proper place which it deserves.

THE TIMING OF SALVATION AND THE BREAKING OF THE SEVEN SEALS

Up until now, the evidence has clearly indicated that there is something deeply disturbing about the conventional stereotype of Jesus, which continues to be perpetuated through religious and secular culture. This idea stems from the early postbiblical interpretations themselves, and it has not abated over the course of nearly twenty centuries. There is no question that the text is faulting those responsible for entertaining and disseminating such views (1 Tim. 1:3-4; 2 Thess. 2:1-4; 2 Tim. 2:17-18; 2 Pet. 3:15-16). One such fallacy maintains that Christ has already accomplished his earthly mission and has thus satisfied the promises of scripture. However, as we shall see, Judaism's rejection of this stereotypical Christ-Messiah on the grounds that he did not fulfill the prophecies of the OT may be closer to the truth.

Within a lengthy and cumbersome sentence (NASV), the author of the epistles of Peter reveals the divine plan, namely, that *the day of the Lord* shall come to pass during the *last days* of the cosmos. In order to comprehend the author's excessively long thought and to mitigate the verbose tension that it creates, we will omit certain extraneous elements from this phrase, which will allow us to gather pertinent information in regard to the precise timing of Christ's salvation. We are not editing the sentence, but rather stripping it of its nonessential components. The result is a concrete and straightforward thought:

> *Blessed be God the Father of our Lord Jesus Christ, who in his great mercy has given us a new birth into a living hope . . . through faith until the salvation which has been prepared is revealed at the final point of time*

> *(1 Pet. 1:3-5, New Jerusalem Bible).*

Once more, we present a scriptural passage with such a crystal clear message that we cannot improve on its words. As we hearken to the prophet's utterance ringing down from the past, we can sense that the ripe moment for his message has arrived. We can finally come to an understanding that we have faith in, and hope for, a *salvation,* which will be *revealed at the final point of time!* Moreover, it is generally agreed among scholarly circles that there can be no salvation without Christ shedding his blood (Heb. 9:22; cf. Lev. 17:11). To that extent, the time period concerning the Messiah's *salvation* could not have been more conspicuous.

By comparison, the New American Standard version of the Bible notes that Christ's *salvation* is *ready to be revealed in the last time* (1 Pet. 1:3-5) or in the last age of human civilization. The author of the epistles of Peter then appends his aforementioned thought with a follow-up explanation concerning the scriptural prediction of a future salvation. Bear in mind that the OT prophets never once mentioned Christ by name, except in latent language, whereas this NT author exclusively presents the oracles pertaining to Christ. To that end, we must assume that the subsequent quote refers mainly to the NT prophets. Following the style of Paul, whose prose comprises extraordinarily long sentential structures, the author of the *First Epistle of Peter* writes,

> *You greatly rejoice . . . that the proof of your faith . . . may be found . . .*
> *at the revelation of Jesus Christ; and though you have not seen Him, you*
> *love Him, and though you do not see Him now, but believe in Him, you*
> *greatly rejoice. . . . As to this salvation, the prophets who prophesied of the*
> *grace that would come to you made careful search and inquiry, seeking to*
> *know what person or time the Spirit of Christ within them was indicating*
> *as He predicted the sufferings of Christ and the glories to follow.*

> *(1:6-11).*

This extraordinary extract convincingly demonstrates that we have not yet encountered the historical Jesus. And yet the evidence of our faith will be verified on the day of his revelation. Furthermore, concerning the *time* of Christ's *salvation*, we are told that the prophets sought the assistance of the *Spirit* before accurately documenting this event within the books of the NT. Why would *the prophets who prophesied of the grace* to come, which is Jesus, need to make a *careful search and inquiry* and ask *the Spirit of Christ* that dwelt inside (within) them if they supposedly had a firsthand experience of the Messiah already? Obviously, it is because these prophetic writers never actually met the Messiah in person. What is more, since "the Spirit . . . predicted the sufferings of Christ and the glories to follow," "this salvation"—which is effected "through the resurrection of Jesus Christ from the dead" (1 Pet. 1:3)—is foretold as a future event. Hence, we can properly speak of a *salvation* that has been thoroughly *predicted* by the NT scriptures. Notice the language Paul employs to denote the death of the Messiah:

> *For I delivered to you . . . what I also received, that Christ died for our*
> *sins according to the Scriptures, and that He was buried, and that He was*
> *raised on the third day according to the Scriptures.*

> *(1 Cor. 15:3-4).*

That said, *the sufferings of Christ* (1 Pet. 1:11), as well as his death and resurrection, are *delivered* to us not according to the historical record of eyewitnesses, but according to the scriptural *predictions*. It is also possible that the word "died," in the previous quote (1 Cor. 15:3), may be expressing a conditional statement, which would indicate the likelihood of an imagined situation or event that is devoid of the concepts of past, present and future. Rather than viewing this term as a past participle, its inclusion in the main clause, "Christ died for our sins," could mean that Christ "died" at some unspecified point in history—whether in the past or in the future may not be indicated—which we should accept by faith. Furthermore, Paul admits that he has *delivered to* us the selfsame knowledge that he *also received,* presumably from the early Christian oral and as yet underdeveloped written traditions! Most people assume that Paul is implying that the *scriptures* came after the fact of Jesus's resurrection and ascension. But we shall see that Paul's entire oeuvre indicates the exact opposite, so this is not the meaning he intends to convey. Besides, after all of his alleged spiritual encounters with the risen Christ, why would he resort to a mere repetition of the phrase, *according to the Scriptures?* He certainly received many divine gifts according to his writings (cf. Acts 9, 1 Cor. 13, 2 Cor. 12:1-4). Yet he claims that all he knows about Christ and all that he *delivered* to us are based on the words *according to the Scriptures.* The only way to understand the aforesaid quote (1 Cor. 15:3-4) is if we accept what the Bible itself is telling us, namely, that the prophetic writers of scripture were informed solely by the knowledge they obtained from the Holy Spirit:

> As to this salvation, the prophets who prophesied of the grace that would come to you made careful search and inquiry seeking to know what . . . time the Spirit of Christ within them was indicating as He [the Holy Spirit] predicted the sufferings of Christ and the glories to follow.

> *(1 Pet. 1:10-11, emphasis added).*

Since our main focus is on Christ's future incarnation, we must embark on a study of certain related end-time events. One such paradigm can be found in the *Apocalypse of John,* commonly called the "book of Revelation," where we find *a book . . . sealed up with seven seals,* which has yet to be opened (Rev. 5:1). Teeming with fantastic glimpses of the coming apocalypse, the *seven seals* represent the great signs of the *last days* on earth. The *book* in question appears to hold all the secrets concerning these prophetic events and is itself connected to them. There are a number of references to this mysterious book spanning several chapters (cf. Rev. 5-10). In the book of Revelation, it is cited as "the little book" (10:9-10), hence *the little book* of *revelation* (Rev. 10). More importantly, the unveiling of its mysterious contents is somehow associated with the commencement of *Armageddon,* the last great battle of human history. Here is an example featuring *a strong angel* who puts forth a profound question:

> *Who is worthy to open the book and to break its seals?*

> *(Rev. 5:2)*

An incorrect answer will ultimately lead to an utter misinterpretation of the entire Bible and its oracles. Fortunately, the correct answer is made explicit:

> *The Lion . . . has overcome so as to open the book and its seven seals.*

> (Rev. 5:5)

Notice the phrasing of the previous sentence: *"The Lion . . . has overcome so as to open the book."* In other words, *"the Lion"*—*"the Root of David"* (Rev. 5:5; 22:16)—is Christ, whose victory over death has something to do with the opening of this book of signs (Fruchtenbaum, 117). It will become increasingly clear that the content of the aforesaid quote is a metaphor for the Messiah *initiating* the final events on earth.

After the aforesaid question is proclaimed, we encounter a scene taking place in heaven where *"a Lamb [is] standing, as if slain, having seven horns and seven eyes, . . . sent out into all the earth"* (Rev. 5:6). Implicit in this eerily evocative phrase is the idea of "a resurrected individual" (Fruchtenbaum, 117). The following verse reads:

> *And He [Jesus] came, and He took it [the little book] out of the right hand of Him who sat on the throne.*

> *(Rev. 5:7)*

Pay particular attention to the fine print, as it were: *And He came*, but whence did he come? If Christ was already in heaven, as most people believe, he would have been holding *the little book* in advance. In contradistinction, we are first exposed to the powerful image of a slain lamb that is *sent out into all the earth,* and then we become privy to the information that Christ arrives in heaven in dramatic style to take the little book *"out of the right hand of Him who sat on the throne"* so as to *initiate* the coming apocalypse. The foregoing scriptural imagery is haunting in its directness as it attempts to disclose that Jesus is not in heaven during the *last days* of the world but on the earth as the slain sacrificial Lamb of God (cf. Rev. 13:8). In addition, *the little book,* which he obtains from the Father, anticipates how the final apocalyptic events will eventually unfold once Christ *initiates* or breaks the seven seals (Rev. 6, 8). This scenario fits well within the overall apocalyptic context of the "great sign" in which an expected child was born, devoured (killed), and later "was caught up [ascended] to God and to his throne" (Rev. 12:1-5).

Then Christ "broke one of the seven seals" (Rev. 6:1):

> *Immediately I saw a white horse appear, and its rider was holding a bow; he was given a victor's crown and he went away, to go from victory to victory.*

> *(Rev. 6:2, New Jerusalem Bible).*

The biblical term *victory* is intimately associated with Jesus Christ's resurrection from the dead, which ultimately results in the conquering of death itself (1 Cor. 15:54, 57), while the metaphor of the *bow* represents God's covenant with the human race. The background to the latter symbol can be found in the writings of the OT. In the wake of the great flood, the Deity declares to *Noah*, the apparent savior of the human species:

> *I set My bow in the cloud, and it shall be for a sign of a covenant between Me and the earth.*

> *(Gen. 9:13)*

The New King James version of the Bible translates the word *bow* as *rainbow* (Gen. 9:13). The image of the *rainbow* is closely associated with the biblical story of *Joseph*, a savior type figure who wore "a coat of many colors" (Gen. 37:3, cf. 49:22-24, *King James*). For all intents and purposes, all these stories of God's covenant with the world share many common traits and culminate in the apocalyptic Messiah who is crowned with a rainbow ("bow") upon his head:

> *And I saw another strong angel coming down out of heaven, clothed with a cloud; and the rainbow was upon his head, and his face was like the sun, and his feet like pillars of fire; and he had in his hand a little book which was open.*

> *(Rev. 10:1-2).*

Therefore, the first horseman of the *Apocalypse* (6:2), who is in possession of *a bow* (the covenant), is evidently none other than Christ himself (cf. Rev. 14:14). *Irenaeus*, a second-century theologian, held the same view, namely, that the first rider of the white horse who is depicted as a peacemaker represents Jesus Christ (Mounce, 141). Here is another passage that introduces the prelude to this same event; it represents a deeply unsettling episode in world history:

> *And I saw heaven opened; and behold, a white horse, and He who sat*
> *upon it is called Faithful and True; and in righteousness He judges and*
> *wages war. . . . And He is clothed with a robe dipped in blood; and His*
> *name is called The Word of God.*

> *(Rev. 19:11-13)*

The above phrase—"and behold, a white horse"—is identical to the one used in the book of Revelation chapter 6 and verse 2, concerning the first horseman of the Apocalypse. Just as the latter horseman conquered death, the former horseman (from Rev. 19:11-13) is "dipped in blood," as both scenarios imply that he has been slain. Essentially, Revelation 6:2 and Revelation 19:11 appear to be two sides of the same coin. The composite biblical message indicates that Christ will be the first person to be revealed in the final days of the coming apocalypse. In point of fact, Revelation 19:11 provides more in-depth details into the specifics of Revelation 6:2. This portent is not dissimilar to the sign that depicts Elijah as arriving "before the coming of the great and terrible day of the LORD"! (Mal. 4:5).

The notion that God will be incarnated at the end of the world defies all expectations. Yet it is mysteriously encoded throughout the Bible. For example, why does *Revelation* describe the end-time dissolution of the universe after the breaking of "the sixth seal" (6:12-17) while adding a startling prediction of an ascending Christ? We read,

> *And I saw another angel ascending from the rising of the sun, having*
> *the seal [anointing] of the living God; and he cried out with a loud voice*
> *to the four angels to whom it was granted to harm the earth and the sea,*
> *saying, "Do not harm the earth or the sea or the trees, until we have sealed*
> *the bondservants of our God on their foreheads."*

> *(Rev. 7:2-3)*

The fact that this is Christ, and that he is often depicted as an angel, can be ascertained from the previously mentioned passages (Rev. 7:2-3; 10:1-2). We will produce a list of citations that will provide the backstories to the rich imagery that we encountered in the last few quotes: (cf. Exod. 13:21; Isa. 59:19; Mal. 4:2; Rev. 1:7, 4:3, 12:1). The purpose of this documentation is to show that these imagist idioms have indisputable symbolic ties to Christ. We can gain a better understanding of this connection by weaving together the bulk of scriptural metaphors that define him. For instance, some biblical passages include the following idioms: *the rising of the sun, the sun . . . will rise, a woman clothed with the sun, a rainbow around the throne [of God], HE IS COMING WITH THE CLOUDS, a pillar of fire,* and so on. Sometimes, however, the narrative portrayal of Jesus is far too close to ignore:

I saw another angel coming down from heaven, having great authority, and the earth was illumined with his glory.

(Rev. 18:1)

But a question needs to be addressed at this point: if Jesus died and was raised from the dead two millennia ago, then why is he portrayed in Revelation 19 as if he were slain at the time of the apocalypse? And more than that, how can the image of a slain Christ from ancient times be reconciled with the glorious figure who returns to earth at the end of time? In other words, to what end are these two figures assimilated in the book of Revelation? And how can they be explained? The assertion made by *New York Times* best-selling author *Rod Parsley* epitomizes the prevailing Christian view. This most powerful communicator was once quoted as saying that Jesus's "robe, dipped in blood, was his own blood on the cross of Calvary. He will wear that robe in the end times because he shed his blood in Roman times." There is a certain irony in this description because it employs a mixed metaphor, which represents a pragmatic anomaly, if not a decidedly anachronistic impossibility. Not only does this statement fail to adequately explain *Revelation's* image of a slain end-times Messiah, but it is also deficient in establishing a direct relationship between that image and the so-called Christ figure of ancient times (cf. Rev. 19:11-15). Thus its conclusion makes no sense at all, scriptural or otherwise. It exemplifies the basic discrepancies of Christian Doctrine. And yet many of us believe this groundless assumption as we have been the unfortunate recipients of unscrupulous stories down through the ages.

A REDEMPTION ESTABLISHED IN FAITH PRIOR TO THE COMING OF JESUS

By grace you have been saved, . . . in order that in the ages to come He [God] might show [reveal] the surpassing riches of His grace . . . in Christ Jesus.

—*Eph. 2:5-7*

In legal terms, prophecies and omens are the initial signatures of God, so to speak, on a binding contract: the *New Covenant* (New Testament). They represent the divine oaths that were promised to mankind since ancient times (Heb. 6:16-19), the most important of which is Christ's salvation that was said to arrive at the end of days:

The hope of eternal life, which God, who cannot lie, promised long ages ago, but at the proper time manifested.

(Tit. 1:2-3)

This is the reason why, in the book of Revelation, the angel "swore" by God that the promise of Christ's coming will no longer delay (cf. Hab. 2:2-3). Indeed, it will arrive at the appropriate time (Rev. 10:5-6).

Lest anyone assume that their personal relationship with God is invalidated as a result of this unexpected turn of events, the apostle *Peter* reassures us that the promise of Christ's redemption is meant for all generations to be saved (Acts 2:38-41). And yet, we "have been saved through faith" (Eph. 2:8) alone! That is to say, we are delivered solely through faith in the promise of Christ's death and resurrection because "faith is the assurance of things hoped for, the conviction of things not [yet] seen" (Heb. 11:1). This is precisely why God "put his Spirit in our hearts as a deposit, guaranteeing what is to come" (2 Cor. 1:22, *New International*). Thus we place our trust in this "promise . . . until the redemption" of our souls is actually accomplished (Eph. 1:13-14, *New King James*). In other words, God first sends us the "Holy Spirit of [this] promise" (Eph. 1:13, Luke 24:49, John 14:26) so as to establish our salvation in faith prior to the coming of Jesus! But how can we be sure that Christ will die for us in order to affect our salvation? We are told that everything will go according to plan (as foretold in the Bible), and that the Deity abides by his word (Isa. 40:8):

> *I am God. Even from eternity I am He; and there is none who can deliver out of My hand; I act and who can reverse it?*

> *(Isa. 43:12-13)*

The promise of Christ's future sacrifice is the underpinning of the biblical message in its entirety:

> *God . . . has caused us to be born again to a living hope through the resurrection of Jesus Christ from the dead, as to obtain an inheritance which is . . . protected by the power of God through faith for a salvation ready to be revealed in the last time.*

> *(1 Pet. 1:3-5).*

Once again, the message is clear-cut: we are saved through a promise, a *hope* in Christ's resurrection, and *through faith,* we wait "for a salvation ready to be revealed in the last time" or in the last age (cf. Gal. 5:5). For this reason, scripture encourages us "to wait for what the Father had promised" (Acts 1:4), namely, the coming of the spirit of God (Christ) upon the earth *"IN THE LAST DAYS"* (Acts 2:17-21), specifically during "the day of Pentecost" (Acts 2:1-2). The disciples' reaction to Jesus's words illustrates this point:

And so when they had come together, they were asking Him, saying,
"Lord, is it at this time [of your coming that] You are restoring the kingdom
to Israel [the reestablishment of modern Israel]?" He said to them, "It is not
for you [the public] to know times or epochs which the Father has fixed by
his own authority."

(Acts 1:6-7)

But had Christ not become revealed as a future promise, scripture might never have amounted to anything insofar as prophecy is concerned. To demonstrate this, notice that when the church celebrates the *Eucharist* (also known as "Holy Communion"), it does so as a memorial of this promise (Luke 22:19). Jesus himself calls to our attention that he will not "eat it [partake of it] until it is fulfilled" (Luke 22:16). In other words, the salvific event to which the Eucharist points has not yet been fulfilled, but will be accomplished "at the end of the last age" (Heb. 9:26, *New Jerusalem Bible*). Similarly, Christ says that he will most certainly not drink from the cup of sufferings (John 18:11), so to speak, "until that day when I drink it new [initially] with you" (Matt. 26:29). According to these insights, it becomes fairly easy to decode Jesus's cryptic revelation concerning the time of his coming. He claims, "I am with you always, even [especially] to the end of the age" (Matt. 28:20). This is a dark and esoteric sentence whose meaning can only be deciphered in this fashion: *"I"* will be *"with you"* at *"the end of the age."* All these sayings indicate that Christ had not yet fulfilled these promises at the time when the NT scriptures were composed. This is precisely why Jesus says,

If I tell you [the truth], you will not believe.

(Luke 22:67)

The setting of Christ's story leads to further fundamental misunderstandings. For instance, according to the time and place in which Jesus entered Jerusalem, just prior to his crucifixion, those who saw him supposedly cried out,

BLESSED IS HE WHO COMES IN THE NAME OF THE LORD.

(Matt. 21:9)

Scripturally speaking, his actual crucifixion is somehow related to this earlier event when the multitudes had uttered this very specific saying. It is important to note that this particular idiom is mentioned several times in connection to Christ's crucifixion (Ps. 118:26, Mark 11:9, Luke 13:35, John 12:13). But an intriguing question arises: if this is what took place, historically speaking, then why does Jesus say something entirely different in another verse? He says,

> *For I say to you, from now on [henceforth] you shall not see Me until you say, "BLESSED IS HE WHO COMES IN THE NAME OF THE LORD!"*

(Matt. 23:39)

Two things come into play here. First, if this so-called historical event to which the idiom refers already occurred just prior to Christ's crucifixion, then why is Jesus repeating the idiom as if it represents a prophecy that has not yet happened? Second, why does Jesus say *"From now on"*—that is to say, from the Roman times onward—*"you shall not see Me until you say, 'BLESSED IS HE WHO COMES IN THE NAME OF THE LORD!'"*? The text is clearly suggesting that Christ will not be seen by anyone until a unique age arrives when astonished crowds, gripped with wonder and awe, will appropriately express some such idiom after witnessing "remarkable things" (Luke 5:26). But there is a problem.

We have two apparently conflicting accounts. Either "the literary Jesus" is giving us the correct version in the sense that this event has not yet come to pass, or the aforementioned verse (Matt. 21:9) embedded in the prepassion narrative is representative of the authentic account by giving us a historical record of what took place in Roman times. Either way, these accounts still pose an ostensible incongruity with the presupposed Doctrine of *biblical inerrancy*, which states that scripture is self-consistent and exempt from error insofar as its coherence and textual integrity are concerned. But how can we resolve these seeming contradictions that have introduced so much tension in the text? Once again, Paul comes to our rescue. He warns us to beware of "contrary . . . teachings" because "they deceive the hearts [and minds] of the unsuspecting" folk (Rom. 16:17-18). Paul finally offers us a solution while insisting that his teaching epitomizes the authentic version of the truth "according to the revelation of the mystery which has been kept secret for long ages past" (Rom. 16:25). And what is this untold and unknown secret? It is simply this: Christ is the glory of the Gentiles (Col. 1:26-27), whose incarnation occurs "at the consummation of the ages" (Heb. 9:26). But this need not concern you at this point of the discussion.

This mystery, however, has certain implications; the most important of which is that scripture gives us neither a record of history nor an interpretation of history; rather, it gives us prophetic history! From this viewpoint, there is no contradiction between the aforesaid accounts. In other words, the prepassion narrative—set just prior to Christ's crucifixion—gives us an authentic version of this event (Matt. 21:9). But the other account, in Jesus's own words, puts it in proper chronological perspective; that is to say, "You shall not see Me until," this idiom— *"BLESSED IS HE*

WHO COMES IN THE NAME OF THE LORD!"—is pronounced at some future time (Matt. 23:39). For this reason, there is a cryptic scriptural allusion to the generations who came before and to those that would come after who would repeat and recite the same idiom until the time of its fulfillment:

> *And those who went before, and those who followed after, were crying out, . . . "BLESSED IS HE WHO COMES IN THE NAME OF THE LORD; blessed is the coming kingdom."*

> *(Mark 11:9-10)*

But has the world witnessed and conceded that Jesus *"truly . . . was the Son of God"* (Matt. 27:54) as scripture attests? If we are to be absolutely forthright, we must confess that this has not been the case. Question: is it even possible to say with any degree of certitude that *"the Son of Man"* has come *"in His glory"*? (Matt. 25:31). Of course not! One need only look at the Bible's prophetic timetable to realize that the above verses actually refer to end-time events, which are said to occur *after* the resurrection and ascension of Jesus (cf. Matt. 24:30-31; 1 Cor. 15:23-24; Rev. 7:2). Therefore, *Anno Domini* (AD), the "year of our Lord," has not yet arrived. We are still living in the BC era: "before Christ"!

What it really comes down to is that the church has simply preached "another Jesus, whom" Paul did not preach (2 Cor. 11:4, cf. Gal. 2:2). They were "carried away by their hypocrisy" and "were not straightforward about the truth of the gospel" (Gal. 2:13-14, cf. 1 Tim. 4:1-3). Paul warns, "Let no one in any way deceive you" by misinforming you "that the day of the Lord has come" (2 Thess. 2:2-3). More specifically, "the day of the Lord" refers to the last transitional phase of all creation (Acts 3:20-21), appointed by God (Acts 17:31), in which the Lord Jesus will be revealed (2 Thess. 1:10). How, then, did the church arrive at the idea of Christ's past visitation? They simply turned prophecy into history! Besides the fact that the text paints a richer and much more complex picture than their simple and literal viewpoint could appreciate, they intentionally posited the existence of *Jewish myths* while neglecting the mystery thereof (Tit. 1:14). Paul retorts,

> *Their talk will spread like gangrene; . . . men who have gone astray from the truth saying that the resurrection has already taken place, and thus they upset [confuse] the faith of some.*

> *(2 Tim. 2:17-18)*

Paul's rhetoric verifies that Christ's resurrection has not yet been historically realized. In a concerted effort to get his point across, he says in another verse, "For now our salvation is nearer [to us] than when we first believed" (Rom. 13:11, *New*

King James). Some experts agree, at least insofar as this verse is concerned, that Paul is pointing to an eschatological event; "for this salvation is viewed as future" (Fruchtenbaum, 105-106). Moreover, how can Jesus's resurrection be a past event if scripture prophesies that "the last enemy that will be abolished is death"? (1 Cor. 15:26). This feat can only be accomplished by Christ in the aftermath of his resurrection from the dead. We wish to underscore this point since our tradition has clearly "gone astray from the truth" concerning this awesome and momentous event!

In discussing the vision of Christ's advent, Paul refers to himself as being born way too early insofar as the temporal order of this event is concerned (cf. 1 Chron. 15:13; 1 Cor. 15:23, *King James*). The word used in the original Greek text is *ektroma*, which means a premature birth. He says,

> *Then last of all He [Christ] was seen by me also, as by one born out of due time [prematurely].*

> *(1 Cor. 15:8, New King James)*

To put this in perspective, Paul says that if we have misunderstood the divine message and have mistakenly expected Jesus to arrive during this lifetime, we are the most pitiful among men (1 Cor. 15:19). He raises another hermeneutical issue, that of *scriptural authority*. In other words, who gets to decide what the Bible means? Paul seems to say that we are guided predominantly by *Sola scriptura* ("by scripture alone" in Latin) as he invokes anachronism to attain ironic effect in addressing the so-called experts of his time. By means of the following rebuttal, he implies that they are not to be trusted. That Paul is very outspoken in his opposition to false doctrines can hardly be doubted. He rightly asks, where are the scholars of this epoch? (1 Cor. 1:20). For "we do speak wisdom . . . , a wisdom, however, not of this [current] age, nor of the rulers of this age, . . . but we speak God's wisdom in a mystery [in secret], the hidden wisdom, which God predestined before the ages" (1 Cor. 2:6-7). Who could have thought that Christ, who has been preached for two millennia, would be revealed for the very first time at the end of the world?

CHAPTER 2

THE DIVINE ALCHEMY OF RESURRECTION

*We eagerly wait for a Savior, the Lord Jesus Christ; who will transform
the body of our humble state into conformity with the body of His glory, by
the exertion of the power that He has even to subject all things to Himself.*

—Phil. 3:20-21

There is no clearer example of Christ's future incarnation than Paul's own words of hope and expectation: "We eagerly wait for a Savior." His heightened anticipation of a savior speaks volumes about the precise timing of mankind's salvation. This inspiring passage also articulates how Christ's transmutation of the human form into a celestial entity will take place at a remote point in time. It is prophesied that this feat will be the end result of the Messiah's resurrection from the dead! Scripture outlines the precise end-time sequence of events that ensues following Jesus's foretold demise:

In Christ all shall be made alive. But each in his own order: Christ
[is resurrected first] the first fruits, after that those who are Christ's [are
resurrected] at His coming, then comes the end.

(1 Cor. 15:22-24)

This lucid passage verifies the initial quote (Phil. 3:20-21) which states that Christ shall implement the regenerative process of the elements (Matt. 19:28)—the transformation of all matter—through his personal resurrection from the dead. Consequently, Jesus is said to be *"the first and the last"* (Rev. 22:13) not only because he has "neither beginning of days nor end of life" (Heb. 7:3) in the divine sense but, more importantly, because "He is the beginning, the first-born from the dead" (Col. 1:18), whose resurrection will not occur *until the day of Christ* (Phil. 1:6, 10) arrives. Scripture also tells us that the "perishable body" will be resurrected into a mode of being equivalent to that of imperishability, after which it will be "raised in glory" (1 Cor. 15:42-43). Please note that the above quote (1 Cor. 15:22-24) appropriately employs the future tense "shall" to suggest that this event is in the foreseeable future. For how can this resurrection be a past event if none of the accompanying phenomena have yet to happen? For instance, mortals will evolve into a state of immortality as death itself will be ultimately vanquished (1 Cor. 15:54). Furthermore, notice that this event is then followed by judgment day: "then comes the end" (1 Cor. 15:24-26, cf. Heb. 9:26-27). That is why Paul instructs scriptural interpreters not to err in their judgments by imputing the resurrection of Christ to past ages (2 Tim. 2:17-18).

THE TRANSFORMATION OF THE UNIVERSE

Man is the meeting-point of various stages of Reality.

—Rudolph Eucken, qtd. in Underhill

The prophecies—a book comprising a collection of oracles with the first published edition appearing in 1555 AD—earned its author *Michel de Nostradamus* instant critical acclaim. However, it was to take several centuries before his prophecies would become more relevant and receive the global recognition that they deserved. All Quatrain quotes, unless otherwise noted, are from *The Prophecies of Nostradamus*, compiled by *John Bruno Hare* (hereafter referred to as "The Prophecies"). Here, following, is a brief treatment of one of Nostradamus's messianic prophecies:

> *The Divine Word will give to the substance [will be incarnated],*
> *That which contains heaven and earth, occult gold in the mystic deed:*
> *Body, soul and spirit are all powerful,*
> *Everything is beneath his feet as at the seat of heaven*

(The Man who Saw Tomorrow, *Century 3, Quatrain 2*).

This quatrain is particularly striking as it predicts a historic event: the embodiment of God on earth. The Nostradamus text helps clarify the Bible as it appropriates the *Divine Word*, a well-known term found in the *gospel of John*:

> *In the beginning was the Word, and the Word was with God, and the Word was God.*

(*John 1:1*)

The prophet attests that the Messiah's body "contains heaven and earth." This is a poetic metaphor used to express the notion that underneath the hazy aura of the human form, Jesus possesses a divine nature. By comparison, scripture writes that in Christ "all the fullness of Deity dwells in bodily form" (Col. 2:9). Nostradamus's phrase "occult gold in the mystic deed" complements Paul's earlier account of a mystical transmutation that will result from Jesus's resurrection, which will not only reconcile the diametrically opposed forces within man (Eph. 2:15-16), but will ultimately abolish death itself (Rev. 20:14). It is nothing less than a *divine alchemy*: the transformation of physical matter into a splendor of eternal spirit and energy (Phil. 3:20-21):

> *But when this perishable [body] will have put on the imperishable, and this mortal will have put on immortality, then will come about the saying that is written, "DEATH IS SWALLOWED UP in victory."*

(1 Cor. 15:54)

Since ancient times, God has foretold that the end of human history will comprise "the period of restoration of all things" (Acts 3:21). *Haggai*, one of the so-called *minor* prophets of the Hebrew Bible, attests,

> *For Yahweh Sabaoth [God] says this: "A little while now, and I shall shake the heavens and the earth, the sea and the dry land."*

(2:6, New Jerusalem Bible)

This constitutes a divine declaration that the universe will soon come to an end:

YET ONCE MORE I WILL SHAKE NOT ONLY THE EARTH, BUT ALSO THE HEAVEN.

(Heb. 12:26)

The scriptural explanation for this apocalyptic end has to do with God seeking to eliminate the impermanent from the eternal nature of things (Heb. 12:27). This final period of world history marks the end of all finite dimensions and the beginning of infinity. Since the Deity promises to end it all "YET ONCE MORE," this laconic phrase implies that the universe must have been destroyed at least once before! Moreover, the *many-worlds interpretation* of quantum mechanics—an idea popularized by the 1986 book *On the Plurality of Worlds*—finds an interesting parallel in the story of creation described in the *book of Hebrews*:

> *GOD, who at various times and in different ways spoke in time past to*
> *the fathers by the prophets, has in these last days spoken to us by His Son,*
> *whom He has appointed heir of all things, through whom also He made*
> *the worlds*

> *(1:1-2, New King James, emphasis added).*

In answering the astrophysicists' age-old question of whether the universe will end with a bang or with a whimper, the divine architect replies,

> *The heavens will pass away with a roar and the elements will be*
> *destroyed with intense heat, and the earth and its works will be burned*
> *up.*

> *(2 Pet. 3:10)*

Evidently, the universe will end with a bang! Even so, the demiurge informs us that shortly thereafter, a new universe will emerge (2 Pet. 3:13). After the great conflagration, there will ultimately be a *"restoration of all things"* (Acts 3:21; cf. Matt. 19:28). In this regard, *John of Patmos*, credited with being the author of the book of Revelation, beholds a vision:

> *And I saw a new heaven and a new earth; for the first heaven and the*
> *first earth passed away, and there is no longer any sea.*

> *(Rev. 21:1)*

The end of days will reveal the greatest mystery of all time, incomparable in terms of depth and scope. The approaching transformation of all matter is initiated at the micro level by a unique metamorphosis of the *One*, Jesus Christ, through his personal resurrection![1] In other words, his divine power to overcome death will first activate the process of transfiguring matter within Christ himself. The God man will then be capable of altering all of reality and existence. Strange, yes; impossible, no! Thus, paradoxically, we hold to the teachings of scripture, which offer an otherworldly explanation for the transformation of the universe: an almost surreal account that bears little resemblance to the world we know.

Jesus says, "And I, if I be lifted up from the earth, will draw all men to Myself" (John 12:32). That we would "be [or become] like Him" and see the divine Christ "just as He is" was certainly prophesied by *John the Evangelist* a long time ago (1 John 3:2). But the final disclosure of the supreme mysteries of God is seldom referenced by contemporary thinkers:

THINGS WHICH EYE HAS NOT SEEN AND EAR HAS NOT HEARD, AND which HAVE NOT ENTERED THE HEART [spirit] OF MAN, ALL THAT GOD HAS PREPARED FOR THOSE WHO LOVE HIM. For to us God revealed them through the Spirit; for the Spirit searches all things, even the depths of God.

(1 Cor. 2:9-10).

CHRIST'S RESURRECTION IS FOLLOWED BY JUDGMENT DAY

There is nothing covered that will not be revealed, and hidden that will not be known.

—Matt. 10:26.

The proof of Jesus's future incarnation, death, and resurrection is furnished in one simple sentence, which might otherwise be ignored if it were not for its inspired and unfailing certainty:

Men will go into caves of the rocks, and into holes of the ground before the terror of the LORD, and before the splendor of His majesty, when He arises to make the earth tremble.

(Isa. 2:19)

In this verse, the term *arises* refers to a resurrection from the dead. Here is a case in point:

For this reason it [scripture] says, "Awake, sleeper, and arise from the dead, and Christ will shine on you."

(Eph. 5:14)

Needless to say, in order to be dead, one must have lived a human life. Moreover, Isaiah's quote (2:19) garnishes the Messiah's resurrection with further apocalyptic details to show that it is closely followed by judgment day. But here is the question we need to ask: was such an event even possible during the time of antiquity? Definitely not! If Isaiah's prophecy is referring to "the last days" (Isa. 2:2, 12) of the world when *the Lord* will arise from the dead "to make the earth tremble," then we must concede that this event has not yet occurred in human history. In fact, Isaiah equates the time frame of the resurrection with that of Judgment day: "The LORD *arises* [from the dead] to contend, and stands to *judge* the people. The LORD enters into *judgment* with . . . His people" (3:13-14, emphasis added). After all, according to Paul's second letter to Timothy, resurrection must be an event that will transpire at the end of time (2:18).

Jesus has numerous names in the Bible; he is called "Prince of Peace" (Isa. 9:6), "Immanuel" (Matt. 1:23), "the Word of God" (Rev. 19:13), "the bright morning star" (Rev. 22:16), and so on. *Daniel* the prophet receives an oracle from an angel (Dan. 10:18) who seems to depict the Messiah as a "great prince" named "Michael":

> *Now at that time Michael, the great prince who stands guard over the*
> *sons of your people, will arise [from the dead]. And there will be a time of*
> *distress such as never occurred since there was a nation until that time.*

> *(12:1)*

As enduring as these oracles are, it is helpful to remember that they are consigned to "the end of time" without exception (Dan. 12:4, 9). Moreover, the aforementioned quote (Dan. 12:1) reveals that prophecy has the capacity to predict coming events. That which it foresees is nothing less than Christ's resurrection followed by a series of great calamities that befall the earth. Ultimately, we will all be caught in the middle of this turmoil. However, according to the scriptures themselves, Christ's startling resurrection has not transpired historically, but is brought to light only *through the gospel*:

> *According to the promise of life . . . which was granted us . . . from all*
> *eternity, but now has been revealed by the appearing of our Savior Christ*
> *Jesus, who abolished death, and brought life and immortality to light*
> *through the gospel, . . . I am not ashamed; for I know whom I have believed*
> *and I am convinced that He is able to guard what I have entrusted to Him*
> *until that day.*

> *(2 Tim. 1:1-12)*

Paul, the author of this *second epistle to Timothy*, composed using long and typically involved sentential structures. In the above segment, we have omitted certain parts that appear to have little consequence so that we can begin to glean the information pertinent to its inner core. This methodology does not alter the text; it simply clarifies it. To our amazement, Paul mentions emphatically that the ubiquitous biblical *promise of life* is Christ himself; for he says, "The promise . . . has now been revealed by the appearance of our Savior." He goes on to say that this salvation was *granted* to *us from all eternity*, which means that the promise of redemption was offered to us prior to its actual accomplishment. Yet Paul concludes that he is *not ashamed* since he is deeply *convinced* that Christ will not fail him, meaning that he will *guard* (or protect) Paul's salvation *until that day* when he will surely establish it. As far as the story is concerned, notice that *Jesus, who abolished death and brought life and immortality to light,* brought this about only *through the gospel,* owing to its vast array of oracles and predictions. This means that Christ's advent is not a past historical event, but one that has now been disclosed "through the gospel." Therefore, it is fair to say that Christ's legend precedes him. Christ's salvation has not yet materialized except insofar as it has been heralded *according to the Scriptures.* All too often, however, the Bible's dire warnings went unheeded:

> *And if anyone takes away from the words of the book of this prophecy,*
> *God shall take away his part from the tree of Life and from the holy city,*
> *which are written in this book.*

> (Rev. 22:19)

There is no question that prophecies predict forthcoming events. An angel tells Daniel,

> *I have come to give you an understanding of what will happen to your*
> *people in the latter days, for the vision pertains to the days yet future.*

> (10:14)

If this is not an oracle concerning the prediction of a *"future"* event, then nothing is. Our research indicates that there is no shortage of such forecasts within scripture. In fact, there are multiple prophetic references pertaining to the *last days* or the *last hour* of time (cf. 2 Pet. 3:3, 1 John 2:18). Jesus himself exclaims,

> *I am coming quickly. Blessed is he who heeds the words of the prophecy*
> *of this book.*

> (Rev. 22:7)

Any one acquainted with the Bible will confirm that it incorporates prophetic content. For instance, we are told that "the testimony of Jesus is the spirit of prophecy" (Rev. 19:10). To be sure, Christ uses the concept of *prophecy* in no uncertain terms, which is why scripture emphatically says,

> *Do not despise prophetic utterances.*

> (1 Thess. 5:20)

However, there are certain long-standing religious institutions, most notably the *church of Peter*, who refute the prophetic conditions set by God, thus diluting the biblical message. But their criticism of prophecy has a religious axe to grind. Historical records indicate that the church of Peter persecuted, and in some cases killed, anyone who spoke about prophecies, whether biblical or otherwise. Punishment was brought to bear on all who dared to defy their public edicts and decrees. The reason for their divisive suppression of *prophecy* is that they have always been privy to a number of oracles that are evidently casting an aspersion on them. For instance, one such prophecy is contained within a brief descriptive account of the *"QUEEN"* called *"BABYLON THE GREAT"* (Rev. 17-19). The aforesaid biblical vignette conforms to this church's history to an astonishing degree (cf. Matt. 7:22-23, Judg. 2:17).

In contradistinction to the words of Jesus, the official position of the church of Peter is based on the pretext that the meaning of prophecy refers only to the people of that age (2000 years ago) and does not reflect any future predictions. They espouse the commonly called *Preterist* viewpoint, which holds that biblical prophecies represent incidents that have already been fulfilled at the close of the first century. How convenient! But if all Bible prophecy has been fulfilled, then it is of no use to us at all. For one reason or another, all the prophetic biblical documents are negated while the book of Revelation is entirely disregarded as nothing more than a historical composition of its time. Good grief. What an absurd and outlandish conclusion; it flatly contradicts scripture. Therefore it should be considered as a heretical view!

THE POSTRESURRECTED JESUS AND
THE FIERCE WRATH OF GOD

> *In the beginning was the Word, and the Word was with God, and the Word was God. He [Christ] was in the beginning with God. All things came into being by Him, and apart from Him nothing came into being that has come into being. . . . There was the true light which, coming into the world, enlightens every man. He was in the world, and the world was made through Him, and the world did not know Him.*

> —*John 1:1-10*

Through a sudden breakthrough, a spiritual vision envelops the gospel writer *John* who encounters the surpassing radiance of the divine. Rapt in this ecstatic experience of *Dasein*—Heidegger's existential sense of *being*—John exceeds the Platonic *Forms* of the *Intelligible Realm* and invokes the enchanted reciprocation of the deity. Entranced in a fleeting moment of transparent lucidity, John beholds Christ's preeminent nature! This mystical vision would certainly explain the seer's ethos, describing Jesus as "the true light" (John 1:9-10) of the world. Likewise, *Nahum*, an OT seer, records the following premonitory vision:

> *The sun rises and they flee.*

> *(3:17)*

His thought is as lengthy as his remark is brief. The apocalyptic ramifications of this sentence are immense, even if not immediately discernible. The picture Nahum paints evokes certain messianic images, especially that of a "woman clothed with the sun" (Rev. 12:1) who actually gives "birth to a son" (Rev. 12:5), and the like. We are immediately reminded of the prophecy that "the sun of righteousness will rise with healing in its wings" (Mal. 4:2). Thus there's a good reason why the term *sun* is substituted for the word *son* (of God) in the book of Nahum because the former term appears in other portions of scripture as a highly charged messianic theme that builds on the analogy of Christ's radiant countenance whose "face was like the sun" (Matt. 17:2; Rev. 1:16, 10:1).

Like so many prophets before him, Nahum indicates that *the sun* will rise. You may recall that the term *rise*—especially in the context of an end-time scenario—invariably refers to the concept of being raised from the dead. In fact, in one verse, God declares, *"Now I will rise, . . . Now I will be exalted, Now I will lift Myself up"* (Isa. 33:10, *New King James*). This is traditionally viewed as a sign of his divine resurrection and ascension into the heavenly realm. In the larger scheme of things, this event will then trigger the general resurrection of the dead (cf. Matt. 27:50-54). At this point, however, Nahum adds a literary twist; a turning point which tips the scales toward the possibility of a future messianic incarnation. The prophet interpolates a non sequitur: "and they flee." Presumably, the prophet is referring to humanity as a whole. But why would people flee in the aftermath of Christ's resurrection? Crowds usually flee a situation that is fraught with danger. According to the scriptural account, this event is no different:

> *The LORD will go forth like a warrior, . . . like a man of war. He will utter a shout, yes, He will raise a war cry.*

> *(Isa. 42:13)*

These developments represent the inception of God's administration of *Judgment*.

> *From His mouth comes a sharp sword, so that with it He may smite*
> *the nations; . . . and He treads the wine press of the fierce wrath of God,*
> *the Almighty.*

> *(Rev. 19:15)*

From these images we get the impression that mankind is on a collision course with God: a confrontation with doomsday. The foreboding tone of these passages grips the reader and carries him through a series of horrors that are about to descend upon the earth. *Zechariah*, an OT augur, also warns of a coming apocalypse:

> *You will flee just as you fled before the earthquake. . . . Then the*
> *LORD, my God, will come, and all the holy ones with Him! . . . For it will*
> *be a unique day.*

> *(14:5-7)*

Notice the relationship between this passage and the following one from the book of Revelation:

> *His [Christ's] name is called The Word of God. And the armies which*
> *are in heaven, clothed in fine linen, white and clean, were following Him*
> *on white horses.*

> *(19:13-14)*

Consider how the images of *holy ones* on *white horses* turn up time and time again in the text to convey their association with Christ and with divinity (cf. Rev. 6:2). But more importantly, these images represent the prelude to the coming apocalypse. *Malachi*, an OT prophet, manages in his book to voice the Bible's main concern for humanity:

> *But who can endure the day of His coming? And who can stand*
> *when He [the Messiah] appears? . . . Then I [God] will draw near to you*
> *for judgment.*

> *(3:2-5)*

Nahum's prognostication tells us that when "the sun rises" from the dead, the unsaved will quickly "flee" his wrath (3:17). Therefore, it clearly shows that Jesus's resurrection is intimately connected with Judgment Day! (cf. Isa. 2:21, Dan. 12:1). *Joel*, an unsung hero of the OT prophets, similarly declares,

*The Day of the LORD is coming; surely it is near, a day of darkness
and gloom, . . . there has never been anything like it, nor will there be again
after it; . . . the earth quakes, the heavens tremble, the sun and the moon
grow dark, and the stars lose their brightness. . . . The day of the LORD is
indeed great and very awesome, and who can endure it?*

(2:1-11)

Tradition paints the serene picture of a gentle Jesus who came to earth, died,
was resurrected, and then quietly went away, never to be seen or heard from
again. This is a far cry from the truth! In fact, there is nothing quiet about Jesus's
coming. A close reading of the text indicates that Christ's one and only coming is
contemporaneous with a great world war (Matt. 24:7-8, Rev. 12:5-7, Dan. 12:1) that
is immediately followed by *Judgment day* (Matt. 24:21, 31; Heb. 9:26-27); something
that did not occur during his purported advent two millennia ago. And if the
so-called "first coming" of Christ has accomplished anything throughout the
centuries, whatever else it might be, it is certainly not our salvation. We devised
the myth of the historical Jesus "because we did not consult Him [God] about the
proper [temporal] order" (1 Chron. 15:13, *New King James*) of this event. Why
else would "we eagerly wait for a Savior" (Phil. 3:20) if the Messiah already came?
These oracles indicate why we can no longer accept the watered down version of
Jesus, which tradition has handed us.

CHAPTER 3

ISRAEL: THE PREEMINENT SIGN OF THE COMING APOCALYPSE

There is an enormous amount of preliminary information we wish to impart concerning the sequence of end-time events, so we will state it as concisely as possible. In order to show that the "great sign" of "a woman clothed with the sun" is a future event, scripture presents a secondary sign, inserted in-between the continuing descriptions of the first sign:

> *And another sign appeared in heaven: and behold, a great red dragon having seven heads and ten horns, and on his heads were seven diadems. And his tail swept away a third of the stars [angels] of heaven, and threw them to the earth. And the dragon stood before the woman who was about to give birth, so that when she gave birth he might devour [kill] her child.*

> *(Rev. 12:3-4)*

The meaning of the *dragon having seven heads and ten horns* is elucidated in another passage where we learn that the *seven heads* actually represent seven succeeding empires:

> *They are seven kings; five have fallen, one is, the other has not yet come; and when he comes, he must remain a little while. . . . And the ten horns which you saw are ten kings, who have not yet received a kingdom.*

> *(Rev. 17:10-12)*

The widely accepted theory among biblical scholars is that the seventh empire, represented by the kingdom that "has not yet come," is Russia (cf. Ezek. 38), which supplanted the mighty Roman Empire by calling itself the *Third Rome*. Its coat of arms still bears the *double-headed eagle* of the Byzantine Empire while its leaders were once bestowed the title of *tsar,* which translated literally reads, *Caesar.* Scripture also discloses that ten leaders will emerge from this empire (Rev. 17:12-14)—presumably starting from the time period when communism began—and so we get the *red dragon having seven heads and ten horns,* which attempts to kill Jesus as soon as he is born (Rev. 12:4). This would be the atheist empire of *"the Nicolaitans"* (Rev. 2:6, 15) that began when its founder *Nikolai Lenin* led a revolution in 1917. In essence, the Bible is attempting to throw some light on the specific succession of empires that culminate in the final empire of the *red dragon having seven heads and ten horns.* Thus it denotes that the omen of the *woman clothed with the sun* is indeed contemporaneous with the sign of the *great red dragon.*

Obviously, this Russian Empire did not exist two thousand years ago, during the supposed lifetime of Christ. The recorded empire of that time was the Roman. By inserting this future empire into the aforementioned quote (Rev. 12:3-4) and displaying its coincidence with the messianic birth sign, the book of Revelation is clearly trying to establish that Christ's future incarnation is concurrent with this seventh kingdom of ten kings. Within the text itself, the sign of the woman who gives birth to Christ and the omen of the dragon appear to converge. Specifically, the woman is about to give birth, and all of a sudden there is an editorial montage, as it were: a menacing red dragon unexpectedly appears. After veering off the subject, the text returns to the birth narrative, and again the dragon gives chase after the woman, and so forth (Rev. 12). Given that they are simultaneously juxtaposed, the reader's impression is that the two signs are intrinsically connected: they are contemporaneous!

According to Revelation 12, the woman wore an emblematic crown with twelve stars. The "crown of twelve stars" represents Jesus's birth after twelve successive centuries have run their course. But when is the starting point of this prophecy? We can ascertain the answer to this question if we can determine the particular epoch during which the twelve centuries will expire. There is a plethora of biblical oracles that clearly point to one significant event, which will usher in the end-times. It comprises the return of the Jewish people to their homeland after being dispersed among the nations for nearly two thousand years (Ezek. 38:8, cf. Dan. 9:25). This momentous event occurred in 1948: the reestablishment of the State of Israel! It represents the fulfillment of one of the most accurate prophecies in all of scripture.

THE BIRTH OF THE MESSIAH
AFTER TWELVE CENTURIES OF PERSECUTION

> *When the Mahammedans will distress the people of Kashmeer [this prophecy was fulfilled in 1948], a son will be born in the house of Bishen Dutt Brahman. He will be an incarnation of Deity and shall be called "Kulgee Awtar."* . . . *At that time* . . . *the Kuliyuga [the last age] will pass*

away. . . . I have revealed this secret about the future, whoever will read or
hear it, will come to me.

—Sakhee 15th, qtd. in Singh 38-39

The woman who wore the *crown of twelve stars* (Rev. 12:1) is said to flee from persecution *for one thousand two hundred and sixty days* (Rev. 12:6). Elsewhere, the Bible uses a different phrase to indicate 1,260 days: "a time and times and half a time" (Rev. 12:14, Dan. 12:7). This time frame is described in the book of Revelation:

And when the dragon saw that he was thrown down to the earth [was
incarnated], he persecuted the woman who gave birth to the male child.
And the two wings of the great eagle were given to the woman, in order that
she might fly into the wilderness to her place, where she was nourished for a
time and times and half a time, from the presence of the serpent.

(12:13-14)

The concept of the 1,260 days has a double meaning: it can depict either actual days or solar years to account for various prophetic time intervals. There is a hermeneutical method applied to biblical prophecy aptly known as the *Day-year principle*. The way it works is that we can substitute actual years in place of days when carrying out calculations (cf. Ezek. 4:5). Isaac Newton, a learned theologian and one of the founders of modern science, also realized that the 1,260 days must be converted to years in this particular context (*Portsmouth Papers*). As we allow the Bible to interpret itself, it indicates that the *crown of twelve stars* represents 1,260 years or twelve centuries. That is to say, *Mary*, the mother of God, gives birth to the Messiah after twelve centuries of persecution! (cf. Rev. 11:3).

But twelve centuries from when, you might ask? If you deduct 1,260 years from 1948, you will arrive at the year 688 of the Common Era. This date represents the outset of the twelve-century time interval:

But as at that time he who was born according to the flesh [Ishmael]
persecuted him who was born according to the Spirit [Isaac], so it is now
also.

(Gal. 4:29).

It is a historical fact that from approximately 688 AD onward, Judaism and Christianity began to face persecution from the Moon religion, intensifying into the crusades of the Middle Ages and beyond. Paul, the author of the aforesaid *epistle to the Galatians*, writes that just as it was then, "so it is now also" to indicate that he is referring to the end of time. For most of the biblical prophecies address events that will be taking place during *the day of the Lord*. In other words, the birth of the Messiah signifies that God will eventually put an end to the persecution of Christians and Jews: the believers. This does not mean that Christ is born in 1948. But scripture does suggest that he is born sometime thereafter. Hence, the rebirth of Israel represents, to use a popular phrase, the prophetic clock that started ticking on 14 May 1948 and which continues to wind down to zero so as to proclaim the appointed time of *the Lord's Day* (Rev. 1:10).

THE SEVENTY-WEEK PROPHECY OF DANIEL

The rebirth of Israel marks a turning point in apocalyptic expectations, and Christ's message concerning end-time events seems to point toward this 1948 prophetic countdown:

> *Truly I say to you, this generation will not pass away until all these things take place.*

(Matt. 24:34)

But what on earth does he mean by this? In order to comprehend this terse remark, we must inquire into the standard time limit of a biblical generation. The book of *Psalms* makes known that a generation is equal to seventy actual years (90:10). Similarly, a noteworthy Hebrew soothsayer named *Jeremiah* exclaims that the deity will intervene in earthly affairs after a seventy-year period has elapsed (25:12). *Daniel*, one of the most prominent seers of the Jewish scriptures, also claims that the deity has appointed a portent which consists of a seventy-week interval until the conclusion of all things is finalized (9:24). Among scholarly circles, this prophecy is known as *the seventy weeks of Daniel*.

What follows is a more detailed examination and comparison between the prophecy of Jeremiah and the vision of Daniel. Although the term *week* typically implies seven years (Gen. 29:27-28, Lev. 25:8), in this particular context, the seventy *weeks* oracle does not refer to a seventy times seven (70 x 7) calculation, but rather to a time period which comprises seventy solar years (Dan. 9:2). The proof is found in a revered text called the *book of Daniel*. In a vision, "the man [named] Gabriel" appears before Daniel to grant him "insight with understanding" (9:21-22). The angelic man imparts a cryptic scriptural clue which, in effect, equates the *seventy weeks* of Daniel with the *seventy-year* oracle revealed to Jeremiah (Jer. 29:10). This is why Gabriel hints that the divine *message* was already issued at the time when Daniel first started to inquire about Jeremiah's oracle with prayers and supplications. He says to Daniel,

At the beginning of your supplications the command was [already] issued.

(Dan. 9:23)

Daniel's invocations were made for the purpose of asking God to help him in deciphering the vision revealed to Jeremiah, an earlier prophet:

I, Daniel, observed in the books the number of the years which was revealed as the word of the LORD to Jeremiah the prophet for the completion of the desolations of Jerusalem, namely, seventy years.

(Dan. 9:2)

Gabriel is basically showing us that the seventy years of Jeremiah's prophecy must continue to be calculated as *years* within Daniel's seventy weeks' oracle. Clearly, more specific details are ultimately furnished by Daniel's seventy-week vision, but the reason why Jeremiah's seventy *years* are now termed as *weeks* is for the purpose of allowing us to perform calculations using *weeks* as the standard of measuring time in addition to using actual *years*. Taken together, both prophecies refer to an actual seventy-year period whose completion will signal the end of the world (Dan. 9:24). But the details at the micro level entail calculations, which combine measurements in both *weeks* and *years*.

This seventy-year time line also points to Christ's incarnation because after its completion God himself vows to walk the earth. Jeremiah prophesies, *"For thus says the LORD, 'When seventy years have been completed . . . , I will visit you and fulfill My good word to you'"* (29:10). This implies that somewhere toward the end of this lengthy time interval, the Messiah will appear and intervene in human affairs (Dan. 9:25). The terminology of Daniel's prophecy suggests that we must use both *weeks* and actual *years* in calculating the Messiah's advent within the overall context of the seventy-year time period. We should also note that these oracles are not referring exclusively to *Jerusalem* (Israel), but to *"all the nations"* of the world (Jer. 25:13). Many experts have erred in their interpretations by either attributing the starting date of these prophecies to the period of time when the Jews returned to Palestine from their *Babylonian captivity*—sometime between roughly 538 and 536 BC—or by separating them (Jeremiah's seventy years and Daniel's seventy weeks) as if they are two mutually exclusive oracles that employ different calculation techniques.

At any rate, if we resume our discussion of Christ's prophecy (Matt. 24:34)—as mentioned earlier in this section—the issue of the seventy-year time period will now become immediately apparent. Jesus is indicating that it will take one generation since the rebirth of Israel "until all these things take place" (Matt. 24:34, cf. 1 Thess. 4:15). Modern Israel, then, becomes the preeminent *sign* as regards the end of days. As to what might occur, we refer the reader to peruse certain key biblical sections—(see Ezek. 38; Dan. 7, 8, 9, 12; Matt. 24; Luke 17, 21; Rev. 9, 13, 19, 20)—among others, so as to gain a more comprehensive view of end-time events. Suffice it to say that a great war is headed our way.

Up until now, we have examined the *seventy weeks* prophecy of Daniel, which has furnished specific *end-time calculations* concerning the end of the world. But from this point on, we begin to investigate a number of distinct measurements that refer exclusively to the messianic Advent. For the sake of clarity, we will refer to these latter equations as the *Messianic calculations*. Gabriel announces the famous "seventy-week" prophecy:

> *Seventy weeks have been decreed for your people and your holy city,*
> *to finish the transgression, to make an end of sin, to make atonement for*
> *iniquity, to bring in everlasting righteousness, to seal up [end] vision*
> *and prophecy, and to anoint the most holy place. So you are to know and*
> *discern that from the issuing of a decree to restore and rebuild Jerusalem*
> *until Messiah the Prince there will be seven weeks and sixty-two weeks; it*
> *will be built again, with plaza and moat, even in times of distress. Then*
> *after the sixty-two weeks the Messiah will be cut off.*

(Dan. 9:24-26).

Most biblical symbols typically have multiple layers of meaning. This passage is no exception. The symbol of *"Jerusalem"* also has a double meaning. On one level, it refers to the earthly Jerusalem (Israel); but on another level, it also denotes the heavenly Jerusalem, namely, God himself. That is to say, the "decree to restore and rebuild Jerusalem" refers both to an authorized worldly injunction regarding the restoration of Israel as well as to God's preordained decree concerning the future incarnation of Christ. Actually, it refers to both simultaneously. This is why Daniel offers two calculations: "seven weeks and sixty-two weeks."

The former calculation is measured in *weeks* of years (cf. Gen. 29:27-28, Lev. 25:8) whereas the latter is calculated using only actual *years* (cf. Dan. 9:2). They also have two distinct starting points. The *"seven weeks"* commence with the birth of Jesus whereas the *"sixty-two weeks"* begin with the rebirth of the Jewish nation. The interesting thing about this setup is that if we execute the correct calculations, the results will turn out to be identical. Even though the variables and starting points are different, the conclusion remains the same; both the "seven weeks" and the "sixty-two weeks" end up on the exact same date! Knowing the result of one calculation will give you the sum of the other. Since we discuss the calculation pertaining to Christ's birth later in this book, we will now deal exclusively with the "sixty-two weeks" measurement. But how precise might these calculations be? One could argue that they are accurate and *close approximations* of future events encrypted within scripture. In fact, no one has effectively deciphered the seventy weeks prophecy until now.

First of all, the aforesaid quote (Dan. 9:24-26) predicts the return of the Jews to Israel, which as far as we know has already occurred (cf. Isa. 11:11). It also forecasts the atoning sacrifice of a forthcoming Messiah, an event which, according to the Danielic text, has not yet occurred. Furthermore, this quote informs us that "the Messiah will be cut off," which in biblical terminology means *slain* (cf. Prov. 2:22, Ps. 37:9). For these reasons, it confirms our premise of the forthcoming incarnation of Christ while relegating his formerly reputed advent as untenable. We also know that Jesus is implied in the previous quotation (Dan. 9:26) because the NT gospels reveal him as the *Christ*, which means the anointed one or the *Messiah*:

> *We have found the Messiah (which translated means Christ) [sic].*

> *(John 1:41)*

In working out these calculations, one comes to realize the approximate date signifying the epoch of the forthcoming Messiah:

> *Then after the sixty-two weeks the Messiah will be cut off . . . and the people of the prince who is to come will destroy the city [Jerusalem] and the sanctuary. . . . And he will make a firm covenant [treaty] with the many for one week.*

> *(Dan. 9:26-27)*

Since Christ will appear prior to the end of the world, it stands to reason that the *Messianic calculations* should be shorter—(7 weeks plus 62 weeks = *69 weeks*) (Dan. 9:25)—than the *end-time calculations*, which comprise *seventy weeks* (Dan. 9:24). There is, however, an additional week that must be added to the *Messianic* equation. As per the aforesaid quote, this accompanying interval of *"one week"* represents the so-called seven years of tribulation (Matt. 24:21, Dan. 9:27), which coincide with the appearance of the beast of *Revelation* (the antichrist) or "the prince who is to come" who "will destroy the city and the sanctuary" (Dan. 9:26). Similar to the two converging signs of Revelation 12, the two princes of Daniel's prophecy are juxtaposed to suggest that they are contemporaries (9:25-27). Notice also that one of the two typesetting formats for *prince* is in upper case— *"Messiah the Prince"* (9:25)—while the other is not: *"the prince who is to come"* (9:26). As a scriptural rule, capitalized pronouns not found at the beginning of a sentence are generally understood to be references to God.

In order to account for this missing week within the *Messianic calculations*, we must first add the original *seven* weeks to the *sixty-two* weeks, which amounts to sixty-nine weeks (9:25). Given that there is one additional week involved (*"one week"*) to account for the arrival of the antichrist (9:27), we are required to add one more week to the *Messianic* equation (69 + 1 = 70). Thus we arrive at the figurative seventy-week (Dan. 9:24) *"generation"* that will not pass away until all the prophecies are fulfilled (Matt. 24:34). This means that Christ's visitation is certainly imminent in our lifetime! We are now in a better position to comprehend the association of the two oracles—between Daniel 9, *"a decree to restore and rebuild Jerusalem,"* and Revelation 12, *and on her head a crown of twelve stars*—in connection with the newly established state of Israel and its relation to end-time events. Both refer to the year 1948. Whereas the former prophecy commences on that date, the latter terminates therein while predicting the future birth of Christ. According to the book of Daniel, the close relation between the modern restoration of Israel and the anticipated death of the Messiah is undeniable (9:24-26). Moreover, Daniel's seminal edict presents the restoration of the state of Israel as a *sign* of the period of time when the prophetic clock will begin its irrevocable countdown to the coming apocalypse.

ISRAEL'S REBIRTH HERALDS
THE COMING REIGN OF THE MESSIAH

> *He [Christ] has made his appearance once and for all, at the end of*
> *the last age, to do away with sin by sacrificing himself.*

> —*New Jerusalem Bible, Heb. 9:26*

This startling verse presents a dead-on prediction pertaining to the future embodiment of God. It epitomizes everything we have said thus far by stating categorically and unequivocally that this is Jesus's first appearance on earth: *once and for all!* Its transparent message reveals the purpose of Christ's mission on earth: to abolish *sin by sacrificing himself,* which is another way of saying, "to reconcile all things to Himself, having made peace through the blood of His [mysterious] cross" (Col. 1:20). Based on the aforesaid quote, the time of his appearance is utterly indisputable: "at the end of the last age"! This verse constitutes the discovery of a lifetime because it not only redefines the history of the last two thousand years but also reinterprets one of the central tenets of Christianity: the Jesus of antiquity.

We cannot emphasize enough the importance of the last days, also known as *the final days* of the world, since they represent the specific time period during which the Messiah will fulfill all the scriptural prophecies concerning him (Heb. 1:1-2, *New Jerusalem Bible*). Inasmuch as the biblical oracles predict the incarnation of a forthcoming Christ, they indicate that the argument for a *Jewish Jesus,* as traditionally understood, is realistically indefensible. In its creative portrayal of a freely embellished *Jewish Messiah,* scripture's use of metaphor is something like a Kantian *imperative,* which endeavors to connect the Jewish scriptures to the Greek

New Testament. Apart from the allegorical and literary devices that provide an ancient Hebrew backdrop for the story, the true origin of the Messiah remains elusive and essentially unknown. *Carl Jung*—a prominent twentieth-century thinker and founder of *analytical psychology*—writes,

> *It is only natural that I should constantly have revolved in my mind the question of the relationship of the symbolism of the unconscious to Christianity as well as to other religions. Not only do I leave the door open for the Christian message, but I consider it of central importance for Western man. It needs, however, to be seen in a new light, in accordance with the changes wrought by the contemporary spirit. Otherwise, it stands apart from the times, and has no effect on man's wholeness.*

(210)

In accordance with Carl Jung's suggestions, we have presented the *Christian message* from a contemporary perspective so that it can *be seen in a new light*. In the process of doing so, we have not tampered with the evidence, and we certainly have not withheld any proof to the contrary. We have allowed the Bible to define itself and recommended that readers should consult the scriptural sources in question for a more detailed and comprehensive understanding of this discussion. In fact, our work demands that readers should *actively participate* in this research by examining and verifying the documentation as opposed to merely *reading* and passively accepting our views. On the whole, our strange new findings show that much of what we think about the *Christian message* is not based on scriptural evidence at all but rather on hearsay.

For example, there is a chronological connection between the birth of the Messiah and the return of the Jews to Israel that can also be found in the apocalyptic writings of *Micah* the prophet:

> *"One will go forth for Me to be ruler. . . . His goings forth are from long ago, from the days of eternity." Therefore, He [God] will give them up [forsake the Jews] until the time when she who is in labor has borne a child. Then the remainder of His brethren [the Jewish Diaspora] will return to the sons of Israel. And He will arise and shepherd His flock . . . because at that time He will be great to the ends of the earth.*

(5:2-4)

We see, then, that the return of the Jews to their homeland coincides not only with the birth of the Messiah but also with his resurrection: Micah predicts that the newborn child—whose origins "are from long ago, from the days of eternity"—*will arise* from the dead during this general time period. This end-time prophecy concerning the return of the Jewish people to Palestine (cf. Ezek. 36:24) can only refer to 1948, when they came back to their ancestral place of origin after being dispersed among the nations for nearly two thousand years. The aforementioned excerpt clearly indicates that the Jewish *return* is a *sign* pointing to the birth of the Messiah. By contrast, the popular story of Jesus regarding his formerly reputed advent contains no specific mention of the reestablishment of Israel, and thus it cannot be the fulfillment of this prophecy. To this extent, the return of the Jews to Israel in 1948 is said to herald the coming of the Messiah!

FIRST COMES CHRIST; THEN COMES THE ANTICHRIST

> *Keep the commandment . . . until the appearing of our Lord Jesus*
> *Christ, which He [God] will bring about at the proper time— . . . whom*
> *no man has [ever] seen.*

> —*1 Tim. 6:14-16.*

On the authority of this fascinating passage, we come to realize that Jesus is not revealed according to the pseudohistorical period of the gospel narratives, but instead, he is manifested *at the proper time*: a forthcoming event frequently alluded to by the NT epistles. The last part of the quote, *whom no man has seen*, is often acquiesced in biblical exegesis to illustrate the imperceptible depth of God's presence or the *unapproachable light* of the divine abyss (1 Tim. 6:16). On the other hand, given that there is considerable evidence to suggest that Christ will make his first appearance in the *last days* of creation, it is both permissible and legitimate to take this clause, *whom no man has seen*, at face value. After all, Paul's words are quite explicit: *no man has [ever] seen* Christ! Granted that this prophecy employs a straightforward matter-of-fact approach, the *insight into the mystery of Christ* (Eph. 3:4) must be that he has not yet been revealed:

> *And they read from the book . . . translating to give the sense so that*
> *they understood the reading . . . that they might gain insight into the*
> *words.*

> *(Neh. 8:8-13)*

In one of his letters, Paul outlines the precise order of coming events:

> *Now, brethren, concerning the coming of our Lord Jesus Christ and*
> *our gathering together to Him, we ask you, not to be soon shaken in mind*
> *or troubled, either by spirit or by word or by letter, as if from us,* as though

the day of Christ had come. *Let no one deceive you by any means; for that Day will not come unless the falling away comes first, and the man of sin is revealed, the son of perdition, who opposes and exalts himself above all that is called God or that is worshipped, so that he sits as God in the temple of God, showing himself that he is God. . . . And now you know what is restraining, that he may be revealed in his own time. For the mystery of lawlessness is already at work; only He [Christ] who now restrains will do so until He is taken out of the way. And then the lawless one [the antichrist] will be revealed, whom the Lord will consume with the breath of His mouth and destroy with the brightness of His coming. The coming of the lawless one is according to the working of Satan, with all power, signs, and lying wonders*

(*2 Thess. 2:1-9, New King James, emphasis added*).

Before we begin our analysis, it is imperative that we provide a definition for what Paul refers to as *the day of Christ*. As the preceding segment maintains, this unique *day* concerns *the coming of our Lord and our gathering together to him*. This kind of language is used consistently throughout scripture (cf. Acts 2:1, Matt. 24:39-42) to represent the concept of the *rapture*: the ascent of the living and the dead into heaven (1 Cor. 15:51-52, 1 Thess. 4:16-17). Hence, Paul is not simply indicating the human manifestation of Jesus on the world scene; rather, he is emphasizing Christ's postresurrection activities that begin to have a real and substantial impact on life as we know it. By implication, *the day of Christ* primarily signifies the risen Messiah.

Now let us paraphrase the previous segment from 2 Thessalonians 2:1-9 so as to gain a certain degree of scriptural insight. First, Paul implores us not to be deceived by any rumors claiming that Jesus has already appeared, *as though the day of Christ had come*! Contrary to popular belief, Paul's disclaimer insists that these conventions are divisive because they profess to be biblically based, *as if from us*, even though this is not the official message of scripture. Second, there seem to be two important figures that appear to coexist during the end-times, namely, the *lawless one* or the *man of sin* (the antichrist) and a mysterious figure (Christ) who is portrayed as a rather sketchy character and about whom Paul gives us the following description: *He who now restrains will do so until He is taken out of the way.* In other words, the antichrist will not be revealed unless the Messiah's death precedes this event: until *the falling away comes first*.

The biblical concept of *falling away* has two primary meanings: it can be rendered as either the falling away from the faith or the end of life. Actually, both options may be applied since Christ will be rejected (Luke 17:25) by apostates as well as experience the horror of death. Take the story of Creation wherein a symbolic death came over *Adam*, whose name means "of the earth" in Hebrew, after which God formed *Eve*, a term that means "life giving" in the language thereof:

> *And the LORD God caused a deep sleep to fall on Adam, and he*
> *slept*

> *(Gen. 2:21, New King James).*

Because of this, scripture informs us that *it is impossible to renew . . . again to repentance* those who *have fallen away*, for they are in the *ground* (Heb. 6:4-7) and not among the living; otherwise they would have had ample opportunities to repent. Wherefore the term *fall* denotes sleep, which in turn refers to death in this particular context:

> *Behold, I tell you a mystery: we shall not all* sleep *. . . for the [last]*
> *trumpet will sound, and the dead will be raised imperishable, and we shall*
> *be changed.*

> *(1 Cor. 15:51-52, emphasis added).*

On the whole, the segment from 2 Thessalonians 2:1-9 suggests that someone must fall, must die, before the antichrist can be brought to the forefront of the world stage. This mysterious person *restrains* or prevents the coming of *the lawless one* by his implied presence. In spite of this situation, we are told that this person will eventually be *taken out of the way*. The biblical term *taken* refers to the concept of ascension into the heavenly sphere:

> *He [Jesus] was taken up, and a cloud received Him out of their sight*

> *(Acts 1:9, New King James).*

In the context of prophetic end-time literature, to be *taken* is tantamount to being *caught up* (1 Tim. 3:16, Rev. 12:5). We find the latter term being used in a verse that further elaborates on the concept of the rapture:

> *We who are alive and remain shall be caught up together with them*
> *[the resurrected believers] in the clouds to meet the Lord in the air*

> *(1 Thess. 4:17, New King James).*

So as we continue to decipher the lengthy segment from 2 Thessalonians 2:1-9, we come to realize that the mysterious pronoun "He" represents Jesus who delays (*restrains*) the antichrist's arrival from transpiring until his death comes to pass. Notice that the subject pronoun "He" is capitalized to imply that the reference is to

God. The implication is that the antichrist will be fully disclosed only after Christ is *taken out of the way.*

The only way that the aforementioned quote (2 Thess. 2:1-9) can become intelligible and substantiate the rest of the prophetic passages presented thus far is if we follow the order of events that the Bible itself is prescribing, whose underpinnings lie in the forthcoming advent of Jesus. This piece of evidence—namely, of a certain person (*He*) who dies and is *taken*—fits well into the big picture of the scriptural puzzle we are trying to solve. The only person capable of fulfilling such an extraordinary event must be Christ himself, who appears to be identified with both *Elijah*—the one sent *"before the . . . terrible day of the LORD"* (Mal. 4:5)—and *Michael,* who rises from the dead to shake the earth (Dan. 12:1). Given that he is the Messiah, it is difficult for any other biblical figure to measure up to him. The implications are staggering: the Messiah must come first on the world stage!

Christ, then, must be the first horseman of *Revelation*, whose *robe* (body) was *dipped in blood* (Rev. 19:11-13, cf. Rev. 6:2). This episode marks the first of several incidents that lead up to the cosmic apocalypse. We already know that the anticipated child born during the end-times is clearly the Messiah (Rev. 12:1-5). And more than that, we are now in a better position to understand the preceding events leading up to his foretold ascension: being *caught up* into heaven (Rev. 12:5). These include his incarnation, death and resurrection, when he "will arise" from the dead (Dan. 12:1) "to make the earth tremble" (Isa. 2:19). We are also told that the antichrist "will be revealed" during the interim in which Christ will be *taken out of the way* (2 Thess. 2:7-8). Hence, it was very much the scriptural intention to instill insight in its advocates so that they might firmly distrust those who claim "that the day of the Lord has come" (2 Thess. 2:2). In fact, we find strong evidence of Christ's forthcoming incarnation in an end-time prophecy extracted from the book of Revelation:

> *And I heard a loud voice from the throne, saying, "Behold, the tabernacle of God is among men, and He [Christ] shall dwell among them, and they shall be His people, and God Himself shall be among them "*

> *(21:3, emphasis added).*

CHAPTER 4

THE PENTECOST: AN OMEN OF THE MESSIANIC VISITATION

In Greek, the word *Pentecost* means *the fiftieth day* (Acts 2:1). It is more or less synonymous with the apocalyptic term known as *the Day of the Lord.* But whereas the *day of the Lord* can be measured (calculated) from the starting date of the *earthly Jerusalem* (Israel) as well from the birth of the *heavenly Jerusalem,* the *Pentecost* is measured only in relation to the heavenly Jerusalem, which represents Christ, because of its association with the *seven-week* prophecy of Daniel. The calculations are made from these two different points of departure so as to facilitate the understanding of end-time prophetic events. According to the text itself, these forecasts are very reliable! (Dan. 2:45).

Daniel's prophecy sheds some light into these two distinct kinds of measurements:

> *So you are to know and discern that from the issuing of a decree to restore and rebuild Jerusalem until Messiah the Prince there will be seven weeks and sixty-two weeks; it will be built again, with plaza and moat, even in times of distress.*

> *(Dan. 9:25)*

We have already calculated the *sixty-two weeks* measurement from the starting date of the earthly Jerusalem. Now we must calculate the *seven weeks'* prophecy, which begins with the incarnation of the heavenly Jerusalem: the *birth* of Christ. In this case, the *seven weeks* are calculated as seven weeks of years or as seven Sabbaths. Since a typical biblical *week* signifies seven years, *seven weeks* are equal to forty-nine actual years. But in order to fully appreciate this concept, we must first impart some necessary prerequisite information. So let us back up just a moment.

In the *book of Genesis,* the sun and moon are the *days* and *nights,* which are to be set for "signs, and for seasons, and for days and years" (1:14). Simply put, God has appointed various signposts through certain religious festivals in the Jewish calendar that will reveal prophetic epochs. For instance, when the deity instructs the Jews to begin instituting *Sabbaths* after they first enter their homeland, it is not merely for the purpose of ritual worship. Rather, there is prophetic value invested in this process; *signs* of divinely appointed times will be bestowed upon these important feasts and festivals. It is with this view in mind that the Godhead speaks through Moses, instructing the Jews to institute the following *Jubilee* year:

> *When you come into the land which I shall give you, then the land shall have a Sabbath to the LORD. . . . You are also to count off seven Sabbaths of years for yourself, seven times seven years, so that you have the time of the seven Sabbaths of years, namely, forty-nine years. . . . On the day of atonement [symbolizing Christ's sacrifice] you shall sound a horn all through your land. You shall thus consecrate the fiftieth year and proclaim a release through the land to all its inhabitants. It shall be a jubilee for you.*
>
> (Lev. 25:2-10)

There is an extra added year that is joined to the original forty-nine, thus making it essentially a fifty-year jubilee cycle. In the NT, this extra year is symbolically referred to as the day "after the Sabbath" (Matt. 28:1) or as *the eighth day* (Phil. 3:5). These concepts will be given separate treatment in the forthcoming chapters. Anyhow, the *seven weeks* of Daniel's prophecy, quoted earlier, refer to a specific fifty-year Jubilee cycle that transpires at the end of days. The same can be said for *the day of Pentecost* (Acts 2:1, 20:16; 1 Cor. 16:8), which means "fifty" in Greek. It is on this *day* that the promise of God's spirit, embodied in Christ, will be revealed upon the earth (cf. Acts 2:1-4, 17-21).

The *phraseology* used by the text to describe various prophetic events remains consistent among many diverse passages. Scripture is replete with examples of this kind. For instance, the disciples *had come together* and were asking questions concerning the coming of Christ (Acts 1:6). Elsewhere, we are informed that "when the day of Pentecost had come, they *were all together*" (Acts 2:1, emphasis added). Another verse reads, "We who are alive and remain shall be *caught up together* with them in the clouds to meet the Lord in the air" (1 Thess. 4:17, emphasis added). Therefore, during the Pentecost, the believers had either *come together* or *were all together* or were *caught up together* or were *gathering together* (2 Thess. 2:1) and so on and so forth. Textually, the consistent use of biblical terminology throughout seemingly disparate passages is a strong indication that these events are meaningfully related. And this is precisely what we find among other kinds of evidence within the biblical sources, namely, that *the day of the Lord* (2 Thess. 2, cf. Acts 1:6), the *Restitution* of all things (Acts 3:20-21, cf. 1:6-7), *the day of Pentecost* (Acts 2:1-21), and the *Rapture* (1

Thess. 4:16-17, Matt. 24:40-41) constitute a series of related events that occurs *at the consummation of the ages*! (Heb. 9:26).

But bear in mind that the countdown to the fifty-year Pentecostal period cannot begin from 1948. The former time interval refers exclusively to the birth of the Messiah. According to Daniel's prophecy, fifty years (*seven weeks*) must be calculated from the time of Christ's *birth*, just as sixty-two symbolic weeks are used to determine events from the time of Israel's *rebirth* (9:25). This is precisely why certain characters in the gospels react to Jesus by asking an inquisitive question:

> *You are not yet fifty years old, and have You seen Abraham?*

> *(John 8:57)*

What an astonishing revelation this is! We finally recognize and understand why this verse was written in the first place: to establish the time frame of the Pentecost. This is why we are urged by scripture "to inquire in His [God's] temple" (Ps. 27:4, *New King James*), which turns out to be none other than Jesus Christ himself (John 2:19). It is an allusion to God's spirit that will appear (or dwell in the earthly temple, the body; cf. John 2:21) in human form (Mal. 3:1, cf. 1 Cor. 6:19). Scripture encourages us to meditate on God's temple so as to instill in us the necessity of measuring or calculating the time of his arrival (cf. Rev. 11:1-2). Most people are under the wrong impression that the "heavenly" temple, as prophesied by Ezekiel (cf. 40-48), is the *third temple* that will supposedly be rebuilt in Jerusalem at some future time. But according to the *gospel of Matthew*, Christ is greater than any temple ever built by human hands! (12:6). This perfectly explains why the Messiah *"is Lord of the Sabbath"* (Luke 6:5), for the *Sabbath* represents *the day of Pentecost*. Because of the prophetic signposts that are given, scripture declares that "when the Sabbath had come, He [Jesus] began to teach" the masses (Mark 6:2).

There are a number of biblical signposts that point to this *Pentecostal* imagery of the *seven Sabbaths*. For example, the "seven" loaves of bread which Jesus multiplies (Mark 8:5), since forty-nine is a multiple of seven, or the *"five barley loaves and two fish"* (John 6:9), which symbolize the *seven weeks* of Daniel's oracle (Dan. 9:25). In the book of Micah, God raises "seven shepherds" to fight against the antichrist (5:5). In *Revelation*, we find a book "sealed up with seven seals" (5:1). Elsewhere, we read of "the seven stars [which] are the angels of the seven churches" (Rev. 1:20). Then there is the mystery of the seven angels holding seven trumpets (Rev. 8:2, 6). In fact, Christ himself is depicted as having seven horns and seven eyes (Rev. 5:6). Later, we also discover that there are seven angels who are ready to unleash seven plagues (Rev. 15:1) upon mankind, and so on and so forth. Thus, this fifty-year Pentecostal prophecy is a recurring theme throughout scripture! It represents the one and only dispensational time period of divinely appointed events in which God's human intervention does not simply bring about one thousand years of relative peace, as is mistakenly assumed, but "everlasting" harmony (cf. Dan. 7:14, 27, 9:24, 12:2; 2 Thess. 1:9; Jude 1:6; Rev. 5:13, 21:4).

All throughout the scripture, from the book of Genesis to the book of Revelation, we find the same Pentecostal theme repeated over and over again, but presented under the apparent guise of distinct and dissimilar narratives that seem to be working out the underlying prophecy of the end of days by giving us more and more details. From Jacob's service to Laban, implying seven times seven years (Gen. 29:20-28) to the period of abundance and famine in the Joseph story, suggesting two periods of seven years (Gen. 41:29-30), to the *seventh* march around the walls of Jericho (Josh. 6:16), we encounter visionary "dreams [that] are one and the same" (Gen. 41:25): an unending litany of corresponding stories that culminate at the end of time with the opening of the seven seals of *Revelation* (5:1, 6:1). Therefore, the Messiah's *seventh-day* advent is a weighty sign of recognition that signals the expiration of time on earth. It represents the epoch when all "vision and prophecy" will cease, and "everlasting" life will begin (Dan. 9:24). When all these prophecies begin to materialize in concrete forms during the period known as the great tribulation, it means that all the previous ages have reached the final point of time:

> The end of all things is at hand.

> (1 Peter 4:7)

THE CONCEPT OF THE PENTECOST IN LITERATURE AND MYTHOLOGY

The Bible is a collection of stories, which describe prophetic events in figurative language. The Greeks also have a collection of stories that insinuate gods among men through the nomenclature of symbols; they are called myths. But is it possible to compare Greek myths to the stories of the Bible? And if so, do these myths represent prophetic truth or historical fiction? This topic concerning the validity of mythology and its relation to the Bible has been a bone of contention for thousands of years.

For the better part of five thousand years of recorded history, the mythmaking process (*mythopoeia* in Greek) has attempted to turn the contents of oracular vision into works of literature, thus putting a face on various aspects of prophecy. It is the stuff of which fables are made. Before the dawn of the Christian experience, sometime around 500 BC, across the far reaches of ancient Greece, a pivotal body of work was produced; its mystical themes were steeped in myth. It is one of the oldest surviving poetic oeuvres to date. Few have taken to calling the rich tapestry of this mythopoeic output as prophetic literature. Its author was *Pindar*, the celebrated ancient Greek poet who composed prophetic and mystical victory poems called the *Nemean Odes*. In one of these poems, he proclaims an oracle through the veil of mythology that appears to correspond to scriptural prophecy:

Graces, sing of the city of Danaus and his fifty daughters on their splendid thrones, Hera's Argos [a city in southern Greece], a home suitable for a god; it blazes with countless excellences because of its bold deeds.

(Nemean 10)

Pindar has all the embellishments of the book of Revelation. Fifty daughters are sitting on radiant thrones around a Greek god whose profound glow shines forth in the wake of his heroic accomplishments. It is a vision akin to the laudable oracles of Delphi that resonates and complements the *Pentecost* of scripture in that it reveals the *seven Sabbaths* of the Apocalypse. The number *fifty*—a unit of biblical measurement shrouded in mystery—is intimately associated with the reign of God on earth, whose people will eventually sit on shining thrones. Similar to Pindar, Jesus says,

He who overcomes, I will grant to him to sit down with Me on My throne, as I also overcame and sat down with My Father on His throne.

(Rev. 3:21).

Throughout history, these prophetic mysteries have been recorded and handed down under the guise of the mytho-poetic narrative. Such an account is the Greek myth of "Theseus and the Minotaur." According to the myth, *Theseus* was the founder of Athens and the legendary hero who slew the Minotaur of Crete. Having been defeated by his battle-hardened armies, Athens made a pact with King Minos of Crete that involved sending him seven men and seven women, each year, as a form of sacrifice. They were to be devoured by his stepson, a hideous monster called the *Minotaur*, who is described as half-man and half-bull. But Theseus, disguised as one of the seven men, cleverly killed the Minotaur and freed his people. The key to the story is the implied prophetic calculation of *seven times seven*, which is akin to the biblical fifty-year period, after which the atonement of God's sacrifice will liberate mankind. Theseus says to his father, "The gods will assist me." It could have been a story taken straight out of the pages of the Bible. Even so, it is still a powerful spiritual account of liberation and redemption that expresses a profound apocalyptic oracle, similar to the biblical concept of the Pentecost. To that extent, these ancient Greek prophecies can be added on to other mystical literary traditions, which disclose similar apocalyptic visions concerning the end of the world.

Whatever our speculations may be about mythology, one thing is certain. Its widespread biblical use was for the purpose of setting the stage for the end-times. No one can deny that the biblical story of *Sodom and Gomorrah* is a myth (Gen. 19). As you probably know, it is a story about *Lot* and his wife who try to escape the approaching judgment of God that comes in the form of a consuming fire from heaven (Gen. 19:24). Unfortunately, Lot's wife is curious enough to turn and look back, and she is instantly turned into "a pillar of salt" (Gen. 19:26). It is not dissimilar to the Greek myth of *Medusa* in which all who dare to behold her eyes are promptly turned to stone. Yet Jesus is inclined to use myths, such as the myth of Sodom and Gomorrah, to indicate that they contain prophecies concerning the end of the world (Luke 17:28-32). In the gospel of Luke, what is most interesting is that Jesus appears to insinuate himself into the story as a literary character, prophesying his own incarnation:

> *Now having been questioned by the Pharisees as to when the kingdom of God was coming, He [Jesus] answered them and said, "The kingdom of God is not coming with signs to be observed; . . . The days shall come [centuries will pass] when you will long to see one of the days of the Son of Man and you will not see it. . . . For just as the lightning, when it flashes out of one part of the sky, shines to the other part of the sky, so will the Son of Man be in His day.* But first He must suffer many things and be rejected by this [implied, future] generation. *And just as it happened in the days of Noah, so it shall be also in the days of the Son of Man: they were eating, they were drinking, they were marrying, . . . until the day that Noah entered the ark, and the flood came and destroyed them all."*

> *(17:20-27, emphasis added).*

What conclusions can we draw from this lengthy segment? First, that our view of the historical Jesus is speculative at best. We seem to have confused literature with history. Thus we falsely conclude that "the historical Jesus" must be discussing his second coming. However, if "the literary Jesus" of Luke's narrative is being asked "as to when the kingdom of God was coming," then obviously we cannot assume that it already came prior to the writing of the gospels, as is commonly believed! What is more, the above quote makes clear that Christ's advent and "the kingdom of God" are quite inseparable; you cannot pry them apart.

Second, if anything approaching a consensus is to be found, it cannot be based on the two speculative comings of Christ. During his discourse on the end of days, the Jesus character of the gospels promulgates a prophecy which most scholars attribute to his second coming: "For just as the lightning, when it flashes out of one part of the sky, shines to the other part of the sky, so will the Son of Man be in His day" (Luke 17:24). What is surprising, however, is that this omen is then expanded by a most intriguing appendage to the previous verse: "But first He must suffer many things" (17:25). In other words, while "the literary Jesus" is predicting his supposed second coming, according to the common view, this terse statement shockingly reveals that his incarnation must necessarily precede his coming from the sky! And since the entire prophecy is set in the future, the sentence pertaining to Christ's suffering and rejection "by this [chronologically implied] generation" cannot possibly be understood in any other context except as a reference to a future event. Otherwise, we would be dislocating this sentence from the end-times setting of the prophecy, thus creating a bizarre anachronism. After all, Jesus prophesies that a long time will pass before we behold "the Son of Man" (Luke 17:22), an idiomatic phrase that is deeply tied to his incarnation (Ps. 8:4; Ezek. 2:1, 12:27; Matt. 9:6, 17:9, 24:44; Gal. 4:4). Thus, the latter portion of the oracle paints Christ's coming in a very different light and calls for a reexamination of scripture. It sets the prophetic time line in its proper chronological perspective as it supplies fresh new insights into the future incarnation of Christ: what ought to be called, "the first coming of Jesus"!

Notice also that *"the kingdom of God,"* which Christ represents (cf. Luke 11:20; Mark 9:1, 13:26), *"is not coming with [visible] signs to be observed"* (Luke 17:20). That is to say, Christ will come in a concealed human form (cf. Luke 17:37) as one of whom "the world did not know" (John 1:10) much less observe. This explains why *on the road to Emmaus* (Luke 24:13-35), two of his disciples failed to recognize him until well after his *death*, symbolized by "the breaking of the bread" (Luke 24:16, 35; cf. 22:19). The messianic character of the gospels then went on to describe the prophetic myths of Noah and Lot, using them as analogies of the end of days, as these became the focal point of his apocalyptic message (Luke 17:26-32). Hence, any claim to the effect that explorers have found missing fragments of Noah's ark is like saying that they have found the remains of Lot's wife who turned into "a pillar of salt"; it is absolute nonsense. And yet surprisingly, the Jesus story itself has taken on mythic proportions.

Take the story of *Perseus*, whose mother was impregnated by Zeus, the father of the gods. This is not unlike what happened to *Mary*, the mother of Jesus. She was herself inseminated by God the Father, not in a literal sense, but through the spirit of Christ. Legend has it that Perseus was then cast into the sea, similar to the story of Moses (Exod. 2:3). *Hermes*, the angelic messenger of the gods, helps Perseus obtain winged sandals, a magic staff and a sword from the divine spirits called the *nymphs*. Perseus finally has enough protection and courage to slay the *Gorgon Medusa*. We are at once reminded of the magical staff of Moses (Exod. 4:2-4) and the ascension of Christ (Acts 1:9), stories that seem to have some bearing on the myth of Perseus. Indeed, at the end of the coming apocalypse, Christ will also slay the great sea monster with a fierce and mighty sword:

> *In that day the LORD will punish Leviathan the fleeing serpent, with His fierce and great and mighty sword, even Leviathan the twisted serpent; and He will kill the dragon who lives in the sea.*

> (Isa. 27:1)

If we did not know better, we might have attributed this verse to *Poseidon*, the god of the sea. But this is not a myth. Or is it?

Regrettably, history has dusted off the last vestiges of mythology, dismissing its import and relegating it to the status of superstition and folklore. Yet its tremendous input is religious in every sense of the word! Moreover, mythic poetry was at that time the highest possible form of artistic expression and the most dependable way to record and transmit visions of a prophetic nature because these divine communications were not only inexpressible through any other medium, but they were also devoid of scientific concepts and principles (see the only known work of *Parmenides*, a Greek philosopher of the sixth century BC, which is a poem "On Nature"). It is for this reason that *Eusebius of Caesarea*—variously known as *Eusebius Pamphili*, a Roman historian and prolific Biblical scholar—writes,

> For as the Supreme God gave oracles to the Hebrews through their prophets, . . . so also He gave them to the other nations through their local oracles. For He was not only the God of the Jews, but of the rest of mankind as well.

(Pamphili Book V)

All these cultural tales are intrinsically religious by nature, thereby making it difficult to discriminate between Greek myths and the collection of stories known as the Bible. As we see it, both compilations are worthy of being noted as prophetic literature. It also appears that both of these traditions describe more or less the same prophecies! However, we must qualify these assertions. Although the sacred texts of many world religions remain valid insofar as "inspired" prophecy is concerned, it is our ever-increasing conviction that the Judeo-Christian scriptures present the most detailed and accurate information to date.

Given the plethora of evidence, which we have gathered, there is something credible in all these prophecies worthy of serious consideration at the very least. As we consult the literary archives of various spiritual traditions, we discover that they all exhibit prophetic visions and dreams in one form or another. We also find the same Pentecostal themes running through much of their writings. From the occultic poems of Pindar and Nostradamus to the prophetic mysticism of Greek mythology, we find a mixture of myth and science, truth and legend. Essentially, they are all declaring the same divine message as though it were written in the stars themselves: the time pertaining to the coming of the gods!

There have always been secret societies in search of mystical knowledge. Since the time of the Delphic mysteries in ancient Greece, such groups have sprung forth everywhere in search of divine wisdom. Gnostics, Freemasons, Alchemists, Kabbalists, and the Illuminati are but a few of these societies. But the mystical wisdom they sought after can only be attained through the *Spirit*. It is for this reason that the latter is said to precipitate the alchemical metamorphosis of the universe at the end of time (cf. 1 Cor. 15:51-53, Heb. 12:26-27). This is precisely why the "people of the book" await the end of the world with such eager anticipation: to experience the transmutation of all *matter* into *spirit*.

In the book of Revelation, from chapter 5 to chapter 10, there is a direct reference made to a mysterious book, which is said to be *sealed up with seven seals*. As we clarified earlier, the *seven seals* represent the seven weeks of Daniel's prophecy: the appointed day of the *Lord*, who will be manifested during the seventh Sabbath. It is also true that the seven seals indicate seven apocalyptic events that will surely take place (cf. Rev. 6-8:1, 8:6). Nevertheless, the number *seven* is the expedient forecaster of the signs of the times during which the knowledge of God will ultimately transpire (Rev. 10:7). The opening of this book gives the reader a glimpse into the mysteries that have been kept hidden from "past ages and generations" (Col. 1:26).

But why is this book so closely linked to the coming of Christ? And why is this text the only one capable of revealing these age-old secrets? Indisputably, this mysterious document is identical to an arcane *scroll*, as mentioned in the *book of Ezekiel*, since the directive to "take it, and eat it" (eat the book) is common to both the book of Revelation (10:8-10) and the Ezekiel (2:9-3:3) texts. The implication is for the reader to consume or digest its contents. More information is furnished in Revelation 10 where we are told that it is actually *a little book*; one could even coin it *the little book* of *Revelation* (Rev. 10:9, 10).

Eschatology is the theological study of the final events of human history. The term is derived from the Greek word *eshatos*, which means "last." It entails the study of prophecy concerning the end of days. A good many experts believe that the intensification of recent social unrest will culminate in an apocalyptic global conflict while the earth itself will be subjected to an unprecedented degree of devastation. But these developments will also denote the high point of the evolutionary process: the physical and spiritual transformation of the human species and of all life. Curiously enough, the forthcoming apocalypse seems to be concurrent not only with the coming Messiah but also with the arrival of *the little book of Revelation*! (Rev. 10:1-2, 10-11).

THEY WHO HAD NO NEWS OF HIM SHALL SEE,
AND THEY WHO HAVE NOT HEARD SHALL UNDERSTAND.

(Rom. 15:21)

PART II
The Greek Jesus

CHAPTER 5

THE FIGURATIVE TEXT

In the Greek language, the word *Bible* means "the books" (*ta biblia*). It is a matter of public record that the original NT was written in Greek, not in Hebrew. This fact in and of itself bears profound implications for the story of Jesus since it is a sign of the literary medium through which the divine message is proclaimed. No early writer of the Judeo-Christian Bible has described Christ's true identity and advent more forcefully than Paul. He is credited with being the author of manifold NT *epistles,* and his writings have become the cornerstone of our study. Paul is at once unpretentious, disarmingly honest, and disturbingly provocative. The effectiveness of his approach stems from the primacy he gives to the subject of prophecy. And the fulfillment of all biblical prophecy culminates in the last book of the *Apocalypse,* variously known as the "book of Revelation."

This author, whom we have come to know as Paul, wrote all of his epistles in the Greek language (cf. Acts 21:37). Paul is born a Roman citizen (Acts 22:28), and as he claims, "To the Jews I became as a Jew" in order to save them (1 Cor. 9:20). In fact, Paul gives us an exact definition of what it means to be a *Jew* within the NT context:

> For he is not a Jew who is one outwardly; neither is circumcision that which is outward in the flesh. But he is a Jew who is one inwardly; and circumcision is that which is of the heart.
>
> (Rom. 2:28-29)

According to Paul's stunning definition, the biblical term *Jew* does not denote a race or an apparent physical birthright but rather an inner essence or, more precisely, an indwelling spirit pertaining to God. This descriptive terminology certainly illustrates a radical new way of approaching, reading, and interpreting the sacred text. *William Barclay*, a world-renowned New Testament scholar, rightly emphasizes that Paul's message must have infuriated the Jews:

> *To a Jew a passage like this must have come as a shattering experience.*
> *He was certain that God regarded him with special favour, simply and*
> *solely because of his national descent from Abraham and because he bore*
> *the badge of circumcision in his flesh. But Paul introduces an idea to*
> *which he will return again and again. Jewishness, he insists, is not a*
> *matter of race at all; it has nothing to do with circumcision. It is a matter*
> *of conduct. If that is so, many a so-called Jew who is a pure descendant of*
> *Abraham and who bears the mark of circumcision in his body, is no Jew*
> *at all; and equally many a Gentile who never heard of Abraham and who*
> *would never dream of being circumcised, is a Jew in the real sense of the*
> *term. To a Jew this would sound the wildest heresy and leave him angry*
> *and aghast.*

(47)

Paul entertains a most peculiar thought that is so critical to his message: the Bible as metaphor. He sets forth the idea that the amount of divine knowledge revealed in scripture is directly related to the decryption of its metaphorical significance. In other words, the more metaphors you uncover, the greater the knowledge. The followers of Moses stumbled over this figurative trap by taking scriptural metaphors at face value as they interpreted everything from an exclusively literal point of view. By contrast, Paul points out that the two sons of Abraham—one according to the flesh and the other according to the promise—are really *allegorical devices* suggesting the two covenants of God: the Old and New Testaments (Gal. 4:22-28). In effect, the same type of metaphor regarding the "two stone tablets" of Moses on which the Ten Commandments were written (Exod. 34:4) can equally be applied to describe the two Testaments of the Bible.

Another biblical example depicts Jesus illustrating that the term *bread* is a figurative concept that represents the *word* or the *teaching* of an individual or a group; Christ urges his disciples to "watch out and beware of the leaven of the Pharisees and Sadducees" (Matt. 16:6). In contemporary terms, it is tantamount to saying be careful of what your church or congregation teaches you. In this particular case, Jesus warns his followers to be wary of the literal interpretations of the Jews (Matt. 16:12). A perfect example is when Christ prophesies, "Destroy this temple [my body], and in three days I will raise it up" (John 2:19):

> *The Jews therefore said, "It took forty-six years to build this temple,*
> *and will You raise it up in three days?"*

(John 2:20)

This exemplifies the kinds of errors that have hampered Jews and Christians alike. The oversight of scriptural interpretation can also be assessed from the erroneous attribution of *historical* and/or *Hebraic* value to the NT story, as is evident from a verse which states that Christ is actually crucified in "the great city which mystically is called Sodom and Egypt" (Rev. 11:8) and not in Jerusalem as most people presume! In response to the constant misconceptions that plague biblical interpretation, the deity insists,

> *YOU WILL KEEP ON HEARING, BUT WILL NOT UNDERSTAND;*
> *AND YOU WILL KEEP ON SEEING, BUT WILL NOT PERCEIVE; . . .*
> *let it be known to you therefore, that this salvation of God has been sent to the Gentiles.*

> *(Acts 28:26-28).*

The meaning of the above clause— *"salvation . . . has been sent to the Gentiles"*—can suggest two distinct ideas. Interpreters must draw one of two conclusions: either it refers to God's redemptive plan being extended to mankind (non-Jews), or it means that Christ— *"this salvation of God"* (Luke 2:25-30; cf. Ps. 62:2, 6; Isa. 12:2)—has been *"sent"* to earth through the Gentiles. If our methods are unfettered by *biblical literalism*, then the choice to appropriate the latter explanation will allow us to blow the divine secret wide open.

GALILEE OF THE GENTILES: A METAPHOR FOR A NON-JEWISH MESSIAH

> *GALILEE OF THE GENTILES—THE PEOPLE WHO WERE SITTING IN DARKNESS SAW A GREAT LIGHT, . . . UPON THEM A LIGHT DAWNED.*

> —Matt. 4:15-16

The historical record indicates that the *Assyrians* invaded and subsequently stamped out the *Northern Kingdom* of Israel in 722 BC. The district of *Galilee* was among the captured territories (2 Kings 15:29). As a result, foreign peoples settled there—as well as in neighboring *Samaria*, the capital—"and lived in its [Israel's] cities" (2 Kings 17:24). This Northern Kingdom was entirely wiped out, never to be heard from again. As it disappeared into obscurity, it was thereafter inhabited by Gentiles.

In retrospect, when the NT describes the Savior by way of unusual and unconventional symbols—which indicate that he will be a *Samaritan* (John 8:48-49), or that he will come from *"GALILEE OF THE GENTILES"* (Matt. 4:12-16)—it casts him as an outsider who clearly does not belong to the Jewish heritage. Galilee is no longer presented as a district of the former Northern Kingdom of Israel; rather, it becomes a metaphor for the Gentile nations per se. The word *Galilee* means *circle*, and as such it implies all the nations of the earth (1101, *New King James*). Perhaps this is the meaning behind Jesus's parable of the *Good Samaritan* (Luke 10:29-37). Although Jews were not in the habit of interacting with Samaritans, since the latter were Gentiles, Christ (the Good Samaritan) shows compassion toward them in their dire time of need.

There is unanimity among biblical scholars that scripture uses the idiomatic terms *nations* and *peoples* to refer to the heathen, otherwise known as the Gentiles (Gen. 10:5, *New King James*). In the context of our study, the definition of a Gentile is simply a person of non-Jewish descent. Here is an important passage pertaining to Paul's calling and mission to the *Gentiles*, the non-Jewish peoples. Paul makes an effort to plead his case that Christ's salvation is a prophecy:

> For there is one God and one Mediator between God and men, the Man Christ Jesus, who gave Himself a ransom for all, to be testified in due time, *for which I was appointed . . . a teacher of the Gentiles in faith and truth.*

> *(1 Tim. 2:5-7, New King James, emphasis added)*

Initially, Paul delineates what is traditionally believed to be Christ's act of atonement, but then he suddenly interrupts this thought by stating that the supporting evidence (*to be testified*) for this redemption (*ransom*) will surface *in due time*! By implication, this means that "the cross of Christ" (1 Cor. 1:17) has not yet occurred in the history of time. Next, Paul insists that there is a deeply meaningful connection between Jesus and the Gentiles because it was on account of this mysterious testimony that he was appointed to enlighten the latter.

Interestingly enough, the text is sprinkled with multiple allusions to help us uncover important clues about the Messiah's mysterious identity. For instance, the Jewish multitudes who are supposedly steeped in scripture cannot believe their eyes and ears when they first encounter the Christ; they respond with incredulous amazement,

> "Surely the Christ is not going to come from Galilee [from the Gentiles], is He? Has not the Scripture said that the Christ comes from the offspring of David [from the Jews], and from Bethlehem, the village where David was?" So there arose a division in the multitude because of Him. And some of them wanted to seize Him, but no one laid hands on Him.

> *(John 7:41-44)*

We are beginning to understand why Jesus seems to offend Jewish sentiment. The Jews cannot possibly believe in the idea of a Gentile Christ. Thus, they conclude that the ideal Messiah must conform to their own interpretation of scripture: he must be of Jewish origin. However, as the above quote maintains, Jesus is neither from Bethlehem nor from Jewish occupied territories; he does not appear to come *"from the offspring of David,"* meaning the Hebrew race. This is the chief reason why the crowd became bitterly divided. Actually, the Jews became furious. What do you suppose they wanted to do? They wanted to kill him! (cf. John 8:59, 10:31, 39).

John's gospel makes no secret about addressing the Jewish response in such a way as to suggest that they should reconsider their long-standing messianic assumptions. The author achieves this literary effect by formulating the Judaic views as a series of questions. Nonetheless, the Hebraic ideology persists. In a state of confusion, the Jews ask,

> *No one of the rulers or Pharisees [Jewish ruling class] has believed in Him, has he? . . . Search, and see that no prophet arises out of Galilee.*

> *(John 7:48-52)*

This biblical episode epitomizes the public reactions that will ensue during Jesus's visitation. Some Jews will believe while most adherents of Judaism will despise a Christ derived from the offspring of Gentiles. This kind of Messiah, then, is doomed to be rejected (1 Cor. 1:23, 1 Pet. 2:8):

> *Jesus said to them, "Did you never read in the Scriptures, 'THE STONE [Christ] WHICH THE BUILDERS [of the faith] REJECTED, THIS BECAME THE CHIEF CORNER stone.' . . . Therefore I say to you, the kingdom of God will be taken away from you, and be given to a [different] nation producing the fruit of it.'" . . . And when the chief priests and the Pharisees heard His parables, they understood that He was speaking about them.*

> *(Matt. 21:42-45)*

Therefore, the Bible itself answers the age-old question: "why do the Jews reject Jesus in the gospels?" Because he is a Gentile!

THE MYTH OF CHRIST'S JEWISH HERITAGE

Paul makes a rather unusual confession:

> *To the Jews I became as a Jew, that I might win Jews; to those who are*
> *under the [Mosaic] Law, as under the Law, though not being myself under*
> *the Law, that I might win those who are under the Law.*

> *(1 Cor. 9:20)*

Elsewhere, he deciphers the meaning of the term *Jew* as signifying the inner person, not simply a physical descendant of Israel (Rom. 2:28-29). His primary motive is to uncover the hidden secrets of God that lie deep within the figurative framework of the Bible. By implication, both Jews and Christians have failed in grasping this veiled terminology. Throughout his epistles, Paul continues this forcible argument in defense of his view about scripture's metaphorical language:

> *I urge you . . . in order that you may instruct certain men not to teach*
> *strange doctrines, nor to pay attention to myths and endless genealogies,*
> *which give rise to mere speculation.*

> *(1 Tim. 1:3-4)*

There is no doubt that Paul is referring to scriptural *genealogies,* which are designed to exhibit the uninterrupted lineage of Christ (cf. Matt. 1, Luke 3). But he exhorts us not to take these "strange doctrines" at face value since they will inevitably lead us to erroneous speculations and conclusions. Paul openly describes these genealogies as nothing more than *myths.* He feels so strongly about this that he even deters some Cretan (Greek) disciples from paying any attention to these so-called "Jewish myths" (Tit. 1:10-14, cf. 1 Tim. 4:7). An example of this "mythic" factor can be found in the genealogies of two gospels that appear to contradict themselves. For instance, Matthew's genealogy introduces *Joseph,* the father of Christ, as the son of Jacob (1:16), but in Luke's lineage, he is said to be "the son of Eli" (3:23). Since Joseph cannot possibly have two fathers, this is proof enough that we must not approach the biblical genealogies from a literal, historical perspective. What is more, it seems as though Paul himself does not endorse the notion of a Jewish Messiah, as these myths would have us believe. And there is a clear indication that Paul's view is supported by the gospels. The latter formulate the notion that Christ is not in fact the progeny of Jews, but *supposedly* so for the sake of comparison:

> *Jesus Himself was about thirty years of age, being supposedly the son*
> *of Joseph, the son of Eli.*

> *(Luke 3:23)*

In essence, the story of Jesus is a prophetic myth, not unlike the myths of Jewish literature. For example, consider the OT stories of Joseph and Moses, two great figures of Jewish spirituality who are nevertheless portrayed as if they are living and reigning in Egypt: they are basically depicted as Gentiles. They may be likened to spiritual Jews or even described as biblical patriarchs, but they are Gentiles nonetheless. Oddly enough, God draws an interesting analogy between these figures and Christ:

OUT OF EGYPT DID I CALL MY SON [Jesus].

(Matt. 2:15)

The Gentile component in all these personages is striking even though they reveal their connection to the spiritual Jews, their brothers in the faith, through several means: Joseph is *revealed* to his Jewish brothers (Gen. 45:1) while Moses is disclosed to *a Hebrew, one of his brethren* (Exod. 2:11). Jesus, of course, pays homage to Jewish tradition by being portrayed as a Jewish *Rabbi* (John 9:2). To that extent, it seems as if we are witnessing the transition of messianic descendancy in the figures of Joseph and Moses, whose stories suggest the coming of a Gentile Messiah!

GALILEE: THE EPITOME OF ALL NON-JEWISH NATIONS

Let us now reflect on the gospel of Luke, which recounts the story of a Roman-imposed census to assess the Hebrew population of ancient Palestine. According to some modern scholars, the account's significance is more symbolic than historical (Borg, 24). In an effort to register, Jesus's parents allegedly travel to Bethlehem. However, notice that Luke presents a geographical impossibility insofar as Christ's Jewish origin is concerned; he writes, "Joseph [Christ's father] also went up from Galilee, from the city of Nazareth, to Judea, to the city of David, which is called Bethlehem" (2:4). Yet there seem to be considerable disparities between the biblical and the historical account regarding the location of these two places. The distance from Nazareth to Bethlehem is approximately 80 miles, heading in a southward direction. So how can we explain the gospel record in which Joseph reportedly "went up from Galilee, from the city of Nazareth, to . . . Bethlehem"? We cannot!

We should also mention that the city of *Bethlehem* is variously known as *"Bethlehem Ephrathah"* (Mic. 5:2). According to the scriptures, *"Bethlehem Ephrathah"* did not really belong to the southern kingdom of Judah (cf. Josh. 15), which at that time represented the Jewish nation per se. Furthermore, given that Luke's geographical account of the census-narrative makes no historical sense, the Bible provides an ad hoc allusion in order to uncover the hidden meaning of the text. The sequence of events (or the plot) within Luke's story seems to trace Jesus's lineage back to the region of the Gentiles since Joseph "went up [north] from Galilee," not down (south) toward Judea. These hidden clues purvey invaluable information regarding Jesus's origins, which may not be apparent to the casual reader. The legitimacy of the story is once again affirmed by virtue of the clues that are furnished concerning Galilee of the Gentiles. Therefore, Luke's census-narrative acts as a conceptual metaphor for the Gentile lineage of Christ.

According to the gospels, Jesus appears in *Galilee* to initiate the preaching of his ministry (Mark 1:14-16, 28). One wonders why Christ inaugurates his divine commission by issuing the following statement: *"Let us go somewhere else [away from Judea] . . . in order that I may preach . . . ; for that is what I came out for, "*and then suddenly and unexpectedly, we find him teaching and performing miracles "throughout all Galilee" (Mark 1:38-39). The turning point concerning the mystery of Jesus's non-Jewish mission is summarized in the ensuing sentence:

> *Jesus was walking in Galilee; for He was unwilling to walk in Judea.*

> *(John 7:1)*

Biblically, *Judea* represents the nation of Israel, namely, the southern kingdom of Judah. In stark contrast, Jesus is so far removed from this location that he is only seen in *Galilee*, a term which essentially signifies his non-Jewish origin. The text displaces him in an apparent effort to dissociate him from the state of Israel. During the vivid recount of his crucifixion, we read that many stood by him who had come from Galilee:

> *Many women were there looking on from a distance, who had followed Jesus from Galilee.*

> *(Matt. 27:55)*

And where is Jesus manifested after his decisive resurrection? He is revealed in Galilee! Curiously, the text has a cryptic method of conveying and identifying the Messiah's human origin. We read,

> *He has risen from the dead; and behold, He is going before you into Galilee, there you will see Him; behold, I have told you.*

> *(Matt. 28:7)*

Because of its emphatic reiteration of the place called *"Galilee of the Gentiles"* (Matt. 4:15), the text suggests that our search for Jesus must be confined to the non-Jewish nations. It is tantamount to saying, "Inquire into the region of the Gentiles, and 'there you will see Him'" in the aftermath of his apocalyptic resurrection! Then the text adds the following cryptic dictum: *"Behold, I have told you."* Therefore, there seems to be no question that the term *Galilee* turns out to be the epitome of all non-Jewish nations.

This may be the reason why "there is no distinction between Jew and Greek" (Rom. 10:12) within the text; that is to say, the spiritual designation of one race connotes the other. This inability to distinguish between Jews and Greeks is also relevant to the enigmatic theme of the Messiah. Hence his obscurity! It may mean that the modus operandi of scripture has assimilated these two races to such an extent that their mystical classification has become almost indistinguishable. In other words, they can frequently displace each other within the metaphorical language of scripture. It seems, then, that tradition's indefinite search for a *Jewish Messiah* must inevitably end in utter futility.

ISRAEL: A SCRIPTURAL TERM
DENOTING THE TEN LOST TRIBES

A point worth mentioning is that the scriptural references to *Israel* or to the *Israelites* are not necessarily indicative of the Jews proper, but more often than not, they reflect the *ten lost tribes* of the northern kingdom of Israel that were wiped out by the Assyrians in 722 BCE. Their cities were overrun by the unrivalled Assyrian forces. Conversely, all but two tribes remained in the southern kingdom of Judah—namely, the tribes of *Judah* and *Benjamin* (Ezra 1:5)—which alone, strictly speaking, represent the term *Jews*. Further complicating matters, the tribes of Judah and Benjamin were also considered to be sons of Jacob, who had previously been renamed *Israel* (Gen. 32:28). So when scripture employs the word *Jews*, it is, by definition, referring to the people of Judah and not to *Israel* per se. When Jesus instructs his disciples not to go by way of the pagans—"but rather go to the lost sheep of the house of Israel" (Matt. 10:6)—he is not referring to the Jews, as we are accustomed to call them, but to the lost tribes of Israel. Jesus actually commands the disciples not to take their ministry to the Hebrews but to the long-lost tribes of Israel that dwell amongst the Gentiles (cf. Isa. 11:11, Jer. 31:31). Another example of this kind can be found in the under mentioned passage where the prophet *Simeon* cites the term *Israel* in connection with the Gentiles:

> For my eyes have seen Thy salvation [Christ], which Thou hast prepared in the presence of all peoples, A LIGHT OF REVELATION TO THE GENTILES, and the glory of Thy people Israel.

> (Luke 2:30-32).

We must not jump to the conclusion that the above phrase, "the glory of Thy people Israel," necessarily refers to the Jews per se. Simeon's prophetic encounter with Jesus merely relates to the concept of the spiritual *"people [of] Israel,"* a topic we have discussed on a number of occasions. In keeping with this scriptural image, we must come to realize that by the time the NT books are written, the *Israelites* have already become part and parcel of Gentile culture for the better part of eight centuries. They have intermarried and assimilated into the Gentile way of life for so long and to such an extent that it would be far too ambitious and sentimental to call them Jews in the proper sense of the word. This explains why there is an uppercase reference regarding the people to whom the Messiah will be manifested—*"A LIGHT OF REVELATION TO THE GENTILES"*—suggesting that the appellation *"GENTILES"* is an umbrella term that covers the juxtaposed concept of *Israel*, which is written in lowercase. In fact, whenever mention is made of Christ in connection with the Gentiles, it is usually set in uppercase letters to indicate that these passages represent important OT prophecies (Matt. 4:15, 12:18, 21; Acts 13:47, 15:17-18; Rom. 15:9-12). It follows that we must always exercise caution in the interpretive process because the Bible, especially the Old Testament, is riddled with references to the people of *Israel*.

It is true that God initiated a covenant "with the sons of Israel" (Deut. 29:1), which was supposedly enacted through his servant Moses. But it would take a man of such enormous stature as Paul to elucidate its meaning. Paul was no stranger to the religious history of the Jews. He writes,

> *I . . . wish that I myself were accursed, separated from Christ for the sake of my brethren, my kinsmen according to the flesh, who are Israelites, to whom belongs the adoption as sons and the glory and the covenants and the giving of the Law and the temple service and the promises, whose are the fathers, and from whom is the Christ according to the flesh. . . . But it is not as though the word of God has failed. For they are not all Israel who are descended from Israel; neither are they all children because they are Abraham's descendants.*

(Rom. 9:3-7)

Paul claims that the *Israelites* are his *kinsmen*, his blood-relatives *according to the flesh*; that is, corresponding to Paul's physical birth. But in spite of this statement, we learn that Paul was "born in Tarsus of Cilicia" (Acts 22:3), which was located in modern-day Turkey. In fact, Cilicia takes its name from the Greeks who were its primary inhabitants. It looks as though we may have another one of Paul's cleverly disguised logical equations on our hands. It runs something like this: (a) if the Israelites are "my kinsmen according to the flesh" and (b) if I was born in a Greek city among the Gentiles, (c) then who are the *Israelites?* The answer, of course, is simple: they are the ten lost tribes of Israel who dwell among the Gentiles.

Paul further describes Jesus as if he were an *Israelite* from the ten lost tribes, thereby linking the *Law* of Moses and the covenants of God with the prophecies concerning the Christ. This messianic descendancy is established when Paul makes a peculiar reference to the "Israelites, to whom belongs the adoption as sons . . . and from whom is the Christ according to the flesh." But there is a problem. If the term *Israelites* represents the Hebrews, then the latter would have been considered to be the "natural" sons of God, just like *Isaac* their forefather (Gal. 4:28-29, cf. John 1:12-13, Rom. 9:8). On the contrary, the preceding quotation (Rom. 9:3-7) refers to the Israelites as being adopted sons, thereby demonstrating once and for all that the concept of *Israel* does not denote the Jews per se. From a scriptural standpoint, the concept of *adoption* is a term which is traditionally associated with the Gentiles (cf. Rom. 8:14-15, Eph. 1:5-8); it indicates that the Gentiles are allowed to join God's family as "fellow heirs" with the natural sons of the Hebrews (Eph. 3:6).

In his discourse, Paul pushes the envelope in order to establish a link between the Messiah's lineage and that of the lost tribes of Israel. He takes full advantage of his cogent argument to impress upon us the following notion: just as the Israelites are Gentiles, so also is their descendant *Christ according to the flesh*. We must take heed of Paul's refusal to acknowledge the *Jews* in toto, thereby rescinding their presumed covenants and promises from God. Paul's remarkably perceptive reinterpretation of the OT suggests that scripture has a unique and highly idiosyncratic terminology that is answerable only to itself; it can only be measured according to its own standards. Hence, we should not project our own interpretations on the text. Paul goes on to delineate precisely what the term *Israel* refers to, wherewith he renders further credibility to his premise. He retorts, "But it is not as though the word of God has failed. For they are not all Israel who are descended from Israel [Jacob]; neither are they all children because they are Abraham's descendants [by birth]." In short, God's promises to *Israel* have not failed simply because they are inapplicable to the *Jews* per se; rather, they continue to be valid, although they pertain to another race, namely, the Gentiles! Had it not been for Paul, we would have never known.

Isaiah often calls the Messiah *"the Holy One of Israel,"* even though in one particular passage, the latter is cast as one *"of Tarshish"* (a son of *Javan,* which means "Greece" in Hebrew; Gen. 10:4) who *"will come first"* on the world scene to glorify the sons of Israel (60:9). Similarly, Paul employs a subtle and mysterious logical equation to show that although Christ was prophesied in the Jewish texts, this does not mean that he is a Semite. He writes,

> *The [Mosaic] Law . . . speaks to those who are under the Law [the Jews]. . . . But now apart from the Law the righteousness of God has been manifested, being witnessed by the Law and the Prophets.*

> *(Rom. 3:19-21).*

Biblical concordance indicates that there are many contexts in which the term *righteousness* can be used to refer to Christ (cf. Ps. 85:11, 98:2; Gal. 5:5). For instance, we read that the messianic *"righteous Branch of David . . . shall be called: the LORD is our righteousness"* (Jer. 33:15-16). In the *book of Isaiah*, God declares,

> *You are My servant [Jesus], I have chosen you; . . . My righteous right hand.*

> *(41:9-10)*

Therefore, according to Paul's cryptic equation, if the Law represents the Jews *who are under the Law,* then Christ—who is *the righteousness of God,* confirmed *by the Law and the prophets* (scripture)—is apparently revealed *apart from the Law,* that is to say, Jesus is manifested apart from the Jews! (Rom. 3:19-21).

CHAPTER 6

SIGNS OF A GREEK CHRIST
FOUND AMONG THE GENTILES

There is a topic that Paul continually returns to throughout his letters. In an enigmatic passage, which we will shortly present, Paul uncovers a *mystery* that has long been hidden from all previous generations. Most biblical *exegetes* (those who expound on scripture) believe that this secret either represents God's plan to save the Gentiles, or it reveals Christ as the Savior of mankind, who was never once mentioned by name in the OT. Even so, these interpretations fail to explain a number of things. First, God's design to save the Gentiles was certainly not hidden from all previous epochs and generations (Deut. 32:43, Ps. 2:8, Ps. 22:27, Ps. 72:11, Isa. 42:6). Second, the tremendous impact of this great *mystery* on the concept of Christ's revelation—given that the former is repeated throughout the NT epistles—cannot possibly be explained as a mere reference to the redemption of non-Jews! It is utterly unthinkable to ponder that the God of this universe would initially be interested in saving the Jews and no one else (Rom. 2:11). And to that extent, it does not qualify as a profound mystery to claim that the Deity is now interested to save the world at large. How could this be a prophetic disclosure if the plan of universal salvation has always been the same? (Rom. 3:29, Deut. 32:43, Ps. 22:27). Hence, this closely guarded secret must have an entirely different meaning altogether.

Third, the idea of a coming Savior who would deliver God's people at the end of the world was certainly known, even if it was not well established in the OT (Isa. 62:11, 19:20, *New King James*). As *Job* convincingly testifies in his book, "I know that my Redeemer lives, and that in the end [of the world] he will stand upon the earth" (19:25, *New International*). Furthermore, if the NT letters contain profuse references to "Jesus the Redeemer," then why would these same letters present this concept as if it were a previously undisclosed mystery? They would not. Therefore, the conventional views in regard to this mystery fail to adequately address what was hidden from all previous generations. The only legitimate explanation is that this great mystery pertains to Christ's forthcoming revelation, as we are told in one

letter after another (1 Cor. 2:6-7, 4:5; Col. 2:2, 3:4; 1 Tim. 3:16; Heb. 1:1-2, 9:26).
For this reason, Paul not only abandons the concept of salvation entirely, in the
under mentioned passage, but he contrasts it with the emphasis he places on Christ
himself and *the glory* of *Christ*, which is said to be found *among the Gentiles*. Unlike
the gospel writers who resort to mythic narratives in order to illustrate the messianic
prophecy, Paul takes it upon himself to reveal the authentic mystery of Christ:

> *The mystery which has been hidden from the past ages and*
> *generations . . . has now been manifested to His saints, to whom God willed*
> *to make known . . . the glory of this mystery among the Gentiles, which is*
> *Christ . . . the hope of glory.*

> *(Col. 1:26-27)*

The mystery that underlies this powerful revelation does not warrant the
aforesaid claim to universal salvation. Nor is it a literary introduction to Jesus as the
Savior. And what is the profound secret which Paul reveals? That *the glory of this mystery*
[found] among the Gentiles . . . is Christ himself! Simply put: it is the prophecy that Christ
will be found among the Gentiles. The passage does not indicate which particular
nation is implied, only that it is certainly not Jewish. This statement best explains why
the Gentiles "began rejoicing and glorifying the word" (Acts 13:48)—namely, Jesus:
"the Word of God" (Rev. 19:13, Ps. 107:20)—once they received the exhilarating
news of this mystery (Acts 13:47). They were excited and honored that God would
be born among them. This conclusion should not be surprising. After all, was it not
Paul who established in his epistles that the NT is a closed book, and who once said
that "our gospel is veiled [undisclosed]"? (2 Cor. 4:3).

Though Christ is conventionally depicted as a Jew, he is continuously set in the
context of a Gentile within various messianic references. A divine oracle, repeated
since the time of Isaiah (Isa. 49:6), may help explain this glaring paradox:

> *I HAVE PLACED YOU [Christ] AS A LIGHT FOR THE GENTILES,*
> *THAT YOU SHOULD BRING SALVATION TO THE END OF THE*
> *EARTH.*

> *(Acts 13:47)*

The notion that Christ appears at *the end of the world* to die on the cross—*to put*
away sin by the sacrifice of himself (Heb. 9:26, *King James*)—has already been explored
in part 1 of this volume. Now we will focus our attention on trying to reveal his
identity. As we will see, the promise of a *God among the Gentiles* (1 Chron. 16:24) is
systematically supported throughout the biblical text:

I, the LORD, have called You . . . ; I will keep You and give You as a
covenant to the people, as a light to the Gentiles.

(Isa. 42:6, New King James)

According to scripture's unique terminology, the implication is quite clear: (1) the Messiah becomes the *"covenant"* (the binding agreement) between God and his *"people"* and (2) his manifestation is exclusively linked *"to the Gentiles."* This is not all that surprising given that the Bible portrays Jesus as their *"light"* of illumination (cf. John 1:9). This mystery has hung in the balance for centuries, awaiting its appointed time of revelation to disclose Christ *"as a light to the Gentiles."* If we look at another one of Isaiah's passages, it would seem as though the Deity was prefacing this discussion with a comment of his own:

"To whom would He [the Messiah] teach knowledge? And to whom
would He interpret the message? Those just weaned from milk [new
initiates]? Those just taken from the breast?" . . . Indeed, He will speak to
this people through . . . a foreign tongue.

(Isa. 28:9-11)

The subject pronoun *"He"* is in upper case, suggesting that the reference is to God. This quote also provides a clear indication that the God man, upon his arrival, will not speak in the expected Semitic language of the Hebrews, but rather in *a foreign tongue.*

All through the Bible, one finds evidence of a messianic sacrifice that gives rise to more controversy than it would first appear. Being an interpreter certainly has its challenges, but Paul makes no secret of the fact that Christ's atoning sacrifice pertains to the Gentiles. To understand Paul's account, we must appraise the way in which it was written. For example, Paul writes that he received a revelation from God certifying that Jesus—who is anointed by the Holy Spirit (Isa. 61:1; Luke 4:17-19)—is the acceptable sacrifice of the Gentiles:

I have written more boldly to you on some points, . . . because of the
grace [the gift of revelation] given to me by God, . . . ministering the gospel
of God, that the offering *[sacrifice] of the Gentiles might be acceptable,*
sanctified by the Holy Spirit. Therefore I have reason to glory in Christ
Jesus in the things which pertain to God

(Rom. 15:15-17, New King James, emphasis added).

Contrary to the majority view that belies this scriptural passage by relating it exclusively to the idea of prospective Gentile converts, Paul's terminology is more in line with "Christ Jesus" and "the things which pertain to God" than anything else. This is why he concludes, "Therefore I have reason to glory in Christ Jesus," and in him alone. There are but a few scriptural examples, which contain the aforesaid key words "sanctified" and "offering," but they do confirm that Paul's message refers mainly to Christ:

> We have been sanctified through the offering of the body of Jesus Christ once for all.

> (Heb. 10:10, New King James)

If we drop down to *Hebrews* 10:14, we will encounter these same two words again:

> For by one offering He [Christ] has perfected forever those who are being sanctified.

> (New King James)

From this vantage point, it is not the temporal sacrifices of the Jews (Jer. 6:20, Heb. 10:8), but "the [messianic] offering of the Gentiles" that represents the "acceptable" atoning act of God (Rom. 15:16). But unlike the aspect of "Gentile conversion"—which was actually a nonissue as far as the Roman Gentiles were concerned (to whom the *epistle to the Romans* was addressed) since they were not expected to oppose it—this shocking revelation demands much courage, which helps explain why Paul writes "more boldly" (Rom. 15:15) on these points. Hence, we cannot, and should not, overlook the possibility that a Gentile Messiah is implied in the text.

GOD IS CALLED BY A GENTILE NAME

Scripture informs us as to *"how God first concerned Himself about taking from among the Gentiles [the non-Jews] a people for his name"* (Acts 15:14). As the passage continues to expound on this matter, it becomes a definitive declaration:

> And with this the words of the Prophets agree, just as it is written, . . .
> *"THE GENTILES WHO ARE CALLED BY MY NAME."*

> (Acts 15:15-17)

What a groundbreaking statement that is! It is completely unheard of among Christian circles, or at least misunderstood. This quote affords crystal clear evidence that the Deity's name is not derived from any Hebraic sources but has its origins in the non-Jewish nations. As claimed by God himself, these are the people who *"ARE CALLED BY MY NAME."* If we peruse the *Tanakh*, the Judaic texts, we will encounter similar ideas and motifs:

> *All the Gentiles . . . are called by My name*
>
> *(Amos 9:12, New King James).*

Amos, a Hebrew prophet of old, declares the exact same message that the rest of the NT writers proclaim. Clearly, the divine message is not denominational, but concerns Jews and Gentiles alike.

It behooves us to ask the following question: If *"all the Gentiles . . . are called by"* God's *"name,"* then what exactly is that name? The Deity first revealed himself to Moses as *"I AM WHO I AM"* (Exod. 3:14). This divine expression is conventionally rendered as *Yahweh*, which is construed as *Lord*. But since there is nothing akin to the letter *w* in the Hebrew alphabet, the variant *Yahveh*—pronounced as *yah-va*—may be furnished instead. Among the orthodox sects of the Judaic tradition, the religious adherents are strictly prohibited from vocalizing or pronouncing the divine name. Even the *tetragrammaton* (means "a four-letter word" in Greek) *YHVH*—the abbreviated form of Yahweh, designating God's name—is not allowed to be uttered. For thousands of years, this four-letter word has become an abiding sign of the personal name of God.

To demonstrate our premise, we will not start our exposition from the beginning of the Bible, but rather from the end. We will skip the *Torah*, pass by the prophets, and end up in the book of Revelation where God offers us a full and final disclosure concerning his name:

> *I am the Alpha and the Omega, the beginning and the end.*
>
> *(Rev. 21:6)*

The Deity reveals that he can only be known through the first and last letters of the Greek writing system. Unquestionably, *"the Alpha and the Omega"* constitute *"the beginning and the end"* of the Greek alphabet! The Divine Maker explicitly identifies himself with the language of the Greeks, and this revelation may furnish a clue as to who are *"the Gentiles . . . called by"* God's *"name"* (Amos 9:12, *New King James*).

If our proposition is correct, we must find indications of a Greek linguistic element within the original name of God as it was previously disclosed to Moses. Indeed we do! In the Hebrew language, the term *Yavan*, or its variant *Javan*, represents the Greeks (Josephus *Antiquities* I, 6). So it is easy to see how the phonetic and grammatical mystery of God's name—*Yahveh*, pronounced as *yah-va*—can clearly be solved by attributing its derivation to the Hebrew term *Yavan*, which refers to the Greeks. Upon further inspection, the Hebrew names for both God and Greece (*Yahvah* and *Yavan*) are quite indistinguishable from one another. Not to mention that the original cryptic and unspoken name of God was rendered as *YV* until Masoretic priests added the *H* vowels around the 6th century AD. Therefore it seems that even the derivation of the tetragrammaton *YHVH* from the original *YV* name of God points to *Yavan*, the Hebrew name for Greece!

A name usually signifies a country to which one belongs. Similarly, whenever God renames a biblical character, it is equivalent to relocating him to a new homeland. For example, when Abram the Gentile left ancient Babylon to come to Palestine (Gen. 12:1-5), God renamed him Abraham (Neh. 9:7). The same can be said of Jacob who fled from his father-in-law *Laban* and journeyed from Mesopotamia to Canaan (Gen. 31:3, 18, 21). Upon his arrival, an angel renames him Israel (Gen. 32:28). Along the same lines, Isaiah references the Messiah and prophesies, "You will be called by a new name" (Isa. 62:2). The fact that Jesus himself will be renamed clearly indicates that he will belong to a new nation. The book of Revelation reminds us that the end-time Christ "has a [new] name written upon Him which no one knows except Himself" (Rev. 19:12). This verse drives home the same biblical notion that Jesus is inevitably linked to a foreign (non-Jewish) nation!

BIBLICAL EQUATIONS AND CRYPTIC SIGNS
REVEAL THE GREEK MESSIANIC ORIGIN

*Jews ask for signs, and Greeks search for wisdom; . . . Christ Jesus . . .
became . . . wisdom from God.*

—*1 Cor. 1:22-30*

We have simply removed the written clutter from the foregoing segment to demonstrate what scripture is alluding to: *Jews* are equated to *signs* (Jews = signs), whereas *Greeks* are equated to *wisdom* (Greeks = wisdom). Since *Christ* equals *wisdom* (Christ = wisdom), it follows that *Christ* is equated with the *Greeks*! The above fragment is written in the form of a logical equation that obviously identifies *Christ Jesus* with the *wisdom* of the Greeks. It is like saying, if (*1* = *A*) and (*2* = *B*), and if the unknown variable named *C* turns out to be equal to *B* (*C* = *B*), then it follows that (*2* = *C*). This almost imperceptible scriptural allusion seems to reveal that the Messiah became a Greek God or *the wisdom of God* (1 Cor. 1:24, 30). Why else would Paul articulate it in such a peculiar manner—comparing Jews and Greeks while assigning distinct attributes to each of the two races—except to cleverly expose to which of the aforesaid ancestries Christ belongs. We must also bear in mind that the Deity *made known to us the mystery of His will . . . suitable to the fulness of the times, that is, the summing up of all things . . . in the heavens and . . . upon the earth* (Eph. 1:9-10). This means that Christ's identity is a *mystery* (a secret) that cannot be revealed until "the fulness of the times" has begun, which is otherwise known as the time period concerning the end of all things in the universe (cf. Gal. 4:4).

Curiously, these somewhat explicit passages eventually reveal Christ's earthly origin to the scrupulous inquirer. For example, in *the first epistle of Paul to the Thessalonians,* we know to whom he is writing, namely, to a Greek community located in a city of Northern Greece. In his prefatory salutation, Paul writes,

> *Paul . . . to the church of the Thessalonians . . . : Grace to you and peace.*

> *(1:1)*

As a point of reference, each time Paul uses the plural pronoun *you* in this epistle, he is always referring to this community of Greek believers (2:1, 14). Interestingly enough, while addressing this Greek population, Paul says that we certainly know "brethren beloved by God, His [God's] choice of you; . . . for the word of the Lord has *sounded* forth from you" (1:4-8, emphasis added). Keep in mind that Jesus's "name is called the Word of God" (Rev. 19:13, John 1:1-2). In a biblical setting, the term *sound* is often associated with a heavenly trumpet and represents the announcement of a divine decree concerning both the coming apocalypse and God's visitation (Exod. 19:19, Rev. 8:2). In an effort to achieve some measure of competence in understanding the meaning of the sentence, "The word of the Lord has sounded forth from you," we must compare it to the following verse where Christ's manifestation is defined by a loud shout (sound) that is depicted as a trumpet (1 Cor. 15:51-52; Rev. 1:10, 10:7, 11:15):

> *For the Lord Himself will descend from heaven with a shout, with the voice of the archangel, and with the [seventh] trumpet of God; and the dead in Christ shall rise first.*

> *(1 Thess. 4:16)*

Therefore according to the aforesaid epistle (1 Thess. 1:8), it appears that Christ, the word of God, proceeds from the prophesied nation of Greece because Paul tells the Thessalonians that "the Lord has sounded forth from you"! Moreover, he reassures them that his coterie of prophets (see 1 Thess. 1:2-4 where the term "we" is used in a lengthy sentence) is fully cognizant of God's predetermined plan and "His choice of you" (1:4, 8). Simply put, Paul insists that all of his prophetic contemporaries are fully aware of God's divine plan concerning Greece. In trying to solidify his thought, Paul states in a follow-up letter to the Thessalonians:

> *We should always give thanks to God for you [Greeks], brethren beloved by the Lord, because God has chosen you from the beginning for salvation.*

> *(2 Thess. 2:13)*

This is an unprecedented example of the unthinkable and the unimaginable! Who can believe this? And yet it is right in front of our eyes. It becomes perfectly obvious that Paul has set his eyes on the Greeks, to the exclusion of all other races, and offers his gratitude to God for having chosen them to be the forerunners of Christ. He tells them, "God has chosen you from the beginning [before creation] for [inducing] salvation."

The popular notion that this scriptural reference to the Greeks merely reflects God's plan of salvation to allow additional Gentile converts to join the original Jewish community of believers is completely eclipsed by the impact of Paul's subsequent remarks. His next statement makes it virtually impossible for us to ignore the mysterious Greek element that surrounds Jesus. Paul declares,

> *For who is our hope or joy or crown of exultation? Is it not even you [Greeks], in the presence of our Lord Jesus at His coming? For you are our glory and joy.*

> *(1 Thess. 2:19-20)*

Notice that the *exultation* of the Greeks is exclusively related to Jesus's *coming.* Moreover, God's hidden mystery (identity) is manifested as the *hope* and *glory* of the Greeks, and this is clearly a reference to Christ himself who alone is the "hope of glory" (Col. 1:26-27). Elsewhere, we read that Jesus is "the hope of the gospel that you have heard" (Col. 1:23). The meaning of the concept of *hope* is elucidated as follows: "Faith is the assurance of things hoped for, the conviction of things not seen" (Heb. 11:1). All these scriptural signifiers indicate that Christ is not yet beheld, which explains why the Greek *hope . . . or crown of exultation* takes effect *at His coming.*

The scriptural affinity between the Greeks and the messianic concept pertaining to the *hope . . . of exultation* provides unmistakable proof of the former's intimate relation to Jesus: "For His [the Messiah's] name alone is exalted" (Ps. 148:13). After all, Christ is exclusively known as "the Exalted One" (Isa. 30:18, *New Jerusalem Bible*). As for the *crown of exultation,* this is a direct reference to Christ's much anticipated earthly visitation (cf. Rev. 6:2, 12:1). Equally, the Greeks are described as the people "beloved by the Lord" (2 Thess. 2:13) as well as the *hope . . . or crown of exultation*

(1 Thess. 2:19-20) simply because the Messiah will be manifested among them. One of Isaiah's most direct messianic oracles adds, "The Gentiles shall see your righteousness; . . . you shall also be a crown of glory . . . and a royal diadem . . . , for the LORD delights in you" (62:2-4, *New King James*). On the whole, these direct and credible biblical cross-references prohibit us from remaining oblivious to the Greek messianic element therein.

THE SIGN OF JONAH AND
THE GREEK MAGI FROM THE EAST

All of a sudden, a shocking and extremely provoking idea emerges from the text:

> *Some of the scribes and Pharisees answered Him [Christ], saying,*
> *"Teacher, we want to see a sign from You." But He answered and said to*
> *them, . . . "No sign shall be given . . . but the sign of Jonah the prophet."*

> *(Matt. 12:38-39)*

A *sign* represents and, to a certain extent, reveals some important aspect of coming events. Signs signify momentous occasions; their prophetic value is enormous.

As the story goes, the prophet *Jonah* was in the belly of a great big whale for three whole days (Jon. 1:17), and Jesus uses this analogy to prophesy that he will likewise "be three days . . . in the heart of the earth" (Matt. 12:40). This story has mystified the biblical scholars who assume that *"the sign of Jonah"* merely refers to Jesus's death and resurrection. All the same, a coin always has two sides. The flip side of the coin is that this *"sign"*—which Jesus gave to the Jews and by implication to all future generations—is also a revelation of his earthly origin! As it turns out, the biblical theme of Jonah has central importance as regards the search for the real Jesus.

Jonah is the English form of the Hebrew name *Yona*, which is rendered as *Ionas* in the Greek. A surprising and unforeseen connection is established when we realize that *Yavan*, the Hebrew term for Greece, is the nation that gave birth to the ancient *Ionians* (Josephus *Antiquities* I, 6). In fact, Greece was called *Ion*, the Hebrew equivalent of which is *Yavan*, from where we presumably get *Yahvah*—the name of God. What is more, an ancient citizen of Ion was once called *Ionas*. Likewise, notice that Jonah's name—Ionas, the Greek form of the Hebrew word *Yona*—carries within it the distinct meaning that defines the bloodline of the ancient Greeks. According to the *Wikipedia*, the Web-based encyclopedia, even the antiquated term *Yona* refers to the Greeks:

> *The word "Yona" in the Pali language, and the analogues "Yavana"*
> *in Sanskrit, Malayalam, Kannada, Telugu and Tamil; and "Javanan"*
> *in Bengali, are words used in ancient India to designate Greek speakers.*
> *"Yona" and "Yavana" are both transliterations of the Greek word for*
> *"Ionians" (Homeric Greek: Iaones, Ancient Greek: Iawones), [sic] who*
> *were probably the first Greeks to be known in the East.*

> *(Yona)*

On these grounds, Jonah is, by definition, a symbol and a representation of the Greeks, not to mention a forerunner of Christ. The tale of Jonah, as described in the text, is very suggestive in this regard. The Bible reveals that the ancient peoples of "Tarshish" (Gen. 10:4) were among the descendants of the Ionians or "the sons of Javan," a transliterated variant form of the standard Hebrew *Yavan*. Amazingly, the text validates our premise by stating that Jonah "was going to Tarshish" (Jon. 1:3), the land of the Greeks. Textually, his identification with this OT prophet (Matt. 12:38-40) answers the biblical riddle of Jesus's earthly lineage. Therefore, the Bible offers yet another clue about Christ's connection to the Greeks through the esoteric *"sign of Jonah."*

Our study of Jonah indicates that he is clearly identifiable with the *Iones* of Javan.[1] The text provides enough evidence to support this assertion not only through his name, but also via his purported journey. By decoding Jonah, we decipher Christ. Therefore, the great *"sign of Jonah"* is not only a symbol of Christ's death and resurrection but also the mystery of his person. And who could possibly argue that the metaphorical clues within the Jonah narrative are haphazardly placed there by sheer chance?

Now let us recite the wondrous story of the "magi from the east" (Matt. 2:1) who followed "the star" (Matt. 2:9) that signified the birth of the Messiah. We are told that when these kings had found him, "they fell down and worshipped Him"; then they opened "their treasures" and "presented to Him gifts of gold and frankincense and myrrh" (Matt. 2:11). Apparently, the backdrop for the story is recounted with minor variations elsewhere in the Bible and depicted as being cast in the same mold, except that the *magi* in this version turn out to be Greek kings while the entire nativity scene takes place on the Greek island of Tarshish! Scripture informs us that "the sons of Javan [Greece] were Elishah, Tarshish, Kittim and Rodanim" (1 Chron. 1:7). Accordingly, the oracle declares,

> *Let the kings of Tarshish and of the islands bring presents; . . . and . . .*
> *offer gifts. And let all kings bow down before him, all nations [Gentiles]*
> *serve him.*

> *(Ps. 72:10-11)*

In this passage, we encounter the same nativity story as the one found in the gospel of Matthew, but somehow it turns out to be a curious and contrasting account that portrays Christ as a Greek King. But how can that be? More importantly, which of the two stories is the correct one? If we bear in mind that it is only the essence of the allegory that matters and that the apparent contradictions emerge as mere by-products of the figurative narrative, then we will be able to correctly assess the text. Naturally, the deeper the meaning, the more authentic its message will be. The essence of this tale is the dramatic moment in which the Divine Creator enters the world of time. The obligation of the text is simply to instill this act in the form of an oracle for future generations.

But the embellishing garb of a story can take many forms. In this particular case it has actually taken two distinct and diametrically opposed forms, namely, a rift between a Greek (Ps. 72:10-11) and a Jewish (Matt. 2:1-11) Messiah. If we keep in mind that the words of scripture are really hidden and disguised messages, which are intended to be grasped and fully disclosed only during the time of Christ's revelation, then we will learn to differentiate the apparent from the substantial meaning of the text. The fable of a Jewish Messiah seems rather spurious not only because it leads us to believe that it is based on a record of historical events, which in fact cannot be substantiated outside the Bible, but also because its elements simply do not add up. As impressive as it may seem, its raison d'etre (reason for being) is simply to convey the notion that Christ is the prophesied Messiah of the Jewish scriptures.

On the other hand, the allegory of the Magi treasures that were offered to the Greek Christ is reminiscent of another OT tale where local chieftains subsidized the rebuilding of the temple in Jerusalem with Greek money after the Hebrews returned from the *Babylonian exile* in 538 BCE (Neh. 7:6). What is inextricably perplexing about this story is that the Babylonian exile antedates the rise of the Greek Empire of Alexander the Great. The world has not been Hellenized as of yet. That said, why would the Hebrews contribute Greek money—namely, "drachmas, and . . . minas"—toward the work of rebuilding the Jewish temple? (Neh. 7:71). How did Greek money find its way to Jerusalem? On an apparent level, the story makes no historical sense. But on a deeper level, it illustrates that the underlying scriptural theme behind the façade of the Jewish temple is the promise of God's earthly abode (cf. 1 Cor. 6:19): an incarnate Messiah (a human temple) who is revealed through the metaphor of a foreign currency. It is precisely this highly symbolic element of Greek currency, which ultimately keeps the text both honest and intelligible. As a result, scripture tells us that "the people did according to this promise" (Neh. 5:13) and celebrated the coming of "a great festival, because they understood the words which had been made known to them," having gained "insight into the words" (Neh. 8:8-18).

In the twelfth chapter of Daniel's book, a heavenly messenger addresses the hidden Christ (who is elsewhere symbolized by *"the hidden manna,"* Rev. 2:17) through

God's prophetic dispensation of the temporal order. In other words, he explains how this messianic mystery will play itself out over the next twenty centuries:

> *Daniel, conceal these words and seal up the book until the end of time.*

> *(Dan. 12:4, 9)*

In our vernacular, this verse suggests that the true meaning of scripture is hidden from public view. The angel instructs Daniel to *"seal up the book"* because its contents will not be revealed *"until the end of time."* And therein lies the mystery of Christ.

THE SIGN OF MELCHIZEDEK: A LOGICAL EQUATION OF A NON-JEWISH MESSIAH

Today, Jeremiah's laments can still be heard through the mournful prayers of the devout who stand by the Wailing Wall, the last remnant of the Jewish Temple in Jerusalem. But everything else is gone, as if erased from the pages of history. There is no trace of the aromatic cedarwood altar that once stood in the midst of an imposing display: an inner sanctum overlaid "with pure gold" (1 Kings 6:20-21, 30). The sumptuous curtain of the Holy of holies (1 Kings 8:6) on to which were embroidered angelic mythical figures called "cherubim" has faded from memory. After the Romans destroyed the last epicenter of Jewish worship in 70 AD, the Temple Mount became a perpetually desolate area. In short order, the Hebrew language fell out of use. On that occasion the Israelite priestly caste fell into oblivion.

The temple ritual-sacrifices for the atonement of sins were merely precursors of the "precious blood, as of a lamb unblemished and spotless, the blood of Christ. For he was foreknown before the foundation of the world, but has appeared in these last times for the sake of you who through him are believers in God" (1 Pet. 1:19-21). These are the words of the person we have come to know as Peter the apostle. By the same token, it has often been said that the *"Passover sacrifice"* rite comprising the blood of an unblemished lamb painted on Israel's doorposts during God's judgment on Egypt was a redemptive and, one might add, eschatological sign prefiguring Christ's agonizing ordeal and ultimate death (cf. Exod. 12:1-29). Therefore, Jesus has supplanted the Judaic priests as he himself has "become a high priest forever according to the order of Melchizedek" (Heb. 6:20). But just who is *Melchizedek?* His brief encounter with Abraham is chronicled in the book of Genesis chapter 14 and verses 18-24. In the story, Melchizedek is cast as a high priest:

> *To whom also Abraham apportioned a tenth part of all the spoils, was first of all, by the translation of his name, king of righteousness, and then*

also king of Salem, which is king of peace. Without father, without mother, without genealogy, having neither beginning of days nor end of life, but made like the Son of God, he abides a priest perpetually. Now observe how great this man was to whom Abraham, the patriarch, gave a tenth of the choicest spoils. And those indeed of the sons of Levi who receive the priest's office have commandment in the Law to collect a tenth from the people, that is, from their brethren, although these are descended from Abraham. But the one whose genealogy is not traced from them [Jews] collected a tenth from Abraham, and blessed the one who had the promises. But without any dispute the lesser is blessed by the greater.

(Heb. 7:2-7)

Pay careful attention to the following sentence: Christ was "designated by God as a high priest according to the order of Melchizedek" (Heb. 5:10). So Melchizedek becomes a figurative representation of Christ. And since "it is impossible for God to lie" (Heb. 6:18), there is no deception involved in this portrayal of Christ's identity. Based on these incisive scriptural remarks, we are faced with yet another clue concerning the origin of Jesus. Again, it comes by way of a logical equation. It goes something like this: (a) if Jesus is "a high priest according to the order of Melchizedek" and (b) if Melchizedek's "genealogy is not traced from them," meaning the Jews, then it follows that (c) Jesus's "genealogy is not traced from them" either. The cryptic biblical conclusion: Christ is not a Jew! Unless interpreters do the necessary detective work to determine what is actually going on in the text and what the scriptures are seeking to convey, they will never even take a guess at the paradoxical conclusion that Jesus is not Jewish. All this of course is shocking, but true.

THE COMING OF THE ACHAEAN MESSIAH

Now I urge you, brethren (you know the household of Stephanas, that they were the first fruits of Achaia . . .). [sic] . . . And I rejoice over the coming of Stephanas and Fortunatus and Achaicus; because they have supplied what was lacking on your part. For they have refreshed [quickened] my spirit and yours.

(1 Cor. 16:15-18)

Consider Paul's reference to a mysterious figure named *Stephanas* and the latter's peculiar relation to the *white horseman* from the book of Revelation (6:2) who is said to wear a "stephanos crown" (Fruchtenbaum, 136). The name *Stephanas* is derived from the term *stephanos*, which means *crown* or *crowned* in Greek. More precisely, it is "a victor's wreath" (Morris, 101). Who typically wears a crown? Why, a king, of course (cf. Rev. 14:14, 17:14, 19:12). In other words, Paul is greatly rejoicing "over the coming of Stephanas," the King! (cf. 1 Tim. 6:15, Rev. 19:16). On closer inspection, it appears that Paul is employing the figure of the Achaean *Stephanas* to suggest the promised coming of a kingly Messiah. Nowhere is this more apparent than in the cross-references between *Christ* and *Stephanas*, enough to draw one's attention to the messianic undertones that are being conveyed, including the connotation that both wear the *stephanos* crown of a king. Speaking of which, Christ's identification with the Gentiles is foreshadowed in the book of Isaiah in which *Cyrus*, a heathen king, is called God's "anointed" Messiah! (45:1, 44:28).

Further associations between Christ and Stephanas are established through the allusion that both of them represent "the first fruits" from the dead (1 Cor. 16:15). The term *first fruits* is part of the biblical jargon whose purpose, in this context, is to provide a definitive scriptural explanation of Jesus as the first resurrected man: "the first fruits of those who are asleep" (1 Cor. 15:20). Remember that Paul just finished discussing Christ's resurrection from the dead, one chapter earlier, describing it (in a timeless context) as the first human accomplishment of its kind. He thereby calls the Messiah: "Christ the first fruits" (1 Cor. 15:23). In the process of intimating a scriptural affinity, Paul is tying the entire Stephanas passage that contains the idiomatic phrase "first fruits" back to the chapter that details Christ's resurrection. Moreover, in view of the fact that Paul rejoices "over the coming of *Stephanas*" who, as he claims, "refreshed my spirit and yours," we cannot attribute this mysterious remark to any other human being besides Christ. Clearly, this is a direct reference to the *blessed* Christ (*Fortunatus* means "blessed" in Latin) who alone is capable of renewing a person's spirit (cf. Rom. 6:4, John 3:7, Eph. 1:3).

Let us not forget that the spirit of Christ is symbolized by water that refreshes the soul:

> Now on the last day, the great day of the feast, Jesus stood and cried
> out, saying, "If any man is thirsty, let him come to Me and drink. He who
> believes in Me, as the Scripture said, 'From his innermost being shall flow
> rivers of living water.'" But this He spoke of the Spirit, whom those who
> believed in Him were to receive; for the Spirit was not yet given, because
> Jesus was not yet glorified.

> *(John 7:37-39)*

This quote implies that the *fullness* of the Spirit has not yet come by reason of Jesus's absence. In fact, scripture indicates that Christ will be *glorified* only at the end of time (2 Thess. 1:10). Currently, we are merely "sealed" and given "the Spirit in our hearts as a deposit" (2 Cor. 1:22, *New King James*). However, in the last days

God "gives the Spirit without measure" (John 3:34) or limit due to the expected manifestation of the Messiah.

But in order to communicate exactly what he means, Paul adds more intriguing clues to this brief episode we have been discussing. He states that "the household of Stephanas" became "the first fruits of Achaia." *Achaia* was an ancient province situated in the Peloponnese peninsula of Greece. It is a vibrant city to this day. In effect, Paul is clearly furnishing a missing piece of the puzzle by insisting that Stephanas is a prominent *Achaean*—personified in the figure of "Achaicus," meaning from Achaia, Greece—therefore, a *Greek*. Paul rises above "scriptural dissonance"—a term we use to define the disparity between the apparent and the esoteric meaning of the text—to convey his essential message: "the coming of Stephanas," the Achaean Messiah!

THE SECRETS OF JESUS

The secret things belong to the LORD our God, but the things revealed belong to us and to our sons forever.

(Deut. 29:29)

Moses once made this terse remark to the sons of Israel. This implies that there are prophecies which are revealed, as there are prophecies which are kept secret. We have seen this in the gospel narratives where "Jesus spoke to the multitudes in parables, and He did not speak to them without a parable" (Matt. 13:34), indicating that there were things left unsaid. Those initiated by the spirit were privy to the secrets of God, whereas the public remained clueless as they had not yet received the spirit of truth (Matt. 13:10-11). Similarly, Christ performs a healing and then issues the following admonition: "See that you tell no one" (Matt. 8:4). Scripture clearly indicates that Jesus repeatedly "warned them [his disciples] not to make Him known" (Matt. 12:16), what some scholars call the "Messianic Secret." But what is the purpose of this sovereign warning? Given that Jesus came to earth to reveal himself and his divine secrets, it is completely incomprehensible that he would make such a statement. Thus the reference to the withholding of *secrets* seems contradictory and must have a different meaning altogether. Scripture itself implies that Jesus did not want to be known publically because this revealed secret would precipitate great controversy and dissension.

This conclusion is more or less suggested by Matthew's gospel. Prior to distilling Jesus's profound secret, scripture prefaces Christ's words to emphasize that they reflect the fulfillment of prophecy:

Jesus . . . warned them not to make Him known, in order that what was spoken through Isaiah the prophet, might be fulfilled, saying, "BEHOLD,

MY SERVANT WHOM I HAVE CHOSEN; MY BELOVED IN WHOM
MY SOUL IS WELL-PLEASED; I WILL PUT MY SPIRIT UPON HIM,
AND HE SHALL PROCLAIM JUSTICE TO THE GENTILES. . . .
AND IN HIS NAME THE GENTILES WILL HOPE.

(Matt. 12:15-21)

We cannot emphasize enough the straightforwardness with which the mystery of Christ's identity is revealed in the foregoing excerpt. Jesus warns those who know him not to make him known to the public because of the prophecy which proclaims that "In his name the Gentiles will hope." This revealed secret would turn out to be the most shocking religious scandal of all time, implicating that Christ will be incarnated as a Gentile at the end of days! Therefore, scripture keeps quiet about this knowledge "until" the fulfillment of the prophecy takes place "at the final point of time" (1 Pet. 1:5, *New Jerusalem Bible*). However, the secret of Christ's Gentile identity is borne out in other passages as well:

Simeon has related how God first concerned Himself about taking
from among the Gentiles a people for His name. And with this the words of
the Prophets agree, just as it is written, . . . "I will return, . . . IN ORDER
THAT THE REST OF MANKIND MAY SEEK THE LORD, AND ALL
THE GENTILES WHO ARE CALLED BY MY NAME," SAYS THE
LORD, WHO MAKES THESE THINGS KNOWN FROM OF OLD.

(Acts 15:14-18)

While seeking to bring about an ongoing shift in hermeneutical perception, this prophecy acknowledges the biblical testimony concerning a Gentile Christ. Even so, we might rightly ask the question, who are the Gentiles who are called by God's name; those who are known by the name *Yahvah*? Our earlier discussion strongly indicated that they are the people of *Yavan* (Javan), namely, the Greeks. The Bible's well-kept secret is epitomized by Moses's instruction to the Jews that effectively prohibited them from pronouncing the divine name or even its abbreviated form, the so-called tetragrammaton: *YHVH*. Conveniently, the divine name remains concealed. Involved in this conspiracy is Greece, as these passages clearly demonstrate the presence of a Gentile Messiah within the text. Contradiction notwithstanding, we are told that the Creator "MAKES THESE THINGS KNOWN FROM OLD."

But how can that be? How can *secrets* be simultaneously hidden and revealed? As we have often said, the concealed plan of the Deity is definitely revealed within the Bible, assuming one knows how to find it. It constitutes the paradox of Paul's "unknown yet well-known" (2 Cor. 6:9) mystery. Another way it is declared is via the *Spirit*:

The anointing which you received from Him [the Holy Spirit] abides
in you, and you have no need for anyone to teach you; but as His anointing
teaches you about all things, and is true and is not a lie, and just as it has
taught you, you abide in Him.

(1 John 2:27)

Christ's *Humanity* (the doctrine that God became man) has always been taken
for granted, though it has never been more carefully scrutinized than at the present
time. This is not to say that scholars are currently debating whether or not Jesus
appeared in antiquity or at a subsequent time therefrom. Nor do they argue whether
the Lord's Day represents Christ's first or second coming. Rather, given the arcane
and obscure language in the text, their primary concern is to ascertain whether
such a figure ever existed:

Judas [not Iscariot] said to Him [Jesus], "Lord, what then has
happened that You are going to disclose Yourself to us, and not to the
world?" Jesus answered and said to him, . . . "the Holy Spirit, whom the
Father will send in My name, He will teach you all things, and bring to
your remembrance all that I said to you [in the gospels]."

(John 14:22-26)

The point being made in this inspiring passage is that Christ is not revealed
to the world, but only to those who wish to follow in his footsteps; those who seek
the way which leads onto eternity. Yet even then, he is disclosed to the apostles
only through *"the Holy Spirit"* who *"will teach"* them *"all things"* and remind them
of all that Jesus said in the gospels. Nevertheless, the Messiah's human identity is
disclosed sometimes secretly, and at other times explicitly within the text.

THE MARKAN SILENCE OF JESUS'S BIRTH

There are two sides to every story. We have merely flipped the proverbial coin
to reveal our take on scripture. And yet in undertaking such a formidable task of
searching for the real Jesus, the sheer size of evidence we have amassed speaks for
itself. Despite the onus of public opinion, we have sincerely disclosed untold secrets,
hidden for generations, which inundate the Bible. Let us not forget that these
mysteries were not meant to be concealed indefinitely. The manifold scriptural
references to this "unknown" Christ have certainly called into question the legitimacy
of the traditional view pertaining to a Jewish Messiah. *John Milton*, the celebrated
English poet, captured the obscure mood of the NT in his seventeenth-century epic
poem *Paradise Lost*:

Now had the great Proclaimer [John the Baptist] with a voice
More awful than the sound of Trumpet, cri'd
Repentance, and Heaven's Kingdom nigh at hand
To all Baptiz'd: to his great Baptism flock'd
With awe the Regions round, and with them came
From Nazareth the Son of Joseph deem'd
To the flood Jordan, came as then obscure,
Unmarkt, unknown

(343).

Why is it that when we read the *gospel of Mark*, the origins of Jesus are mysteriously missing from the text? Curiously, the birth narrative is omitted entirely. This literary gap might as well have required a backstory so that we could formulate an opinion about who Christ is and where he comes from. Obviously, in a story of such immense importance, the apparently calculated absence of Christ's lineage must have a special reason. Mark seems to accentuate the covert identity of Jesus by refusing to write anything about it. The reasons for this secrecy are explained by Christ's own words:

> *I speak to them in parables; . . . while seeing they do not see, and while hearing they do not hear, nor do they understand.*

(Matt. 13:13)

Mark is essentially conveying the same idea, namely, that the human origin of Jesus is a mystery even if he does not say it in so many words. In contradistinction to other gospels that portray the formative years of Jesus through biblical language, Mark simply declines to formulate any commentary. He refuses to speak as if the Jewish birth narrative has no business being there. He perpetuates the concept of an obscure and unknown Christ by virtue of his unwillingness to disclose him (cf. Matt. 11:25). If nothing else, the undercurrent of Mark's gospel raises an important question: are the Matthew and Luke birth narratives of a questionable nature?

The veracity behind Mark's deliberate silence is echoed in the rest of his gospel. For instance, we are told that Christ "began to go through Galilee [of the Gentiles], and He was unwilling for anyone to know about it" (Mark 9:30). In fact, the Markan text suggests that just about everyone who comes into contact with Jesus is told not to disclose him! (1:34, 44; 3:12; 5:43; 7:24, 36; 8:30; 9:9). The gospel of John amplifies this illustration with a hint of meaning, indicating that Jesus remained concealed in Galilee for an extended period of time (7:4-9, 12:36). In a figurative sense, John's portrayal would not only explain Christ's Gentile background but also his prolonged two-thousand-year absence. That is why *Albert Schweitzer*—a scholar, theologian, and philosopher—rightly maintains that Christ is essentially an unknown, shadowy figure insofar as the historical method is concerned (*The Historical Jesus*). This is in line with the early Christian view called *Docetism* (derived from the Greek term *Dokesis*, meaning "to seem"), which held that Christ did not really exist in human form:

> *According to Photius [a 9th-century Byzantine Patriarch], Clement of Alexandria held at least a quasi-docetic belief regarding the nature of Christ, namely that the Word/Logos did not became flesh, but only 'appeared to be in flesh,' an interpretation which directly denied the reality of the incarnation.*

> *(Ashwin-Siejkowski 95)*

Yet in deference to biblical usage, we are not denying John's proclamation of "Jesus Christ as coming in the flesh" (2 John 1:7) but rather qualifying it in terms of its chronological relevance. In other words, we deny the timing of this event, not the event itself! Why do you suppose scripture promotes the idea that Jesus's words are continuously misunderstood by everyone? Once again, we read of misapprehension connected to nescience:

> *They understood none of these things, and this saying was hidden from them, and they did not comprehend the things that were said.*

> *(Luke 18:34)*

CHAPTER 7

THE DIVINE REVERSAL

In order to grasp the mystery of this *divine reversal*—namely, the possibility of a Gentile Messiah who defies traditional scriptural expectations—we must turn to the story of *Jacob* (also called "Israel") in the book of Genesis. Jacob was the son of Isaac, whose father was the great Abraham: *"A FATHER OF MANY NATIONS"* (Rom. 4:17). One of Jacob's sons was Joseph, who in a cruel twist of fate was betrayed by his brothers, sold into slavery and carried off to Egypt (Gen. 37). One of the few things we know about him is that he wore "a varicolored tunic" (Gen. 37:3) that symbolized a rainbow, an important image that is often associated with the Messiah. But while he was in Egypt, Joseph rose to power and became a ruler, second only to Pharaoh (Gen. 41:40).

As was the Jewish custom of consecration, at some point Joseph presented his two sons, *Manasseh* and *Ephraim*, to his father Jacob so that they might receive a blessing. A commonly held belief among the adherents of Judaism was that the firstborn males (Exod. 13:12) were entitled to obtain the supreme spiritual blessing (Num. 3:11-13). But quite unexpectedly, Jacob lays his right hand on Ephraim, the younger, and his left hand on Manasseh, the elder, thereby "crossing his hands" (Gen. 48:14). Jacob's mysterious gesture suggests a promissory reversal as he seems to turn the tables on Judaism to imply the unthinkable. Mind you, this *blessing* is of surpassing importance because, first and foremost, it signifies the lineage through which the Messiah would come forth (Gal. 3:16).

The ancestral descent of the future Messiah represents the deeper significance of this *blessing*, which has been conferred on all male heirs since the time that the "promise" of *"an everlasting covenant"* was first made to Abraham by God (Gen. 17:7). Allegorically, Manasseh, the firstborn, signifies the *Tanakh*—the authoritative *canon* (derived from the Greek term *kanon*, which means "rule") of the Hebrew scriptures—while Ephraim symbolizes the Greek NT (cf. Gal. 4:22-24). In short, Manasseh is portrayed as a Jew, whereas Ephraim is depicted as a Gentile. There is biblical evidence to suggest that Ephraim typifies the *nations*, a scriptural term that traditionally denotes the non-Jewish peoples. This is illustrated in a verse taken from the book of the prophet *Hosea:*

Ephraim mixes himself with the nations.

(7:8)

As you can imagine, Jacob's apparent, or perhaps deliberate mix-up infuriates Joseph, who obviously represents the entire Jewish nation!

The vagaries of Jacob's *mix-up* have set in motion a series of puzzling contradictions that have baffled scholars ever since. This symbolic act seems to be impervious to interpretation, thereby prompting much confusion and debate. No one really knows exactly why Jacob ends up "crossing his hands" during the transmission of this prophetic blessing, which appears to be the main theme of the chapter in its entirety (Gen. 48). It is a narrative plot that serves to undercut the reader's expectations while giving rise to profound interpretative conflict. Still, we demand the secret. The idea of a *divine reversal* has not crossed anyone's mind.

The NT texts elaborate on the divine proclamation of a new covenant. If the Deity births a new contract, then by implication, the old covenant becomes obsolete (Heb. 8:13, Jer. 31:31-32). One of the most important conditions of a divine covenant requires, by definition, the death of the person who enacts it (Heb. 9:16-17). In fact, the NT clearly states that "without shedding of blood, there is no forgiveness" from the divine realm (Heb. 9:22). In actuality, the New Covenant represents the oath of God to fulfill his promise, namely, to sacrifice himself as the propitiation for *sin* (rendered as *hamartia* in Greek, which means "missing the mark") in order to exculpate mankind (1 John 2:2). The *first epistle to the Corinthians* explains what happens next. Through the mysterious process of resurrection, Christ will eventually transform the sin of Adam into pure light (1 Cor. 15). The resurrection will initiate a transmutation of all the contrary elements into an alchemical *singularity* or oneness. Therefore, this reversal of fortunes, as was mentioned earlier, suggests that the Gentiles have supplanted the Jews by becoming the heirs to the messianic promises of Christ!

Eusebius of Caesarea (c. AD 263-339), an exegete of the *biblical canon* (the books that are considered authoritative and "divinely inspired"), writes,

> *I hold that the secret prophecies were delivered in a disguised form because of the Jews, as the predictions concerning them were unfavorable.*

(Pamphili Book VI)

Similarly, when Christ does not conform to the Mosaic Law's strict guidelines in keeping the Sabbath holy (Exod. 20:8) and heals someone on the *Sabbath* (Mark 3:2-5), his actions suggest that it is vastly outdated. Evidence that the OT is rendered largely ineffective by the NT (also known as the "New Covenant"; cf. 1 Cor. 11:25) can also be found in Jesus's general approach to, and mistrust of, the Jewish ruling class: the Pharisees and Sadducees. His ideas about God are at odds with Jewish values throughout the gospels (Matt. 16:6). As a matter of fact, Jesus makes a solemn pronouncement concerning this *divine reversal*:

> *Therefore I say to you [Jews], the kingdom of God will be taken away from you, and be given to a nation producing the fruit of it.*

> *(Matt. 21:43)*

This verse is a throwback to an OT motif, which is predicated on the notion that the *Shekinah glory* (Exod. 24:16, 40:35) *"has departed from Israel"* (1 Sam. 4:21).[1] In another view, the *Shekinah glory* signifies the God who dwells among men (Num. 35:34) and, by implication, refers to the *glory* of Jesus Christ (John 1:14). In a related theme, the allegorical connotation suggested by the so-called displacement of the *Ark of the Covenant*—being transferred from the Jews to the Philistines (1 Sam. 4:2-4)—once again resembles a *divine reversal* and signifies that the Jewish messianic promises have now been supplanted by the Greeks and epitomized by the Greek New Testament! In the same vein, the OT *book of Ruth* can be considered as a representative version of the NT in the sense that it is named after a Gentile woman called *Ruth* who ends up marrying *Boaz,* an Israelite (Ruth 4:13). Her wedding symbolizes the spiritual marriage between the OT and the NT scriptures. In fact, according to the gospel genealogies, this Gentile woman turns out to be the great grandmother of *David,* the celebrated Israelite king and supposed forebearer of the Messiah (Matt. 1:5, Luke 3:32).

These stories, then, lend themselves to the obvious interpretation that some kind of a *divine reversal* has been implemented by the deity. This would explain why at some point in time *the tabernacle of the LORD . . . and the altar . . . were [not in Israel but] in the high place at Gibeon* (1 Chron. 21:29), an ancient city, which was located north of Jerusalem and inhabited by non-Jews (2 Sam. 21:2). In keeping with the words of scripture, this occurred because *"the glory has departed from Israel, for the ark of God was taken"* (1 Sam. 4:22). The significance of all these stories is that the glory of God, represented by the Ark of the Covenant, was transferred to the "Greeks" simply because these are the same people to whom Jesus would exclusively reveal himself! (John 12:17-23). The fact that God's glory has *"departed from Israel"* (1 Sam. 4:21) is in itself a cause and a sign of *offense* since it implies that God can longer be found among the Jews. Hence, Israel could not have anticipated that the *divine reversal* would influence them in the way that it did.

As a consequence, Isaiah forewarns the Hebrews not to jump to any conclusions with regard to this promissory displacement that has been effected by God:

For thus the LORD spoke to me with mighty power and instructed me . . . , saying, "You are not to say, 'It is a conspiracy!'"

(Isa. 8:11-12)

Paul builds a similar case: "But it is not as though the word of God has failed. For they are not all Israel who are descended from Israel" (Rom. 9:6). This is yet another indication that scripture has been grossly misinterpreted. Although Eusebius makes a valid point that the biblical oracles were concealed because their predictions were in conflict with Judaic expectations, there are other reasons why these prophecies remained undisclosed. The hidden meaning of these auguries was withheld for the purpose of revelation at the fulness of time (Gal. 4:4). Certainly, the future apocalypse of *"God . . . dwell[ing] on the earth"* (1 Kings 8:27) concerns the entire world, not just the Jewish race (cf. Zeph. 1:14-18, Zech. 14:7-9). For this reason, Paul puts forth a fundamental question:

Is God the God of Jews only? Is He not the God of Gentiles also? Yes, of Gentiles also.

(Rom. 3:29)

For one reason or another, the hidden mystery of Christ remains a secret to the general public, and there is no question that the deity does this of set purpose. To that extent, it may not be inappropriate to say that the Bible contains a divine conspiracy whose message is encrypted. Yet there are noteworthy exceptions where scriptural disclosures are also made: some transparent, others under an apparent biblical camouflage, as it were. So it does not appear that God had a hand in maintaining absolute secrecy regarding the origin and advent of Christ, for he asks:

Who has believed our message? And to whom has the arm [Christ] of the LORD been revealed?

(Isa. 53:1)

In retrospect, we begin to understand why *Noah*—a messianic-type figure who saved humanity from global inundation by constructing an ark—cursed one son, *Canaan* (Gen. 9:25), while blessing the other, *Japheth*. Noah's *blessing* is apparently related to the concept of *the divine reversal*, as mentioned earlier, where Jacob confounds the anticipated *blessings* (promises) that were supposed to be bestowed on Manasseh, a symbol of the Hebrew race, and offers them to *Ephraim* instead. In fact, Noah forcefully exclaims, *"May God enlarge Japheth"* (Gen. 9:27). But what is the meaning of this benediction? There is no other explanation for Noah's unexpected *blessing* except to say that it relates to *Japheth* simply because he is the father of Greece! (Gen. 10:2).

GENTILES HAVE REPLACED JEWS AS HEIRS
TO THE PROMISES OF CHRIST

Now let us take into account what Moses and Isaiah have to say concerning the manifestation of Christ among his people. In his scintillating discussion, Paul—the author of the epistle to the Romans—refers back to these earlier prophets in an effort to demonstrate the replacement of the Jews by the Gentiles in regard to the promises of Christ. He punctuates Israel's ignorance when he writes,

> *But I say, surely Israel did not know, did they? At the first Moses says, "I [God] WILL MAKE YOU [Israel] JEALOUS BY THAT WHICH IS NOT A NATION, BY A [different] NATION WITHOUT UNDERSTANDING [of scripture] WILL I ANGER YOU." And Isaiah is very bold and says, "I [Christ] WAS FOUND BY THOSE WHO SOUGHT ME NOT, I BECAME MANIFEST TO THOSE WHO DID NOT ASK FOR ME."*

> *(Rom. 10:19-20)*

This is yet another passage signifying that the promise of God's incarnation cannot derive from the Hebrew race. It cannot be overstated that Paul continually underscores Israel's incomprehension to one degree or another.

In the above passage, Moses clearly predicts that another nation will eventually supplant Israel, thus alienating and vexing the Jews. In like manner, Isaiah indicates that the Messiah will become *"manifest"* to a nation that did not even expect him, much less seek him. According to Paul, Jesus's life has already been predicted by the Holy Spirit and documented in the sacred scriptures. Moreover, for his name's sake (1 Kings 8:41-43; cf. Mark 9:7), he will dwell among the Gentiles:

> *Christ Jesus . . . [has been] promised beforehand [in advance] through His prophets in the holy Scriptures, . . . who was declared the Son of God with power by [as a result of] the resurrection from the dead, according to the spirit of holiness, . . . to bring about the obedience of faith among all the Gentiles, for His name's sake.*

> *(Rom. 1:1-5)*

This impressive sample contains further evidence that Christ's resurrection is actually ascribed to prophecy, not history. What is more, all these extracts reflect the Deity's change of plans, what we call *the divine reversal*: the displacement of the

Jews by the Gentiles in regard to the inheritance of the messianic promise. These unforeseen developments are epitomized in the confounding story of Jacob's blessing when he precludes the firstborn, Manasseh, from obtaining the Abrahamic *promise* and bestows it instead upon the second-born, Ephraim (Gen. 48:9-19). But make no mistake; Jacob knew exactly what he was doing. He later reveals that Ephraim will not only become more important than Manasseh, but he will also be the progenitor of the Gentiles, for "his descendants shall become a multitude of nations" (Gen. 48:19).

Elsewhere, Paul reminds us that this is in fact what has happened to Israel, as the prophetic destiny of Christ has evidently changed hands; it is now under new ownership:

> That which Israel is seeking for, it has not obtained, but those who were chosen [the non-Jews] obtained it, and the rest were hardened; just as it is written, "GOD GAVE THEM A SPIRIT OF STUPOR [spiritual blindness], EYES TO SEE NOT AND EARS TO HEAR NOT, DOWN TO THIS VERY DAY." . . . But . . . salvation has come to the Gentiles, to make them [Jews] jealous.

(Rom. 11:7-11)

In this passage, we encounter language which is as clear as it is precise. Therefore, according to Paul, the Jews and Gentiles have traded places in the forthcoming plan of God. But there is more.

Later in the same chapter, Paul instructs us so that we do not remain "uninformed of this mystery," namely, "that a partial hardening has happened to Israel until the fulness of the Gentiles has come in; and thus all Israel will be saved" (Rom. 11:25-26).[2] Yet, notice that *the fulness of the Gentiles* also corresponds to a future time period when Christ's sacrifice will *"TAKE AWAY THEIR [Israel's] SINS"* (Rom. 11:27). In other words, the Messiah is actually manifested during the final age, variously known as *the fulness of the Gentiles*, which ultimately transpires "in the end of the world" (Heb. 9:26, *King James*). This is why the aforementioned passage (Rom. 11:25-26) denotes that the Jews will not be saved until this time period occurs. *The fulness of the Gentiles* is a variant of another scriptural expression: *the fulness of the time*. We are told that "when the fulness of the time came, God sent forth His Son, born of a woman [incarnated]" (Gal. 4:4). Both terms represent the coming of Christ (cf. Heb. 1:2). And both represent the year of his coming, which is sometimes rendered as "the full number [year] of the Gentiles" (Rom. 11:25, *New International*). To curtail any further expectations of a Jewish Messiah, scripture uses an analogy to indicate that God will deliver an apocalyptic message to the Jews in a non-Semitic language:

"BY MEN OF STRANGE TONGUES [in a foreign language] AND BY THE LIPS OF STRANGERS [non-Jews] I [Christ] WILL SPEAK TO THIS PEOPLE, AND EVEN SO THEY WILL NOT LISTEN TO ME [but reject me]," says the Lord.

(1 Cor. 14:21)

Paul's advanced knowledge of Christ is imparted to the reader via a semantic blitzkrieg: a prophetic assault on ignorance. He commences his prophetic offensive as follows:

Christ has become a servant . . . to confirm the promises given to the fathers, and for the Gentiles to glorify God . . . ; as it is written, "THEREFORE I WILL GIVE PRAISE TO THEE AMONG THE GENTILES." . . . And again he [the prophet] says, "REJOICE, O GENTILES, WITH HIS PEOPLE." And again, "PRAISE THE LORD ALL YOU GENTILES, AND LET ALL THE PEOPLES PRAISE HIM." And again Isaiah says, "THERE SHALL COME THE ROOT OF JESSE, AND HE WHO ARISES [from the dead] TO RULE OVER THE GENTILES, IN HIM SHALL THE GENTILES HOPE."

(Rom. 15:8-12)

The foregoing excerpt constitutes a collection of OT oracles pertaining to Christ (cf. 2 Sam. 22:50; Ps. 18:49, 57:9, 108:3, 117:1; Deut. 32:43; Isa. 11:10). Why does Paul go through the trouble of quoting these OT prophets? And why does he keep piling up one prophecy after another concerning the Gentiles? He tells us why. Paul does not want us "to be uninformed of this mystery," lest we err in our "own estimation" (Rom. 11:25) and misconstrue the aforesaid passage to mean God's plan of salvation extended to the non-Jews. This latter view pales by comparison to the glorious secrets revealed by the aforementioned oracles. The *mystery* of the Messiah is that he is not praised among the Jews but rather glorified among the Gentiles. Indisputably, Jesus *"ARISES [from the dead] TO RULE OVER THE GENTILES"* not over the Jews! As for the earlier generations of biblical scholars, how could they not have known that these turn of events would so radically change the course of human history? In response to the common misconceptions about the Bible, the author of the epistle to the Hebrews retorts,

For though by this time you [clergy] ought to be teachers, you have need again for someone to teach you the elementary principles of the oracles of God.

(Heb. 5:12).

ISRAEL'S PRECLUSION FROM MESSIANIC INHERITANCE

Every religion is true one way or another. It is true when understood metaphorically. But when it gets stuck in its own metaphors, interpreting them as facts, then you are in trouble.

—*Joseph Campbell*, Power of Myth

Though both Jews and Christians have drawn erroneous conclusions from the holy scriptures, this does not mean that the divine message has been unsuccessful:

But it is not as though the word of God has failed. For they are not all Israel who are descended from Israel; neither are they all children [simply] because they are Abraham's descendants, . . . [despite the saying:] "THROUGH ISAAC YOUR DESCENDANTS WILL BE NAMED." That is, it is not the children of the flesh [by birth] who are children of God, but the children of the promise [that] are regarded as descendants.

(Rom. 9:6-8)

Paul is teaching us the inspired prophetical word of God (2 Tim. 3:16). Yet he turns our interpretative world upside down with his unorthodox treatment of the scriptural sources. He insists that there is a biblical terminology, which we must strictly adhere to.

Paul is saying, in effect, that the oracles regarding the alleged *descendants* of Israel are not indicative of the Hebrew race whatsoever! The added remark pertaining to *the children of the promise* does not denote those who are Jews by birth, thereby excluding Abraham's physical descendants from inheriting the scriptural promises of God. In this sense, only *the children [or the people] of the promise are regarded as [the true] descendants*. Paul's definition concerning the textually ambiguous *people of Israel* also precludes Jews from being heirs to the promises of Christ; that is, they are not part of his genealogy. It appears, then, that the scriptural concept of *Israel* is more of a figurative or spiritual term, rather than one that is literal or concrete.

What about the Christian "men of letters," or the learned scholars of rabbinic Judaism? How is it that they all misinterpreted this surprising turn of events? The answer is that the process of making a simple textual inquiry will not amount to much insofar as scriptural interpretation is concerned. Paul describes the problem in its starkest terms:

Not that we are adequate in ourselves to consider anything as coming from ourselves, but our adequacy is from God, . . . not of the letter [text], but of the Spirit.

(2 Cor. 3:5-6)

Paul is saying that what he lacks in scriptural knowledge, he more than makes up for with his personal revelations. In other words, you can search the scriptures all you want, but if the Spirit of God does not reveal the intended meanings, you will only end up concocting your own fictive aberrations!

In a similar context, Isaiah prophesies that the Messiah will mysteriously come to the land of the Gentiles:

The oracle concerning Egypt. Behold, the LORD is riding on a swift cloud, and is about to come to Egypt.

(Isa. 19:1)

Isaiah's concept of the Lord coming to Egypt—the land of the heathen—is echoed in the *book of Chronicles* where God declares that there is no need to build for him a material temple since his plan already includes the building of a human temple on earth (1 Chron. 17:12-14):

And it shall come about when your days are fulfilled [in the end-times] . . . that I will set up one of your descendants after you, who shall be of your sons; and I will establish his [the Messiah's] kingdom.

(1 Chron. 17:11)

According to Paul, this promise of a messianic son comes forth from the *spiritual descendants* of Israel who curiously turn out to be the heathen: the non-Jewish nations. Here is another passage that references Jesus as a Gentile:

You have kept me as the head of the nations [Gentiles]. A people whom I have not known [non-Jews] shall serve me. . . . Therefore, I will give thanks to You, O LORD, among the Gentiles.

(2 Sam. 22:44-50, New King James)

As we have amply demonstrated, the term *nations* represents the Gentiles. According to Eusebius, a renowned scholar of the Bible, the following verse— *"to him [the Messiah] shall be the obedience of the peoples [nations]"* (Gen. 49:10)—means that "he [Christ] is the expectation of the Gentiles" (Pamphili Book III).

The tables have turned when the Godhead reproves Israel proper:

> *"I am not pleased with you, . . . nor will I accept an offering from you. . . . My name will be great among the nations [Gentiles]," says the LORD of hosts.*

> *(Mal. 1:10-11)*

This constitutes further scriptural proof that the Deity promulgates the origin of the divine *seed* both candidly and beyond measure! In reading the entire first chapter of the *book of Malachi*, one senses the curious sentiment that God rejects the Jewish *expectation* of the Messiah and, like Jacob, blesses a different nation (1:11, 14). On the other hand, the Jews behave like Joseph who thought that Jacob made a mistake in blessing Ephraim instead of Manasseh. Their reasoning is as follows:

> *Is not the LORD in our midst? [Therefore] Calamity will not come upon us.*

> *(Mic. 3:11)*

And yet, in the *book of Micah*, God appears to rebuke them as well as contradict their far-fetched interpretations of his oracles (3:9-12). The Deity declares, "Israel," you "twist everything that is straight" (3:9); that is, you alter the meaning of the oracles to suit yourself! This certainly reflects the traditional position of Jewish religious movements—especially among the more austere sects—that *God* is the exclusive right and most precious possession of the Jews. But this belief is both theologically and scripturally baseless and inaccurate.

By contrast, Isaiah's prophecies cryptically reveal the people who will truly seek the Messiah in their midst:

> *Then it will come about in that [future] day that the nations [Gentiles] will resort to the root of Jesse [Jesus], who will stand as a signal [sign] for the peoples [Gentiles]; and His resting place [grave] will be glorious.*

> *(Isa. 11:10)*

The above quote refers to the famous OT prophecy in which the Messiah is portrayed as a spiritual tree: *a shoot will spring from the stem of Jesse, and a branch from his roots . . . , and the Spirit of the Lord will rest on Him* (Isa. 11:1-2). In the NT, Jesus actually attributes these prophecies to himself (Luke 4:16-21). Accordingly, Isaiah depicts Christ as a tree *branch*, a term which traditionally serves as a sign of the Messiah (Zech. 3:8, cf. Dan. 4:23). This divine symbol is a throwback to *"the tree of life"* in the Garden of Eden (Gen. 3:22, cf. John 14:6).

As noted by Eusebius Pamphili in his book, *Demonstratio Evangelica*, the Gentiles are scripturally implicated as being God's *inheritance*. In ancient times, inheritance was typically transferred from father to son. Within a scriptural context, God the Father says to God the Son,

> *Ask of Me, and I will surely give the nations [Gentiles] as Thine inheritance.*
>
> *(Ps. 2:8)*

The obvious biblical conclusion is that the Gentiles are the true *spiritual* heirs, the mystical *Jewish* progeny who inherit the promises of Christ. Now consider what Paul has to say about a strikingly similar theological idea:

> *By revelation [from God] there was made known to me the mystery, . . . which in other generations was not made known to the sons of men, as it has now been revealed to His Holy apostles [teachers] and prophets in the Spirit; to be specific, that the Gentiles are fellow heirs . . . of the promise in Christ Jesus.*
>
> *(Eph. 3:3-6)*

If Jews and Gentiles are co-heirs with respect to the messianic promises, then the possibility of a non-Jewish Christ is not entirely out of the question.

The book of Acts further relates the wonders and divers miracles of Christ among the Gentiles:

> *And all the multitude kept silent, and they were listening to Barnabas and Paul as they were relating what signs and wonders God had done . . . among the Gentiles.*
>
> *(Acts 15:12)*

According to the prophet Isaiah, one of the Gentile nations, which proclaims God's glory is "Javan," a Hebrew term for Greece (Gen. 10:4):

> And I will set a sign among them and will send survivors [posterity] from them to the nations [Gentiles]: Tarshish, . . . and Javan, to the distant coastlands that have neither heard My fame nor seen My glory. And they will declare My glory among the nations [Gentiles].

> (Isa. 66:19)

It may be remarked in passing that *Tarshish* represents the offspring of Greece (Gen. 10:4). As we will see, Tarshish signifies the Greek coastlands that *"declare"* God's *"glory among the nations."* Notice that Greece does not simply acknowledge God's manifestation on earth, but rather declares it to the world at large!

Have you ever considered why Jesus says to the Jews, *"You shall seek Me, and shall not find Me"*? (John 7:34). It is a direct and straightforward prediction explicating that although they seek a *Jewish* Messiah, they will not find one:

> The Jews therefore said to one another, "Where does this man intend to go that we shall not find Him? He is not intending to go to the Dispersion among the Greeks, and teach the Greeks, is He?"

> (John 7:35)

Why does John's gospel include this episode? Because it is precisely what the Messiah will do. He will not appear among the Jews, as expected, but rather manifest himself *"among the Greeks."* This verse represents a cryptic method through which sacred scripture reveals the mystery of Christ's identity.

THE UNKNOWN GOD OF GREECE

> Then Paul stood in the midst of the Areopagus [the Supreme Court] and said, "Men of Athens, I perceive that in all things you are very religious; for as I was passing through and considering the objects of your worship, I even found an altar with this inscription:

> TO THE UNKNOWN GOD

> Therefore, the One whom you worship without knowing, Him I proclaim to you."

> —Acts 17:22-23, New King James

In all of Paul's travels, never does he point to a specific altar and indicate that it represents the very God that he proclaims. Yet this is precisely what Paul does during his *inspired* homily in Athens, Greece. Paul professes that the altar *"TO THE UNKNOWN GOD"* signifies the unique Deity to whom he is deeply committed: Jesus Christ. As we shall see, the scriptural implication of a Greek God is wholly warranted. As an illustrative instance, notice the capitalization of the term *GOD*, which in a pagan context would not have merited letters in upper case but would have been simply rendered as *god*. This imprint of an *"UNKNOWN GOD"* calls forth the messianic prophecy of Isaiah:

> *I was sought by those [non-Jews] who did not ask for Me; I was found by those [Gentiles] who did not seek Me.*

> *(65:1, New King James)*

And then there is Jeremiah's bone-chilling prophecy, which suggests that a Gentile nation will supplant Israel insofar as the *messianic promises* are concerned:

> *"Behold, I am bringing a nation against you from afar, O house of Israel,"* declares the LORD. *"It is an enduring nation, it is an ancient nation [Greece], a nation whose language you do not know, nor can you understand what they say."*

> *(5:15)*

This oracle was fulfilled by the advent of the Greek New Testament, which displaced the Hebrew language and was henceforth incomprehensible to Jews. In addition, Jeremiah's omen pertains to the concept of the *divine reversal* where another nation supersedes Israel's divine *birthright*.

Scripture uses the term *offspring* primarily in reference to the concept of a divine *seed*; that is, to the promise of a coming Messiah (Gal. 3:16, Gen. 9:9, *King James*). But since Christ must arrive on earth through a certain lineage, the term *offspring* also represents the notion of a messianic descendancy. For instance, Jesus signifies that he is the promised Messiah when he says, *"I am the root and the [spiritual] offspring of David"* (Rev. 22:16). Now consider the earth-shattering news of Isaiah's prophecy that concerns the descendants of the covenant who *"shall be known among the Gentiles and their offspring,"* a lineation that may be said to refer to Christ:

> *I [God] will direct their work in truth, and will make with them an everlasting covenant. Their descendants shall be known among the Gentiles, and their offspring among the people [non-Jews]. All who see*

them shall acknowledge them, that they are the posterity whom the LORD
has blessed.

(61:8-9, New King James)

During his Athenian sermon, Paul indicates that the Greeks have a role to play
in the mystery pertaining to the earthly origin of the divine incarnation. Actually, he
makes a noticeable scriptural intimation to the effect that the *Greeks* represent the
divine *offspring.* He says,

In Him [God] we live and move and have our being, as also some of
your own [Greek] poets have said, "For we are also His offspring."

(Acts 17:28, New King James)

In an effort to validate the aforesaid scriptural conclusion to his Greek audience,
Paul returns to this verse and reasserts that the Greek poets are indeed correct in
saying that "we [Greeks] are the offspring of God"! (Acts 17:29, *New King James*).
If the Greeks are heirs to the divine promises, "the offspring whom the LORD has
blessed" (Isa. 61:9), then they also denote the *ancestry* of Christ, which is tantamount
to saying that they are the *"ancient nation"* of Jeremiah's prophecy (5:15). This
becomes evident from another passage in which God declares that the Messiah who
"will accomplish" his plan does not come from the Jews:

My purpose will be established, and I will accomplish all My good
pleasure; calling . . . the man of My purpose from a far country [not
Judea]. . . . I have planned it, surely I will do it.

(Isa. 46:10-11)

Accordingly, the book of Acts presents a quite different view of "scriptural
meaning" than that of the conventional, Christian hermeneutical approach. For
example, while comparing Jews to Greeks, it switches sides, as if to make a spiritual
statement, by mentioning "the Jews and the God-fearing Gentiles" (Acts 17:17),
having earlier associated the latter with "the God-fearing Greeks" (17:4). In its
depiction, the text portrays Jews as a sort of pagan community while the Greeks are
now characterized as spiritual *God-fearing* believers. All these delicately complex,
and somewhat oblique references, betray what the fifth book of the NT is seeking
to convey, namely, that the inconspicuous, *Greek messianic element* has inevitably burst
through the landscape of scripture. This state of affairs would certainly explain why
"the Jews, becoming jealous and taking along some wicked men from the market

place, formed a mob and set the city in an uproar" (Acts 17:5). Why else would the Jews be *jealous* and take to the streets?

If indeed Jesus was Jewish, this would have been a cause for celebration among the Hebrew people, not a motive for *jealousy* and dissension. Why they were incited to riot in the Greek city of Thessalonica (Acts 17:1, 5) while Paul was preaching to them (17:1-2) remains unknown. What we do know is that Paul was producing evidence based on his mysterious arguments to prove that Jesus is the Messiah (Acts 17:2-3). The text itself suggests that the proclamation of the Messiah to main cities throughout Greece was the tipping point that greatly instigated and infuriated the Jews (Acts 17:13). Given the amount of evidence, which we have gathered—including the deduction that no other motive can possibly account for the enigmatic incitement of the Jews—the most probable explanation for the Jewish revolt can be attributed to the Pauline promulgation of a Greek Messiah, even though this notion is not made explicit in the text. Nevertheless, there are other passages, which lend support to this premise. Paul writes,

> As He [God] says also in Hosea, "I WILL CALL THOSE WHO WERE NOT MY PEOPLE [non-Jews], 'MY PEOPLE,' . . . AND IT SHALL BE THAT IN THE PLACE WHERE IT WAS SAID TO THEM, 'YOU ARE NOT MY PEOPLE,' THERE THEY SHALL BE CALLED SONS OF THE LIVING GOD"

> (Rom. 9:25-26).

Bear in mind that this *"UNKNOWN GOD"* of the "gospel," and "the revelation of the mystery [of his origin] . . . , has been kept secret for long ages past" (Rom. 16:25). In fact, it has been *"HIDDEN SINCE THE FOUNDATION OF THE WORLD"* (Matt. 13:35). But we must also take into account that this *apokalypsis* (disclosure) is not man-made. It is not predicated on any "cleverly devised tales" (2 Pet. 1:16) but rather "received" through "the Spirit who is from God," as this revelation is "taught by the Spirit, [through the process of] combining spiritual thoughts with spiritual words" (1 Cor. 2:12-13). According to Paul, this secret "has now been revealed" (Eph. 3:5) "in order that in Christ Jesus the blessing of Abraham [of the Jews] might come to the Gentiles" (Gal. 3:14). Clearly, this blessing refers to Abraham's promised messianic *offspring*, namely, "to his seed . . . , that is, Christ" (Gal. 3:16). It is reminiscent of the confounding *blessings* bestowed by Isaac and Jacob (Gen. 27:30, 48:14), which in and of themselves indicate a *divine reversal* of sorts. In effect, scripture tells us why the Hebrew people were offended in the preceding passages; because this controversial, messianic blessing (*promise*) "has come to the Gentiles, to make them [the Jews] jealous" (Rom. 11:11). Paul exclaims,

> *For I say that Christ has become a servant . . . on behalf of the truth*
> *of God to confirm the promises given to the fathers, and for the Gentiles to*
> *glorify God for His mercy; as it is written, "THEREFORE I WILL GIVE*
> *PRAISE TO THEE [Christ] AMONG THE GENTILES, AND I WILL*
> *SING TO THY NAME.". . . Isaiah says, "THERE SHALL COME THE*
> *ROOT OF JESSE [the Messiah], AND HE WHO ARISES TO RULE*
> *OVER THE GENTILES, IN HIM SHALL THE GENTILES HOPE."*

> *(Rom. 15:8-12)*

But who exactly are the Gentiles? Greek was the official language of the Gentiles mainly due to the conquests of Alexander the Great which stretched from Egypt to India. The historical record describes this multilateral occupation by employing the term *Hellenization*—the dispersion of Greek culture and language among foreign nations—which is derived from the Greek word *Hellas*, meaning "Greece." This explains why Paul uses the all-encompassing term *Greeks* to refer to the Gentiles. Here is a case in point. Instead of distinguishing between Jews and Gentiles, Paul simply differentiates between Jews and Greeks: "There will be . . . distress for every soul of man who does evil, of the Jew first and also of the Greek" (Rom. 2:9). In another passage, Paul invokes *the Gentiles* in one verse while furnishing the alternative term *Greeks* in the immediately following verse (Rom. 1:13-14). *Albert Barnes*, a noted American theologian and Bible commentator, once wrote, "All those who were not Jews were called Greeks, because they were chiefly acquainted with those pagans only who spake the Greek language." That the two terms are synonymous is evident from Paul's reference to the Greeks under the name of *Gentiles*:

> *Macedonia and Achaia [Greek cities] have been pleased to make a*
> *contribution for the poor. . . . Yes, they were pleased to do so. . . . For if*
> *the Gentiles [these Greeks] have shared in their spiritual things, they are*
> *indebted to minister to them also in material things.*

> *(Rom. 15:26-27)*

Why does John's gospel accentuate the notion that "Jesus . . . hid Himself" (12:36) from the world? To highlight the idea that he is essentially a concealed and *unknown God* as far as the public is concerned. How, then, can the biblical authorities purport to understand Christ when in actuality they issue uninformed statements about him? We think this is due to a blatant neglect on their part to complete the required research. But, most importantly, it is because they have not been divinely *inspired*; hence they err indiscriminately. By contrast, the true knowledge of Christ comes primarily through revelations from God! (Eph. 1:17, Rev. 1:1).

THE GREEK COASTLAND PROPHECIES

In the Bible, the first recorded reference to the term *Gentiles* ("nations") can be found in a verse that comes directly after the *birth* of the Greek coastlands:

> *And the sons of Javan [Greece] were Elishah and Tarshish, Kittim [Cyprus] and Dodanim [Rhodes]. From these [Greeks] the coastlands of the nations were separated into their lands, every one according to his language, according to their families, into their nations.*

> *(Gen. 10:4-5)*

Scripture first cites the sons of Greece in chapter 10 and verse 4 while the next verse traces the Gentile coastlands through Greek descent: "from these" Greeks are derived "the coastlands of the nations [Gentiles]." In other words, the foregoing quote illustrates that all the scattered biblical references to the *ships of Tarshish* (1 Kings 10:22), the *"ships of Kittim"* (Dan. 11:30), and *"the coastlands of Elishah"* (Ezek. 27:7) refer exclusively to the Greek coastlands.

This notion that the *coastland* paradigm alludes to the *Greeks* is verified by way of a revealing passage from the prophet Isaiah:

> *Therefore glorify the LORD in the east, the name of the LORD, . . . in the coastlands of the sea.*

> *(24:15)*

Notice that Isaiah does not say, "Glorify the LORD" in Jerusalem, which would have been the case if the Messiah were actually Jewish. As it turns out, *"the coastlands of Elishah"* (Ezek. 27:7)—belonging to Elishah, the son of Greece (Gen. 10:4)—are the same "coastlands of the sea" alluded to by Isaiah. This recognition has profound implications as we try to piece together the cross-references leading up to the thematic conclusion of the text.

But what does Isaiah reveal through this oracle, and why is it important? He clearly identifies the location from which the *glory* of the Lord will appear. And therein lies the oracle's significance. For in attempting to explain the setting of the divine glory, it severs its ties with Jerusalem while displaying a propensity to gravitate towards a Greek interpretative solution. Furthermore, it has long been known by scholars that the scriptural symbol of "the sea" represents the *Mediterranean Sea*. Therefore, a correct interpretation of Isaiah's prophecy is rendered as follows: "Glorify the LORD in the east, the name of the LORD, . . . in the [Greek] coastlands of the [Mediterranean] sea" (24:15).

According to a number of biblical experts, these *coastlands* (Gen. 10:4-5) can only refer to the Greek islands. Jeremiah puts it in proper perspective as he announces God's *divine reversal*:

> *"Those who handle the [Mosaic] law did not know Me. . . . Therefore I will yet contend with you [Jews]," declares the LORD. . . . "For cross to the coastlands of Kittim [Greece] and see, . . . and observe closely, and see if there has [ever] been such a thing as this [done before]! Has a nation changed gods?"*

> *(2:8-11)*

Not only does this quote vindicate our premise that the *coastlands* represent the Greeks, it includes the additional acknowledgment that God will no longer *dwell* in Israel, but in Greece.

A passage that closely parallels the preceding quote can be found in the book of Isaiah:

> *The time is coming to gather all nations [Gentiles] and tongues [languages]. And they shall come and see [witness] My glory. And I will set a sign among them and will send survivors [descendants] from them to the nations: Tarshish, Put, Lud, Meshech, Rosh, Tubal, and Javan, to the distant coastlands that have neither heard My fame nor seen My glory. And they will declare My glory among the nations.*

> *(66:18-19, emphasis added)*

One thing that is clear from this passage is that the Greek coastlands are among the nations which proclaim the divine splendor of the Deity. Despite several references made to other nations in connection with the eyewitness reports that will declare God's presence to the world, what is most astounding is that the Greek coastlands of *Tarshish* and *Javan* take precedence since they are enumerated as being the *first* and the *last* in the list thereof. It is surely not accidental that this *"sign"* is *"set . . . among"* the nations because it corresponds directly to Jesus's mysterious and tenacious allusion to the Greeks: *"I am the Alpha and the Omega, the first and the last, the beginning and the end"* (Rev. 22:13, emphasis added).

In the attempt to avoid speculation—which is based on a subjective interpretation that takes things out of context—we will furnish additional information that is conducive to this end. Let us call your attention to the following oracle:

> *Pay attention to Me, O My people; and give ear to Me, O My nation; . . . My righteousness is near, My salvation has gone forth, and*

My arms will judge the peoples; the coastlands [isles] will wait for Me, and for My arm they will wait expectantly.

(Isa. 51:4-5)

Who is it that actually represents God's figurative *"arm,"* given that *"the coastlands will wait for [him] . . . expectantly"*? The reference to God's *"arms [that] will judge the peoples"* obviously denotes Jesus who will judge the nations at the end of the world (Ps. 7:8, Joel 3:2, Rev. 19:11). An analogous interpretation of the celestial *"arm"* can be extracted from the book of Psalms, where we read,

I have found David [the Messiah] My servant; with My holy oil [divine spirit] I have anointed him, with whom My hand will be established; My arm also will strengthen him. . . . And in My name his horn [kingdom] will be exalted.

(89:20-24)

There seems to be no question that the reference to God's *"arm"* connotes Christ who, in the aftermath of his resurrection, will ascend to heaven and, metaphorically speaking, sit "down at the right hand of God" (Mark 16:19).

Having this information at our disposal, we can now decode Isaiah's oracle as follows: *"The coastlands [islands] will wait for Me, and for My arm [Jesus] they will wait expectantly"* (51:5). The definitive conclusion drawn from this research is that the awaited Messiah is anticipated to surface in *"the coastlands,"* and not in Israel as previously thought. Given that the biblical *coastlands* have been linked to the Greek islands, we have increased confidence in positing that a *divine reversal* of fortunes has been effected by God in the sense that he will not manifest himself to those who knew him, but rather to a race that not only did not know him, but also one that did not expect him! (Isa. 65:1, *New King James*). Now if the Greek *"coastlands"* are said to *"wait expectantly"* for the Messiah (Isa. 51:5)—or to "eagerly wait for a Savior" (Phil. 3:20)—it stands to reason that the Redeemer must be born among them. This is the reason why Paul says to the Greeks in a figurative sense that we are *eager with great desire to see your face* (1 Thess. 2:17). That is to say, amid this spiritual climate of intense messianic fervor, we wait with great anticipation and deep longing to see Christ's countenance among you.

A related theme can be found in the story of *Elisha*, the foremost disciple and protégé of the prophet Elijah (2 Kings 2:3). The former is best known for performing *great signs and wonders*. Amazingly, Elisha raises the dead (2 Kings 4:32-37), a miracle often associated with Jesus (John 11:43-44). Elisha is also capable of feeding the hungry multitude. In fact, we are told that they *"eat and have some left over"* (2 Kings 4:43). Likewise, Christ feeds a great multitude and instructs his disciples to *"gather up the leftover fragments that nothing may be lost"* (John 6:12). Moreover, Elisha is given the divine power to heal leprosy (2 Kings 5:14), a miracle which the Messiah himself performs in the NT gospels (Matt. 8:2-3). Therefore, the uncanny similarities of these diverse signs and wonders, and the analogous scriptural terms used to denote them, suggest an intimate identification between these two figures. Simply put, Elisha prefigures the Greek Christ, especially since he himself is a son of Greece! (Gen. 10:4).

Taken as a whole, the combined passages pertaining to the mystery of Christ's earthly origin have not only appropriated inimitable meaning, but they have also introduced some recurrent themes that will help us solve this enigmatic riddle. This exposition is based, in part, on a *cross-referential analysis,* which has essentially allowed the Bible to interpret itself. We have neither altered the words, nor added any of our own speculations. Our interpretations have merely followed the dictates of scripture. This is precisely why the supporting evidence is so strong and the conclusions appear to be virtually indisputable!

MESSIANIC SIGNS OF A SEAFARING PEOPLE FROM THE GREEK COASTLANDS

> *Sing to the LORD a new song. Sing His praise from the end of the earth! You who go down to the sea [fishermen], and all that is in it. You islands and those [Greeks] who dwell on them. . . . Let them give glory to the LORD, and declare His praise in the coastlands.*

> —*Isa. 42:10-12*

Time and time again, we encounter passages which foretell of a coming Messiah whose *glory* and *praise* is initially declared *in the coastlands.* These excerpts reveal why Christ's disciples are portrayed in the *NT gospels* as being predominantly men of the sea (cf. Ezek. 47:9-10). It seems that the gospel narratives are seeking to establish a connection between Jesus and *the Greek coastland prophecies,* which would explain why most of his disciples turn out to be fishermen! At least that is the foregoing conclusion of the text. As an illustration, notice how Isaiah's following oracle announces God's incarnation while confirming the latter's ties to a certain cluster of islands:

> *Listen to Me, O islands, and pay attention, you peoples [Gentiles] from afar [not from Israel]. The LORD called Me [the Messiah] from the womb; from the body of My mother He named Me. . . . In the shadow of His hand He has concealed Me, . . . He has hidden Me.*

> *(49:1-2)*

God's incarnation is said to transpire among the *peoples from afar*, who are portrayed as non-Jewish seafarers that dwell in a mysterious archipelago comprising numerous *islands*. By comparison, the New King James version translates the Hebrew term for *islands* with the word *coastlands* (Isa. 49:1; see *King James*, Isa. 51:5 where *coastlands* are rendered as *islands*). But why should the *islands* pay particular attention to the declaration of these prophecies? Since we already know that the *coastlands* represent the Greek *islands*, it appears that the latter are a *sign* denoting the *concealed* earthly origin of the long-awaited Messiah. As a matter of fact, we read elsewhere that "the coastlands will wait expectantly for His [messianic] law" (Isa. 42:4), an image traditionally associated with Moses the lawgiver.

The more we learn about the seafaring people from the Greek coastlands, the more we understand their connection to the NT apostles. For they become yet another *sign* representing not only Jesus's contemporary audience, but also those who will come to believe in his authoritative message that will be confirmed through great miracles, signs and wonders (John 2:11, cf. Matt. 15:31). It is only meet that they would be described in the gospels as figurative fishermen. Since the people of *the coastlands* are the first to *declare* God's *glory* (Isa. 42:10-12), it follows that Christ is born in their midst; that is, "among the Greeks" (John 7:35). Accordingly, the text reveals that Jesus will in fact "teach the Greeks" from the outset of his ministry (John 7:34-35).

Consider Matthew's reference to the region where the light of God is initially revealed. It is not called "Galilee of the Jews" but rather, *"GALILEE OF THE GENTILES"* (4:15-16). Two verses later, we read,

> *And walking by the Sea of Galilee, He [Jesus] saw two brothers, . . .*
> *casting a net into the sea; for they were fishermen. And He said to them,*
> *"Follow [imitate] Me, and I will make you fishers of men." And they*
> *immediately left the nets, and followed Him.*

> *(Matt. 4:18-20)*

It has been shown how these personages, known as the *disciples*, represent the seafaring people of the coastlands. In addition, the "Sea of Galilee" seems to be a representation of what the biblical scholars call *"the Great Sea"* (Ezek. 47:10), namely, the *Mediterranean Sea*. In point of fact, the body of water in the land of Galilee is not a sea at all but rather a lake. Inasmuch as the region of *Galilee* is a metaphor for the Gentiles, so the *Sea* of Galilee seems to be a symbol of *"the [Greek] coastlands"* that are situated within the *Mediterranean Sea*.

The evidence concerning the *fishermen* of the gospel accounts compels us to recognize that all these scriptural passages must refer to *a seafaring people*. According to religious studies professor *Ronald Farmer*, "The Hebrew people never became a seafaring people. They were a land-based culture." Moreover, the only people who are repeatedly mentioned in the text as dwelling near the Mediterranean Sea, and whose livelihood depends on it, are the people of the *coastlands*: "The coastlands which are beyond the sea" (Jer. 25:22). Many biblical scholars associate *the coastlands of the sea* (Esth. 10:1; Isa. 11:11, 24:15) with the Greek islands. For example, "the coastland of Caphtor" (Jer. 47:4) is often associated with the island of *Crete*. In like manner, the Greek island of *Rhodes* (known as *Dodanim* [Gen. 10:4], a variant of *Rodanim* [1 Chron. 1:7]) seems to be implicated in the text as being one among the *"many coastlands"* (Ezek. 27:15) that enjoyed a wide range of commercial trade. It is virtually certain that the coast of *Kittim* represents Cyprus, an island inhabited by Greeks since ancient times. After all, was it not Isaiah who once said, *"The cypress [Cyprus] tree . . . shall be to the LORD for a name, [and] for an everlasting sign"*? (55:13, *New King James*). In fact, many historians suggest that the ancient name *Cyprus* was derived from the island's overabundance of cypress trees!

As we can see, the biblical references to the Greek coastland prophecies are profuse. Another example might be the apocalyptic sign that we encounter in the book of Acts: Paul was on the *Greek coastlands* as the prophetic *day of Pentecost* was fast approaching (20:14-16). This imagery reminds us of John, the author of Revelation, who was also on the *Greek coastlands*—namely, on the island of Patmos—"on the Lord's day" (1:9-10). We already know from prior research that *the day of the Lord* ("the Lord's Day") is synonymous with *the day of Pentecost*. It is yet another *sign* that the revelation of Jesus actually takes place on the Greek island of Patmos, one among the many so-called Greek coastlands. So the previously undisclosed *Greek element* within the Bible seems to reveal the divine plan for the future messianic incarnation. Moreover, the reason why we must *"wait expectantly"* (Isa. 42:4, 51:5; cf. Mic. 7:7; Phil. 3:20) for the end-time Christ is that there is no conclusive historical evidence, trustworthy or not, to support the notion that he ever existed!

A SIGN OF OFFENSE: JESUS THE NAZARENE, THE KING OF THE JEWS

> *When classical Christianity speaks of the madness of the Cross, it is merely to humiliate false reason and to add luster to the eternal light of truth; the madness of God-in-man's-image is simply a wisdom not recognized by the men of unreason who live in this world: "Jesus crucified . . . was the scandal of the world and appeared as nothing but ignorance and madness to the eyes of his time."*

> —*Foucault 79*

But how does history treat this biblical event? Considered even to this day as the preeminent sign of a *Jewish* Messiah is the engraved inscription that supposedly hung above Jesus's cross:

JESUS THE NAZARENE, THE KING OF THE JEWS.

(John 19:19)

We will briefly decipher the first part of the inscription: why Jesus is called the *Nazarene*. It has absolutely nothing to do with the alleged city of Nazareth. We find no mention of this city prior to NT texts, and many scholars suggest that its association to Christ may be a literary device to meet the stipulations of prophecy. Matthew's reference to Jesus, who will fulfill the prophecy, simply states that "He shall be called a Nazarene" (Matt. 2:23). And since then, scholars have been unable to locate the biblical source of this prediction. For this reason, experts propose a different type of inquiry.

Another way to explore the concept of the *Nazarene* is to look at a common biblical symbol: the metaphor of the *olive tree*. Greece, especially the island of Crete, has long been renowned for its olive tree cultivation since ancient times. Its spiritual significance can be seen from the historical record which indicates that the Athenians offered olive trees, as the most sacred of gifts, to their virgin goddess *Athena*. It is not surprising, then, that another cryptic clue, intimating the Greeks, might be hidden within the biblical symbol of the olive tree. In one such paradigm, God's apocalyptic witnesses "are the two olive trees . . . that stand before the Lord of the earth" (Rev. 11:4). Both figures ostensibly represent the incarnated Christ. In addition, the garden of Jesus's arrest is called *Gethsemane* (Mark 14:32), which literally means "oil press" in Aramaic. In the gospel of Luke, it is simply described as "the Mount of Olives" (22:39). We should also point out that the biblical symbol of the olive tree is usually associated with God's reign and splendor (Judg. 9:8, Hos. 14:6), much as it is a sign of his spirit and energy (Ps. 89:20, Heb. 1:9). This is the reason why *Ezra*, a priest of ancient Israel, "taught the people" in such a way "that they might gain insight into the words of" scripture (Neh. 8:9-13); he instructed them,

> Go out to the hills, and bring olive branches, . . . as it is written.

(Neh. 8:15)

Strangely enough, Isaiah makes use of the term *branch* to cite the Messiah (Isa. 11:1); most probably an olive branch is indicated (cf. Gen. 8:11). Zechariah then elaborates on this idea so as to meet the exigencies for further evidence. He prophesies that this *"man whose name is Branch"* will be the incarnation of God (Zech. 6:12). Furthermore, it is widely accepted that the term *Nazarene* literally means "the branch." In this context, the Hebrew words used to denote the term "branch" are *tsemah* and *natser*. Hence, *natser* becomes *natserite* or *Nazarite*. In short, the idiomatic expression, *"Jesus the Nazarene"* (Mark 16:6) can be paraphrased as Jesus *the [olive]*

Branch, or as *Tsemah Natser.* While the former expression seems to reveal a Greek messianic lineage, the latter terms may hold a clue to the mystery of his personal name. Therefore this study suggests that the term *Nazarene* does not denote a Jewish Jesus who is supposedly associated with the city of Nazareth but is rather an esoteric biblical sign of his name and origin. Curiously enough, "Jesus the Nazarene" may simply be another way of saying that he is the proclaimed Greek Messiah!

But what can we make of the second part of the inscription, namely, that he is "the King of the Jews"? If most religious authorities believe that Jesus was Jewish, should we not do the same? Before making up our minds, let's take a look at this brief episode from the gospel of John:

> *And Pilate wrote an inscription also, and put it on the cross. And it was written, "JESUS THE NAZARENE, THE KING OF THE JEWS." Therefore this inscription many of the Jews read, for the place where Jesus was crucified was near the city; and it was written in Hebrew, Latin, and in Greek. And so the chief priests of the Jews were saying to Pilate, "Do not write, 'The King of the Jews'; but that He said, 'I am King of the Jews.'" Pilate answered, "What I have written I have written."*

> *(19:19-22)*

Three inscriptions were apparently written: one in Hebrew, one in Latin, and one in Greek. It is conceivable that the three inscriptions represent the idea that Christ was prophesied by the Jews, killed by the Latins, and revealed by the Greeks. If so, then this scriptural analogy is as brilliant as it is apocalyptically breathtaking. And even from an altogether different standpoint, in the event that Jesus was a local Jewish figure, why would there be a need for a Latin and a Greek inscription as well? In other words, why would the Bible supplant the exclusive Hebraic legacy of Jesus with a global one instead? The point here, then, is that scripture is full of incessant perforations that allow us to peer into the hidden origin of Christ.

We will now explore the mysterious reason why the Jews said to Pilate, *"Do not write, 'The King of the Jews'; but that He said, 'I am King of the Jews.'"* As we have witnessed from previous examples, scripture persistently inserts these types of comments in order to uncover hidden truths. It is also a well-known fact that religious Jews do believe in a *Mashiach,* the variant form of *Moshiah,* which means "Messiah or Anointed One" in Hebrew. But in the scriptures, why do they exude such a deep hostility towards Christ? More importantly, why do they take offense with Pilate's inscription? There can only be one reason to explain all of this; Jesus is apparently not Jewish! There is simply no other explanation that can demonstrate otherwise. The essence of the aforementioned quote can be paraphrased as follows: "do not write that he is a Jew, but write only that he claimed to be a Jew without really being one." The narrative's implication is that if Christ had been a Jew, the Hebrew people would have accepted him. There is no other significant explanation for this *offense* except for the fact that the Messiah is non-Jewish. This offense is prophesied in scripture: "I will stir up your sons, O Zion, against your sons, O Greece" (Zech. 9:13). It is for this reason that God says, *"Behold, I am about to do a thing in Israel at which both ears of everyone who hears it will tingle"* (1 Sam. 3:11).

When everything is taken into consideration, the legitimacy of this event will not be validated until the onset of the apocalypse. The Hebraic proclamation regarding the *"King of the Jews"* was obviously not recorded in the annals of history, but rather in the literary narratives of the gospels so as to address analogous concerns that will arise at some future time period. But in the end, what the Jews said about Jesus mainly reflects scriptural literary devices that are attempting to convey Christ's true identity. Regardless, one thing is certain. Conventional *Judaism* believes in an awaited Messiah and accepts the concept of a forthcoming resurrection.

Although they have given rise to vastly different outlooks, it is curious how both the Judaic and Christian scriptures do not contradict the notion of a divine Messiah. In the OT, God declares,

> *"From you One will go forth for Me to be ruler in Israel. His goings forth are from long ago, from the days of eternity."*

> *(Mic. 5:2)*

In *Leviticus* 26:12, God himself vows to become man and enter human history:

> *I will also walk among you and be your God, and you shall be My people.*

Daniel also has a vision pertaining to the glorious coming of the *"Son of Man"* in which *"he came up [ascended] to the Ancient of Days and was presented before Him. And to Him was given dominion, glory and a kingdom"* so that all the nations of the world *"might serve Him"* (7:13-14). The NT, of course, is replete with references to "the only begotten Son of God" (John 3:16-18, 1 John 4:9, cf. Col. 1:15-16).

For that matter, our thesis is unique in that it integrates the genuine concepts of Christianity with the acknowledged expectation of the Jews regarding the foretold Messiah. Perhaps unbeknownst to them, both religions seek and anticipate one and the same person. And in that sense, Judaism and Christianity are essentially two versions of the same religion. In effect, the Jews have the right timing—but the wrong Messiah. On the other hand, the Christians have the right Messiah—but the wrong timing.

JESUS REVAMPED

Given the *secret knowledge* that is placed at our disposal, the ultimate conclusion of our inquiry seems inescapable. We have hitherto spoken about a fastidious and credible solution to the apparent complications encountered in the Bible. Without the revelation of a Greek Messiah, how else could the various elements of scripture become both comprehended and cohesive? The evidence we have accrued procures nothing less than a complete redefining of the conventional Jesus account. It begs the question whether the popular notion of a Jewish Messiah can be reconciled with the *"Alpha and the Omega"* (Rev. 1:8) God of the NT. The Deity does not introduce himself as the *Aleph* and the *Tav*, employing the first and last letters of the Hebrew alphabet, which would have been the case if he were to be revealed as a Jewish God. Rather, the divine *"I AM"* (Exod. 3:14) is construed through the aforementioned Greek element: *"I am the Alpha and the Omega"* (Rev. 22:13). In fact, this is the official name of God, which is not unlike the original name found in the Jewish sacred writings, namely, *Yahvah*: a transliteration of *Yavan*, meaning Greece! Altogether then, both the OT and NT names of God converge through the Greek component.

Despite the inordinate contradictions stemming from literal hermeneutical analysis, public opinion continues to perpetuate its scriptural myths. This is one of the reasons why the Bible continues to remind us that *"THERE IS NONE WHO UNDERSTANDS"* (Rom. 3:11). Arguably, the Bible warns against such disproportionate errors of judgment by interpolating hints that discredit these aforementioned interpretative endeavors. The newfound evidence of Christ not only shatters our preconceptions about him, but it also seems to offer a peremptory biblical solution. If we advocate the "prophetic" teachings of the NT that foretell the coming of Christ, then we must not interpret the metaphorical story of the gospels as if it were a historical account of this notable event. For instance, the ancient Jewish bloodlines leading to the birth of Christ are nothing more than mythic interpolations, which otherwise suggest something much more profound and infinitely more mysterious.

To this end, we will impart a cryptic clue concerning the arcane genealogy of Jesus. The ancestry of Christ, as recorded in the gospels (Matt. 1:1-17, Luke 3:23-38), is actually a mathematical riddle whose solution reveals the precise year of his birth! The key to solving this puzzle can be found in the gospel of Matthew chapter 1 and verse 17. Notice that there is a constant repetition of fourteen generations throughout the foregoing lineage. We also know from scripture that a generation is equal to seventy years (Ps. 90:10). Do the math.

We begin to realize that the NT genealogies are not actually referring to a literal but rather to a figurative Jewish progeny. The mystery of Jesus, which has been concealed throughout the ages (Eph. 3:5, Col. 1:26), will ultimately be revealed at the appointed time:

But now once in the end of the world hath he appeared to put away
sin by the sacrifice [death] of himself.

(Heb. 9:26, King James)

For one reason or another, biblical commentators have either ignored or attempted to downplay the significance of this verse. What is even more troubling is that they have imposed meanings through "broken contexts, bizarre leaps in chronology, and assumed material that simply is not in the text" (McCallum, 38). On the other hand, we have brought to light the Greek messianic prophecies of the Bible and their consolidating effect at integrating seemingly conflicting accounts. At last, we are beginning to sense that the Bible is steeped in mystery and intrigue. Consequently, we must not revert to the subterfuge of past ages. Now that we have opened Pandora's box, it is up to the experts to sort things out.

CHAPTER 8

NEBUCHADNEZZAR'S DREAM AND THE KINGDOM OF BRONZE

> *The head of that statue was made of fine gold, its breast and its arms of silver, its belly and its thighs of bronze, its legs of iron, its feet partly of iron and partly of clay. You [Nebuchadnezzar] continued looking [in the dream] until a stone was cut out without hands, and it struck the statue on its feet of iron and clay, and crushed them.*

> —Dan. 2:32-34

*D*aniel, a renowned interpreter of dreams and visions (cf. Dan. 1-2), is commissioned to decipher King Nebuchadnezzar's dream. Daniel began to articulate the meaning of the dream and confided to the king that it refers *"to what would take place in the future"* (Dan. 2:29). The composite statue turns out to be a prophecy concerning succeeding empires that would reign upon the earth. In the dream, the first great empire, represented by the head of gold, is *Babylon* (2:38). In that Daniel's interpretation involves an implicit historical time frame for each successive empire, it provides an accurate historical starting-point from which the rest of the oracle can be understood. Then comes *"another kingdom,"* represented by silver, followed by a *"third kingdom of bronze, which will rule over all the earth"* (2:39). Finally, there *"will be a fourth kingdom as strong as iron; . . . it will crush and break all these [previous empires] in pieces"* (2:40). But inasmuch as this fourth empire has feet and toes *"partly of potter's clay and partly of iron, it will be a divided kingdom"* (2:41), which means that *"some of the kingdom will be strong [iron] and part of it [clay] will be brittle"* (2:42). In other words, the latter part of this empire would not endure.

Upon further examination of Nebuchadnezzar's dream, Daniel elucidates that the head of gold signifies the *Babylonian Empire* (2:38). The *"breast,"* with *"arms of silver,"* denotes the kingdom which conquered Babylon. We know from the historical record that this was the empire comprised of Medes and Persians (2:39). The *"belly"* and *"thighs of bronze"* indicate the *"third kingdom"* (2:39) of the prophecy

175

that displaces the *Medo-Persian Empire*. Historically speaking, this was the Greek Empire of *Alexander the Great*, the *Hellenistic Empire*, which subdued and defeated the conglomerate Persian forces. Last but not least, the *"legs of iron,"* standing on *"feet partly of iron and partly of clay"* (2:33) obviously represent the *Roman Empire*, which supplanted the Hellenistic (Fruchtenbaum, 24-25) as the center of world power. In retrospect, the Roman Empire was indeed *"a divided kingdom"* (2:41) since *Byzantium* (Constantinople) endured and continued to thrive while *Rome* fell quickly to foreign invasions.

Evidently, the image of *"clay"* symbolizes the Roman populace—the western part of the Roman Empire—while the concept of *"iron"* indicates the people of the *eastern Roman Empire* (Byzantium). The former were Latin—later followers of the church of Peter—whereas the latter were considered to be Greeks, eventually founding the *Greek Orthodox Church* in Constantinople (Ware, 18-29). Yet both of these divisions were part of the unified Roman Empire. Daniel then proceeds to interpret the conclusion of the dream:

> And in the [final] days of those [successive] kings the God of heaven
> will set up a kingdom which will . . . endure forever.

(2:44)

Where there is a kingdom, there is a king. Therefore, we can surmise that God's *"kingdom"* signifies the appearance of Christ the *King* (Matt. 2:2, Rev. 19:16) who sets up the divine rule at the end of days. Jesus is represented by the *"stone . . . cut out of the [heavenly] mountain without hands . . . that crushed"* the entire statue to pieces (2:45). The implication is that universal peace will eventually ensue as *"nation will not lift up sword against nation, and never again will they learn war"* (Isa. 2:4). This end-time scenario has been foretold in Bible prophecy through the various and sundry tales of many OT patriarchs. For example, there is no more effective way to represent this notion of peace than through the symbol of a dove—a depiction of "the Spirit of God" (cf. Matt. 3:16)—that came back to Noah with an olive branch "in her beak," essentially signifying that the *flood of war* (see Dan. 9:26, 11:22) "was abated from the earth" (Gen. 8:11).

In the end, Nebuchadnezzar's vision turns out to be an ancient portal to the dreaded apocalypse: a divine message hidden deep in the bosom of his dreams. And it is authenticated by Daniel:

> God has made known . . . what will take place in the future; so the
> dream [vision] is true, and its interpretation is trustworthy.

(2:45)

It should come as no surprise, then, that *rabbinic Judaism* anticipates the Messiah's one and only visitation in the last days:

> *If you shall see kingdoms rising against each other in turn, then give heed and note the footsteps of the Messiah.*

> *(Bereshit Rabbah XLII: 4, qtd. in Fruchtenbaum)*

ALEXANDER THE GREAT AND THE LITTLE HORN

In many ways, the preceding and the following visions from the book of Daniel refer to the same empires, but from different perspectives. They are written from varying viewpoints to ensure not only the authenticity of the prophecies but also the historical accuracy of the predictions. In the meantime, let us proceed with our discussion. Daniel has a follow-up vision of a mighty *ram* followed by *a male goat* that attacks and overwhelms it (8:3-7). In time, the goat's *horn [power] was broken; and in its place there came up four conspicuous horns* (8:8). Daniel recounts the oracle:

> *And out of one of them came forth a rather small horn which grew exceedingly great toward the south, toward the east, and toward the Beautiful Land [Israel]. And it grew up to the host of heaven and caused some of the host and some of the stars to fall to the earth, and it trampled them down. It even magnified itself to be equal with the Commander of the host [God]; and it removed the regular sacrifice [Holy Communion] from Him, and the place of His sanctuary [Church] was thrown down.*

> *(8:9-11)*[1]

The angelic messenger named *Gabriel* appears once again and interprets the vision to Daniel (8:16). Surprisingly, Gabriel refers to Daniel as the *"Son of man"* (8:17). As this prototypical title belongs exclusively to Jesus (Mark 14:61-62), Gabriel's nominal sketch of the "highly esteemed" (Dan. 9:23) character named *Daniel* suggests that the last named is an allegorical precursor to the Messiah. Gabriel says,

> *Son of man, understand that the vision pertains to the time of the end.*

> *(Dan. 8:17)*

The celestial being now begins to expound the oracle:

> *Behold, I am going to let you know what will occur at the final period of the indignation [God's wrath], for it pertains to the appointed time of the end. The ram which you saw with the two horns represents the kings of Media and Persia. And the shaggy goat represents the kingdom of Greece, and the large horn that is between his eyes is the first king [Alexander the Great]. And the broken horn and the four horns that arose in its place represent four kingdoms which will arise from his nation [Hellenistic Empire], although not with his power. And in the latter period [in the last days] of their rule, when the transgressors [the succeeding empires] have run their course, a king will arise insolent and skilled in intrigue. And his power will be mighty, but not by his own power, and he will destroy to an extraordinary degree and prosper and perform his will.*

(Dan. 8:19-24)

In chapter 11, Daniel receives additional information concerning the previous vision:

> *But as soon as he [Alexander the Great] has arisen, his kingdom will be broken up and parceled out toward the four points of the compass, though not to his own descendants, nor according to his authority which he wielded; for his sovereignty will be uprooted and given to others besides them [the Greeks].*

(11:4).

In Daniel chapter 2 (the statue vision), the antichrist, who mingles *"in the seed of men"* (2:43), comes from the part of the Roman Empire, which is represented by the symbol of *iron* (2:40-43), namely, the Byzantines. But in Daniel chapter 8, he arises out of one of the four successors of Alexander the Great. As you will see, both lines of succession are correct and coalesce so as to give us a more precise understanding of where the antichrist comes from.

Following Alexander's death, the heirs to the Hellenistic Empire were called the *Diadochi*, which means "successors" in Greek. The four generals alluded to by scripture appear to be *Ptolemy, Seleucus, Cassander,* and *Lysimachus* (Fruchtenbaum, 20), all of whom had ruled over different Hellenistic kingdoms after the partition of the empire. The book of Daniel clearly indicates that the smallest territory in land size, held by one of these four generals, denotes the symbolic *"small horn"* (the antichrist) of the end-times (8:8-9). Interestingly, the text also states that this small territory cannot possibly come from Alexander's *"own descendants,"* namely, the Greeks (11:4). Historically, Greece was conquered by the Romans in the second century BC, and so their empire came to an abrupt end.

On that account, in order to locate the actual place that represents the *little horn*, we must search elsewhere. By implication, Cassander, who controlled Macedonia and most of Greece, must be ruled out of the equation. On the other hand, Lysimachus's terrain, which originally consisted of the tiny area called *Thrace*, is the only one to qualify as the smallest amount of land size in comparison with the other Hellenistic kingdoms. If you recall, Daniel mentioned that the little horn *"grew exceedingly great toward the south"* and *"toward the east"* (8:9). Evidently, after the major *Battle of Ipsus* in 301 BC, Lysimachus gained vast amounts of land to the *south* and to the *east*, as he was awarded *Anatolia* for his decisive allied victory. By that time, General Lysimachus had become a very wealthy and powerful man as he presided over all aspects of life, political and otherwise, within the geographic region we now call *Asia Minor*. He also founded his capital at *Pergamum*, in modern-day western Turkey, where all his wealth was kept.

Anatolia then becomes the seat of the Ottoman Empire, which destroyed the last remaining vestige of the Roman Empire in 1453 of the Common Era. By the late nineteenth century, the Turks were in turn defeated by *Imperial Russia* through various wars, but especially after the *Russo-Turkish War* of 1877-1878. If we trace the succession of empires that supplant one another in the region denoted by the symbol of the little horn—namely, Thrace and Asia Minor—we will notice a sequence that begins with General Lysimachus and continues on with the Byzantine Romans, whose capital (*Constantinople*) was actually situated within the former's domain. Next, the Ottoman Turks come forth from this same territory and are subsequently defeated by the great Russian Empire. Since Lysimachus represents the little horn, we can trace the roots of the antichrist from this foregoing general all the way up to Russia, the so-called *Third Rome*. It is for this reason, no doubt, that the book of Revelation features *"Pergamum"* as the place *"where Satan's throne is"* (Rev. 2:12-13) located, indicating not only the origin of the little horn, but also the succession of empires that lead to his proverbial doorstep. In this respect, the *small horn*, the kingdom of Lysimachus, becomes a key piece of the puzzle that decidedly affirms the link that leads to the antichrist (Dan. 8:9-12). That is to say, the Lysimachaean province gave rise to the Byzantine and Turkish empires, and in the process of usurping the latter, the modern Russian Empire was born.

Ezekiel, a dominant force in Jewish apocalyptic literature, prophesies that *"in the latter years,"* a mysterious *"prince of Rosh"* and *"Meshech"* will come *"from the remote parts of the north,"* from *"the land of Magog,"* to invade Israel, *"whose inhabitants have been gathered from many nations"* (Ezek. 38:2, 8). It is customary for scholars to identify the abovementioned locations with modern-day *Russia*, which will be in league with many nations during its latter-day military campaigns. Historical investigations reveal that the term *"Rosh"* is derived from the tribe of the *Rus* who migrated from Scandinavia and founded Russia (*Kievan Rus*) roughly around the tenth century of the Common Era. By the same token, the term *Meshech* originates with the clan whom the Greeks called *moshoi*, and whence the name *Moscow* is traced.

The earlier Ezekiel quotation referred to *"the land of Magog."* In ancient times, it comprised the lands where the *Scythians* once lived, and thus represents contemporary Russia. In his sobering book, the biblical scholar *Arnold Fruchtenbaum* provides a supplementary elaboration of Ezekiel 38:

> *The identification of Magog, Rosh, Meshech, and Tubal is to be determined from the fact that these tribes of the ancient world occupied the areas of modern day Russia. Magog, Meshech and Tubal were between the Black and Caspian Seas which today is southern Russia. The tribes of Meshech and Tubal later gave names to cities that today bear the names of Moscow, the capital, and Tobolsk, a major city in the Urals in Siberia. Rosh was in what is now northern Russia. The name Rosh is the basis for the modern name Russia. These names, then, cover the modern territories of northern and southern Russia in Europe and Siberia to the east in Asia.*

(70)

In addition, *Ivan the Great* adopted the official emblem of the Byzantine monarchy: the double-headed eagle. He then went on to marry *Sophia Paleologue*, the niece of the final Byzantine ruler *Constantine XI*. In the aftermath of the Ottoman Turks' conquest of the eastern Roman Empire and in an effort to salvage the last vestiges of Christianity, Ivan designated Moscow as the *Third Rome* in 1497 AD. In effect, Moscow became the offspring of the Roman Empire, heirs to the legacy. Russia, then, becomes the link of the little horn (antichrist) to the Roman Empire (cf. Daniel 7:7-8 f.).

The celebrated seer *Nostradamus* confirms this conclusion and gives us an insightful clue in this regard:

> *The great Empire of the Antichrist will begin where once was Attila's empire and the new Xerxes will descend with great and countless numbers.*

(The Prophecies, *Epistle to Henry II*)

Maps that show the extent of Attila's empire reveal that it comprised areas of the former Soviet Union and modern-day Russia. Moreover, Nostradamus calls the antichrist *the new Xerxes*. The differences between Russia and Persia are worlds apart. Nevertheless, Nostradamus pierces through the opaque veil of prophecy to glimpse an intimate alliance built for conquest:

Arabs will be allied with the Poles.

(The Prophecies, *Century 5, Quatrain 73)*

The term *Poles* refers to those who dwell in "the remote parts of the north" (Ezek. 38:6). Here, following, is a prophecy that might lend support to the idea that a military buildup in Asia could ignite the end of the world:

> *When those of the arctic pole are united together,*
> *Great terror and fear in the East*

(The Prophecies, *Century 6, Quatrain 21).*

OMENS THAT TRACE THE IDENTITY OF THE LITTLE HORN

Following his interpretative tasks at the royal court of King Nebuchadnezzar, Daniel has prophetic dreams of his own. He is entranced by visions of *"four great beasts"* that arrive to wreak havoc upon the earth (Dan. 7:3): *"The first was like a lion"* while the *"second one"* resembled *"a bear"* (7:4-5); then *"another one"* appeared, a beast that looked like *"a leopard"* with *"four heads, and dominion was given to it"* (7:6).[2] Finally, *"a fourth beast"* made its appearance, *"terrifying and extremely strong; and it had large iron teeth"* (7:7). This *"mighty nation"* (cf. Isa. 60:22) crushed all of the remaining empires, *"and it was different from"* the previous beasts (kingdoms); *"and it had ten horns"* (Dan. 7:7). According to the Bible's own definition, the concept of a *horn* is a symbolic representation of a kingdom (Dan. 7:24, Rev. 17:12).

The contents of the *"four great beasts"* in Daniel's vision—comprising the lion, bear, leopard, and the fourth creature with the *"iron teeth"*—are essentially identical to those found in the earlier part of his book that refer to the statue of Nebuchadnezzar's dream. Keep in mind that the fourth beast of Daniel's vision in chapter 7, depicted as having *"iron teeth"* (7:7), is the same empire as the one cited in chapter 2 regarding Nebuchadnezzar's dream, namely, the *"fourth kingdom as strong as iron"* (2:40). Both of these specific visions represent the Roman Empire—*"a divided kingdom,"* partly *"strong and part of it . . . brittle"* (2:41-42)—that was split into east (Byzantium) and west (Rome). For one thing, Rome—symbolized by the *"potter's clay"* (2:41)—was considered to be the weak part of the empire as it was sacked in the year 410 AD by *Alaric the Visigoth.* On the other hand, Byzantium—represented by *"iron"* (2:42)—did not fall until 1453 when the *Ottoman Turkish Empire* finally conquered it.

The historical record indicates that the predecessors of the Romans were the Greeks. Appropriately, the Hellenistic Empire of Alexander the Great is denoted by the third beast, symbolized by the *"leopard"* (7:6). By the same token, the Greeks defeated the Persians, and so the figure of the *"bear"* clearly represents the Medo-Persian Empire (7:5). Going farther back in history, we also note that the Medo-Persians defeated the *Chaldean-Babylonian Empire* in 539 BC. In similar fashion, Daniel's vision obviously signifies the Babylonians when citing the first beast: the *"lion"* (7:4).

The fourth and final beast of Daniel's vision is by far the most important. Earlier in this volume, we elaborated on an end-time empire of *a great red dragon having seven heads and ten horns* (Rev. 12:3). We have already illustrated how this kingdom will be associated with a revival of the Russian Empire at the end of the world (Ezek. 38:2-3, Rev. 17:9-14). The disclosed location of this empire is rendered as being in the *"remote parts of the north"* (Ezek. 38:15-16). This empire coincides with Daniel's last beast (kingdom) which *"had ten horns"* (Dan. 7:7). Daniel writes,

> *I considered the horns, and, behold, there came up among them another little horn, before whom there were three of the first horns plucked up by the roots: and, behold, in this horn were eyes like the eyes of man, and a mouth speaking great things.*

> *(7:8, King James)*

The *little horn* that *came up among them* represents the coming of the *antichrist*.[3] Entranced by this vision of unparalleled human arrogance, Daniel *"kept looking because of the sound of the boastful words which the horn was speaking"* (7:11). Exactly how the little horn will seize power is discussed in the book of Daniel:

> *A despicable person will arise, on whom the honor of kingship has not been conferred [he is initially appointed, not elected], but he will come in a time of tranquility and seize the kingdom by intrigue.*

> *(11:21)*

One of the celestial beings explains to Daniel that the *"four great beasts"* (7:3) are really four kings that represent four succeeding empires (7:17). What is more, *"the ten horns"* symbolize ten kings or leaders who proceed from the last of these *"four great beasts"*; *"and another will arise after them [an eleventh leader]"* who *"will speak out against the Most High"* as well as *"wear down the saints [believers] of the Highest One"* (Dan. 7:24-25). Hence, this figure will speak pompous words "against the Most High" God (Dan. 7:8, 25). The Bible says that "he will exalt and magnify himself above every god, and will speak monstrous things against the God of gods; and he will prosper until the indignation is finished, for that which is decreed will be done" (Dan. 11:36). Paul contributes to this discussion by adding the following remark:

*[This is] the son of destruction, who opposes and exalts himself above
every so-called god or object of worship, so that he takes his seat in the
temple of God, displaying himself as being God.*

(2 Thess. 2:3-4)

There are extensive mentions of the "son of destruction" in the Bible, not the least of which is a reference to a despotic tyrant who will aim to conquer the world (Dan. 7:21). The infamous little horn will pursue a course of destruction as part of an effort to eradicate all traces of the Judeo-Christian religion. He will forge an immense military alliance (Dan. 9:26, 11:23, 31; Ezek. 38:4-7) that exacts conformity to his *one world government*: those who show reluctance will ultimately perish (Rev. 13:8, 15). Scripture says that the little horn will rule the world, "but not by his own power" (Dan. 8:23-24), indicating that other governments will "give their power and authority to the beast" (Rev. 17:13). Interestingly enough, the designation "dragon"—who "gave his authority to the beast [little horn]" (Rev. 13:4)—happens to be the national symbol of the *People's Republic of China*. The reference to "the kings from the east" makes it quite possible that China will eventually unite with, and lend support to, the *little horn* (Rev. 16:12). In their unquenchable thirst for power, both the little horn and his allies are ultimately bent on world domination. Nostradamus writes,

*A colonel with ambition plots,
He will seize the greatest army*

(The Prophecies, *Century 4, Quatrain 62*).

According to Bible prophecy, the believers in God *"will be given into his hand for a time, times, and half a time"* (Dan. 7:25). This interim is equivalent to 1,260 days (Rev. 12:6, 14). In this particular context, however, the 1,260-day period does not represent years, as was the case earlier, but actual days. Isaac Newton, one of the founders of modern astronomy and an astute theologian, notes in his unpublished documents—the so-called *Portsmouth papers*, auctioned at London's Sotheby's in 1936—that *"a time, times, and half a time"* equals to three and a half years. Apparently, the antichrist will enjoy success for this particular length of time (Rev. 11:2, 13:5-6). In reference to this specific time period, Jesus warns, *"When you see Jerusalem [Israel] surrounded by armies, then recognize that her desolation is at hand"* (Luke 21:20).

The antichrist's forces will cover the earth, gathering on the horizon to decimate the world (Isa. 60:2, Joel 2:1-2). But according to Nostradamus, first he will feign amity and tranquility:

Peace and semblance the spy will simulate

(The Prophecies, *Century 9, Quatrain 88*).

Likewise, the Bible warns us that the little horn's allied forces *"will destroy many while they are at ease"* (Dan. 8:25); that is to say, in a time of peace. Then all exertions cease. Only the eerie silence remains (Rev. 8:1) as the heavens prepare a punitive response. From the Bible to Nostradamus, the unifying theme that runs across the litany of these texts—like Ariadne's thread guiding us out of a labyrinth of obscurity—is the ubiquitous prophecy of the Messiah who will deliver us from worldwide disaster at the end of time! (Matt. 24:21-22).

The mysterious clues we are promulgating lead to the secret knowledge of the man we call the *little horn*. For instance, when we look at the four horsemen of the Apocalypse, several things become immediately discernible. The *white horse* of the first seal is an omen given by scripture to indicate the conspicuous purity of the first rider, Jesus Christ (Rev. 6:2). There is no hint of a counterfeit symbol anywhere in the Bible. Hence, we must take this sign at face value. On the other hand, the second seal reveals a terrifying *red horse* that "take[s] peace [away] from the earth" (Rev. 6:3-4). It has been traditionally linked to the red dragon that has seven heads and ten horns (Rev. 12:3-9). Therefore the *red horse* turns out to be the sign of the little horn's arrival, which happens to be contemporaneous with Christ's earthly visitation (Rev. 12, 19).

But when we look at the third seal, we are told that there is "a black horse; and he who sat on it had a pair of scales in his hand" (Rev. 6:5). This image may be best explained by Nostradamus's art. He used astrology—the study of celestial bodies that are believed to exert influence over human affairs—and the ancient arts of divination to peer into the future (Cheetham 20, Ward 16). He offers us a sign, similar to the "scales" of *Revelation*, through the use of a cryptic aphorism: "the Dragon's head [is] in Libra" (*The Prophecies*, Epistle to Henry II). In fact, the symbol of the "great red dragon having seven heads and ten horns" (Rev. 12:3) can also lend itself to an astrological interpretation that seems to demystify the identity of the little horn! Do the math.

666: THE NUMBER OF THE BEAST

The signs of the little horn are legion. Of the few and far between literary references which are known, two parallel passages may hold the key to the perennial mystery of the little horn who is said to be incarnated at the final point of time (cf. Rev. 12:9, 13:18; 2 Thess. 2:3-10; John 14:30; Dan. 7:8, 25-26, 8:10-11). One passage—well known, but not fully explored—is found in the book of Revelation:

*And he causes all, the small and the great, . . . to be given a mark on
their right hand, or on their forehead, and he provides that no one should
be able to buy or to sell, except the one who has the mark, either the name
of the beast or the number of his name. Here is wisdom. Let him who has
[biblical] understanding calculate [count] the number of the beast, for the
number is that of a man; and his number is six hundred and sixty-six.*

(13:16-18)

Revelation states that this numerical symbol represents "the mark, . . . or the
number . . . [associated with] his name" (13:17). And "his name" clearly signifies
a title or a position of authority (cf. Rev. 19:16). It is also worth noting that some
ancient manuscripts contain the number 616 instead of the more common 666
(*New American Standard*, 863). The other passage, equally popular, is encountered
in the Nostradamus text:

*The year 1999, seventh month,
From the sky will come a great King of Terror:
To bring back to life the great King of the Mongols,
Before and after Mars [Roman god of war] to reign by good luck*

(The Prophecies, *Century 10, Quatrain 72*).

Nostradamus tells us the precise year in which the little horn will make his
first public appearance: nineteen hundred and ninety-nine. According to popular
culture, this was not only the last year of the twentieth century (cf. Dan. 10:13),
but it also marked the end of the thousand-year period that is said to coincide with
Satan's release from prison, when he will gather the armies of "Gog and Magog" for
a final great battle while "the beloved city" of Jerusalem will come under siege (Rev.
20:7-9; cf. Rev. 19:19; Luke 21:20-22; Ezek. 38:8-9, 15-16; Ps. 83:2-8). But the most
interesting part of Nostradamus's quatrain is that "the year 1999" confirms biblical
prophecy. How do we know this? If we simply invert the four-digit year *1999*, we get
the number *1666*. This equation confirms the quintessential sign, indeed, the actual
number of the beast that is embedded in the book of Revelation, namely, the coded
trilogy of *666!* In the process of inverting the date *1999* into the cryptic number
1666, notice that the numeral *1* remains a constant. By comparison, the ancient
biblical manuscripts that cite the variant number 616 provide further evidence as to
the mystery of the triple-digit *666;* that is to say, the latter numerical riddle can also
be rendered as *1666.*

Nowhere does the text indicate an *alphanumeric* explanation: the idea that one
must use both numbers and letters to crack the code (cf. Ps 90:12-13). Therefore,
the shrewdness of the biblical calculation method lies in the realization that the

coded number *666* must undergo a simple numerical inversion. Accordingly, the year *1999* becomes the all-important sign of the little horn; not only a very critical date in human history, but also one that bears a conspicuous similitude to *the number of the beast: 666.* Just because that date has elapsed does not make this sign any less significant. It simply means that the antichrist has already stepped on the world stage. Nostradamus insists that his prophecy accurately describes the year of the king of terror's impending reign. But the connection between the Bible and the Nostradamus text does not end there. There is more.

Nostradamus clearly identifies the *great king of terror* with *the great king of the Mongols.* It is said that the former will resurrect the latter. Without question, the symbol of *the great King of the Mongols* is *Genghis Khan.* He is famous for his brilliant military achievements and for the creation of one of the greatest empires of all time. It was in fact the largest contiguous empire in recorded history. But he was also notorious for his great ruthlessness and terror. It is these traits of cruelty, no doubt, that inspired Nostradamus to associate him with the third and final antichrist who will prove much more formidable than his predecessors (Napoleon and Hitler). In fact, the little horn's allied victory will be as swift as the Mongol Empire's dissolution was lengthy (Rev. 11:2, 12:6).

To understand what all this means, we need to go back in time to a violent period that occurred between the thirteenth and fifteenth centuries, when the territories of the *Kievan Rus* (the early Russians) were conquered by the *Golden Horde,* the Mongol-Turkic western forces of the great *Mongol Empire.* Mongol kings demanded tribute from their Russian subjects, which they did receive promptly. In 1480, however, *Ivan III* (also called "Ivan the Great")—*Grand Prince of all Rus* and *Grand Prince of Moscow*—discontinued paying tribute to the Mongols and subsequently expelled them from Russian lands. Incidentally, given that he was also responsible for adopting the Byzantine legacy after the fall of Constantinople in 1453, Ivan III began referring to himself as *tsar* (Caesar). Hence, we find many parallels between Nostradamus's mantic quatrain and the prophetic book of Revelation in that both strongly suggest a Russian connection to *the number of the beast: 666* (cf. Ezek. 38:2, 15). A number which is as prophetically deafening as it is inaudible and secret. *Hippolytus Romanus* (c. 170-236 AD), a highly prolific theologian of the Roman Church, composed a *treatise on Christ and antichrist* in the early part of the third century. To dispel any notions that the term *antichrist* is a purely metaphorical construct, Hippolytus writes, "The Saviour appeared in the form of a man, and he too [the antichrist] will come in the form of a man."

JESUS: THE GREEK SERPENT

We will now resume our discussion on the Greek messianic prophecies of the Bible from which we have digressed so as to impart indispensable prerequisite information. According to the *book of Numbers,* God instructed Moses to build a *bronze serpent:*

*And Moses made a bronze serpent and set it on the standard [pole];
and it came about, that if a serpent bit any man, when he looked to the
bronze serpent, he lived.*

(21:9)

Curiously enough, Jesus identifies himself with this *bronze serpent*; he exclaims,

*And as Moses lifted up the [bronze] serpent in the wilderness, even so
must the Son of Man be lifted up; that whoever believes may in Him have
eternal life.*

(John 3:14-15)

Jesus's death on the cross turns out to be the fulfillment of Moses's prophetic sign pertaining to the mysterious and remedial *bronze serpent*! (cf. John 5:46). In this respect, we encounter a healing Messiah who is perhaps also prefigured in the ancient Greek myth of Asclepius; most notably in the rod of Asclepius, a snake-entwined staff which heals the sick. This symbol endures to this day as the emblem of the medical sciences. Similarly, by incurring the wrath of God on behalf of humanity's sins, Christ becomes the serpent who hangs on a cross: *"for it is written, 'CURSED IS EVERYONE WHO HANGS ON A TREE'"* (Gal. 3:13; cf. *New King James*, Acts 5:30). Thus, Christ becomes the snake that dies on a staff (pole), the result of which allows him to bestow immortality on mankind. The medieval setting of this divine event is foreshadowed in the alchemist legend of the philosopher's stone.

But why is this serpent made of bronze? It turns out that this *bronze* symbolism pervades many images of Christ in the Bible so that it has come to be intimately associated with him (cf. Ezek. 40:3). The reason we digressed to present the various visions found in the book of Daniel was so that we could clearly understand the exposition that would follow. In all of scripture, the only verses which unequivocally delineate the meaning of the symbol of *bronze* are the ones inscribed in the book of Daniel; a nation comes to be identified with the image of *"bronze,"* namely, *"the kingdom of Greece"* (Dan. 2:32, 39; cf. 8:21). Needless to say, the famous *"statue"* in King Nebuchadnezzar's dream (Dan. 2) will become the foundation of our subsequent study.

In establishing the clear-cut identifying symbol associated with each successive empire in Nebuchadnezzar's dream, we provide a key principle to unlocking the mystery behind the figurative language of the text. Actually, whenever we encounter the term *bronze* within scripture, it seems to be employed with the precision of a surgical scalpel by a master surgeon. Its biblical application is neither coincidental, nor random. In referring to the composite statue of Nebuchadnezzar's dream, the noted scriptural scholar *Arnold G. Fruchtenbaum* writes,

> *The first empire is the Babylonian Empire which included the head
> of gold. . . . The second empire is the Medo-Persian Empire represented by
> the arms and breasts of silver. . . . This is followed by the third empire, the
> Hellenistic Empire represented by the belly of brass [bronze]. . . . It started
> out as a unit under Alexander the Great but split into four divisions at
> his death. This empire is subject to considerable revelation in Daniel 2:39,
> 7:6, 8:7-27; and 11:3-35.*

(24)

However, we must add a word of edification concerning the terminology usage
in the different versions of the Bible. For example, whereas the New American
Standard, the New King James, and the New Jerusalem Bible all indicate the
term *bronze* in Daniel 2:39, the Authorized King James version denotes the word
brass instead. These *inspired* renditions are not considered to be deviations from
the essential meaning of the text. Rather, they enhance it by providing a certain
dimension of depth, amplifying the meaning, as it were. To be sure, the terms
brass and *bronze* refer to similar metallic elements and components which in and
of themselves indicate the interchangeability of the terms used to denote them. Be
that as it may, whether we come across the kingdom of *brass* or the empire of *bronze*,
cross-references between various Bible translations will invariably yield identical
results that refer exclusively to the kingdom of Greece.

Therefore, the transition from Moses's statement to Christ's elaboration marks
a turning point in our ability to decipher the riddle of the *bronze serpent.* If we were
to combine and paraphrase the passages pertaining to both Moses (Num. 21:8-9)
and Jesus (John 3:14-15), they would read as follows: "Moses made a bronze [Greek]
serpent" and lifted it on a pole (cross) so "that whoever" looked upon it and
believed would gain "eternal life." On his part, Christ conveys the notion that he is
in fact represented by Moses's prophetic *serpent* sign, an oracle which, after all, he
must fulfill. And if so, then it stands to reason that Christ is identified with a *bronze
serpent* because that is exactly what Moses lifted on a pole. Following the dictates of
scripture, we are led to the inevitable conclusion that the Messiah must come from
Greece! Even more startling is the Bible's acknowledgment that the secrets of Christ
would not be revealed until the time of the end (Gal. 4:4, Dan. 12:4, 9).

Scripture is perforated with this unique *bronze* image. For instance, we could
almost hear Ezekiel's footsteps pacing excitedly to and fro through the dusty roads
of Assyria (Ezek. 1:1, 3:15) after seeing a vision of a heavenly being that is gleaming
"like burnished bronze" (Ezek. 1:7). This is the person whom the prophet believes
to be "the appearance of the likeness [the image] of the glory of the Lord" (1:28,
cf. Col. 1:15). Not surprisingly, Christ himself is revealed within scripture through
the use of this same striking image. Specifically, there is a direct correspondence
between the *bronze feet* of the incarnated Messiah in the book of Ezekiel (cf. 1:5, 7 f.)

and the *"thighs of bronze"* that clearly symbolize the kingdom of Greece in the book of Daniel (2:32, 39). Another instance of this specific resemblance can be found in the book of Revelation:

> *And on His [Christ's] robe and on His* thigh *He has a name written,*
> *"KING OF KINGS, AND LORD OF LORDS."*

> *(19:16, emphasis added)*

But why is his name written on his thigh? There can be no other scriptural explanation except for the attempt to identify him with the Greek "thighs of bronze"! (Dan. 2:32, 39).

Another paradigm involves *John the Seer*—the author of the book of Revelation—who in his visions beheld an apocalyptic semblance of Christ in which "His feet were like burnished bronze" (Rev. 1:15, 2:18). Bear in mind that all these biblical images are not there by sheer chance. Therefore, one of the constant biblical portrayals of Jesus pertains to the symbol of *bronze*, an image that is deeply associated with the Greeks. Despite the outpouring of scriptural intimations, no one thus far has grasped this imagistic connection to the mysterious origin of Jesus, and indeed there has been little attempt to comprehend it:

> *This figure of speech Jesus spoke to them [Jews], but they did not*
> *understand what those things were which He had been saying to them.*

> *(John 10:6)*

But there is another meaning to the term *bronze*. The Bible provides a good measure of evidence to suggest this word's staggering implications for the modern lexicon of warfare, if for no other reason than to reveal the mystery behind the crucifixion. What is more, few prophecies have been so carefully hidden or so generally overlooked as the ones that refer to Christ's death. These cryptic verses give a whole new meaning to the proverbial nails of the cross. Here are some examples: "The archers bitterly attacked him, and shot at him and harassed him" (Gen. 49:23); *"No hand shall touch him, but he shall surely be . . . shot through"* (Exod. 19:13). You get the idea.

A twentieth-century prophecy has recently surfaced, the so-called *Third Secret of Fatima*, which substantially corroborates our view. The vision took place in the spring of 1917 and is recounted by *Lucia Santos* (1907-2005 AD):

> *And we saw . . . a Bishop [Christ] dressed in white (we had the*
> *impression it was the Holy Father) [sic] . . . going up a steep mountain*
> *at the top of which was a big Cross. . . . Before reaching there, the Holy*

Father passed through a big city half in ruins [from warfare]. And half
trembling with halting step, afflicted with pain and sorrow, he prayed. . . .
Having reached the top of the mountain, on his knees at the foot of the big
Cross, he was killed by a group of soldiers who fired bullets and arrows at
him. Beneath the two arms of the Cross there were two Angels, each with
a crystal aspersorium in his hand, in which they gathered up the blood of
the Martyrs and with it sprinkled the souls that were making their way to
God.

(Haffert, 5-6).

The cross-references we have examined appear to substantiate our claims that there are biblical signs pertaining to the coming of a Greek Messiah. In fact, the text shows how the location of the Messiah's birthplace is not found *"among the clans of Judah"*:

Too little to be among the clans of Judah, from you One will go forth
for Me [God] to be ruler. . . . His goings forth are from long ago, from the
days of eternity.

(Mic. 5:2)

Bear in mind that after the Assyrian conquest of the Northern Kingdom of Israel, at around 722 BC, all that remained to the Jewish people was the southern Kingdom of Judah. If the eternal *"ruler"* (the Messiah) comes from a region *"too little to be among the clans of Judah,"* then he obviously comes from elsewhere and is, by definition, a non-Jew! Correspondingly, the Deity further announces an absolutely spellbinding prophecy: *"I will"* call *"the man of My purpose from a far country"* (Isa. 46:10-11). *"A far country"* indicates a nation and a language other than the one that the Hebrew prophets lived and spoke in. To a certain extent, these verses are largely self-explanatory in that they signify a non-Jewish Messiah. It is also important to note that all of the aforecited oracles stand or fall by their capacity to measure up to the standards of the following axiom:

No prophecy was ever made by an act of human will, but men moved
[inspired] by the Holy Spirit spoke from God.

(2 Pet. 1:21)

MICHAEL: THE PRINCE OF GREECE

Like Ezekiel before him, Daniel confronts a heavenly being whose face "had the appearance of lightning, his eyes were like flaming torches, his arms and feet like the gleam of polished bronze" (Dan. 10:6). These images from the *Hebrew Bible* are then carried forward into the Greek NT. Closely connected with the advent of Christ is the biblical description of *the appearance of lightning*:

> *For just as the lightning comes from the east, and flashes even to the west, so shall the coming of the Son of Man be.*

> *(Matt. 24:27)*

In Daniel 10:6, the arms and feet of *bronze* once again evoke the image pertaining to the statue of Nebuchadnezzar's dream, namely, the kingdom of Greece (Dan. 2:39). With these images in mind, we are confronted with a specific and unique narrative structure that suggests a messianic revelation.

The aforesaid "man" from heaven (Dan. 10:5), whose feet were "like . . . bronze" (10:6, 2:32), tells Daniel that *"the prince of . . . Persia"* withstood him *"for twenty-one days"* (10:13). Similar to the *day-year principle*—a hermeneutical method that is applied to apocalyptic prophecy in which days can correspond to years (Ezek. 4:5)—scripture provides another mathematical formula to help us decipher biblical terminology: the principle that "one day is as a thousand years" (2 Pet. 3:8, Ps. 90:4). In accordance with the latter concept, where biblical days can symbolize longer periods of time, it is our estimation that *"the prince of . . . Persia"* withstood the angelic man, who represents the Messiah, for twenty-one centuries. As a matter of fact, we are currently living in this prophesied twenty-first century! The Divine Being then expounds the oracle to Daniel:

> *Then behold, Michael, one of the chief princes, came to help me, for I had been left there with the kings of Persia. Now I have come to give you an understanding of what will happen to your people in the latter days [last days], for the vision pertains to the days yet future.*

> *(10:13-14)*

Daniel continues recounting the experience of the vision: "Then he said, 'Do you understand why I came to you?'" (10:20). The celestial being raises the question as to whether Daniel has understood the message, for he is clearly elaborating on a messianic prophecy:

> *But I shall now return to fight against the prince of Persia; so I am*
> *going forth, and behold, the prince of Greece is about to come. . . . Yet there*
> *is no one who stands firmly with me against these forces except Michael*
> *your prince.*

(10:20-21)

So then, the dark spiritual forces that are personified by *Persia* delay the arrival of the humanlike angel *"for twenty-one days."* Accordingly, the prophetic milestone of Christ's Advent is predicted to occur during the twenty-first century! What is more, Daniel is told that *"Michael, one of the chief princes, came to help"* the angel battle against the evil kings of Persia. Notice that the angelic-man (10:5) says that he shall go forth *"to fight against the prince of Persia,"* and then quickly adds that, in like manner, *"the prince of Greece is about to come."* We already know from the historical sources that *"the prince of Greece,"* Alexander the Great, fought against the allied Persian forces (cf. 8:3-8, 11:1-4). Therefore, biblically speaking, the prince of Greece fights on the side of the angel. To that end, *Michael* the prince, who came to help the angel contend with the Persian armies (10:13), is like *"the prince of Greece,"* who also comes to his aid as the angel is about to go to war (10:20).

A careful reading of the text reveals more information than we had previously anticipated. Pay particular attention to the words of the angel:

> *I shall now return to fight against the prince of Persia; so I am going*
> *forth, and behold, the prince of Greece is about to come.*

(10:20)

This verse seemingly coalesces the two figures—namely, the angel and the prince of Greece—as if they are one and the same person; they appear to be equated in the sense that both are *"going forth"* to battle Persia or to declare war against these forces. The moment of epiphany comes when the celestial being makes a terse remark about *"the prince of Greece"* who will aid in the fight, and then follows it up with the conclusion: *"no one . . . stands firmly with me against these forces except Michael"* the prince (10:21).

At this critical point we are on the verge of comprehending the omen which will occur *"in the latter days,"* otherwise known as the last days of the world (10:14). Apparently, the oracle pertains to the coming of a *Messiah-Prince* (cf. Isa. 9:6, Dan. 12:1-2) during the twenty-first century. Persia represents the Moon religion whose end-time military alliance will plunge the world into World War III (cf. Rev. 9:13-16). But now that the cryptic identification has been established between Michael and the prince of Greece, it seems that this is the same messianic Prince as the one found in Daniel 9:25 and 12:1. The ultimate conclusion of this analysis is that Daniel gives us just enough information to reveal the hidden origin of Christ, without going into great detail. The obvious implication drawn from the aforecited passages is that *"Michael"* is *"the prince of Greece"*!

Of course, scripture is not implicating *Alexander the Great* per se, but rather the *Messiah* whom the former merely represents by virtue of the latter's Greek ancestry. Nevertheless, the angel instructs Daniel to *"conceal [hide] these words and seal up the book until the end of time"* (12:4, 9). This is why the angel poses the following question: *"Do you understand why I came to you?"* Finally, we recognize that the angel is unveiling a hidden message about the place and time of God's visitation upon the earth. The place of origin is *Greece*, and the timing of this event is said to occur during the *twenty-first century.*

CHRIST WILL RULE THE EARTH
WITH THE ROD OF GREECE

Let us now consider a prevalent symbol associated with the Messiah and metaphorically expressed through the idea that he will rule *"the earth . . . with a rod of iron"* (Ps. 2:8-9). One thing that we can deduce from this imagery is that the figurative *"rod of iron"* does not indicate a rule of "tyranny, as the English idiom might be held to indicate" (Morris, 154). Another illustration of this sign depicts a woman who gives birth to the Messiah, "a male child, who is to rule all the nations with a rod of iron" (Rev. 12:5). This symbol is intimately associated with Christ as it is cited in numerous passages (cf. Rev. 2:27). For instance, during Judgment Day, Jesus will *smite the nations*:

> And He will rule them with a rod of iron.

> (Rev. 19:15)

The symbolism of the kingly *rule* and the *iron* are a throwback to the book of Daniel, the only place within the entire Bible where these terms seem to appropriate considerable meaning. In particular, we are referring to the vision of the imposing *statue* in Nebuchadnezzar's dream. In an earlier annotation, we indicated that the Roman Empire represents the *"fourth kingdom as strong as iron"* (Dan. 2:40). Scripture indicates that this iron empire *"will be a divided kingdom; . . . it will have in it the toughness of iron, . . . mixed with common clay. . . . [S]o some of the kingdom will be strong and part of it will be brittle"* (Dan. 2:41-42). It has been previously noted how the western part of the Roman Empire—namely, Rome—denotes the weak part, which completely collapsed by the year 476 of the Common Era when the last Roman Emperor was deposed by *Odoacer* the barbarian. Conversely, the eastern part of the Roman Empire had *"the toughness of iron"* as it continued to thrive for over one thousand years until the Ottoman Empire overtook it in 1453. Correspondingly, Rome represents the fragile *"potter's clay"* of the *"divided kingdom,"* whereas *Constantinople*, the capital of the *Byzantine Empire*, signifies the portion which is *"as strong as iron"* (Dan. 2:40-41). In point of fact, the religion, culture, and language of Byzantium were Greek (Ware, 18-71). Indisputably, even though it was the empire of the Romans, it came to be known as the *empire of the Greeks*. Under the circumstances, we can ascertain that the symbols of *clay* and *iron*, in Daniel's prophecy, indicate the kingdoms of the *Latins* and *Greeks* respectively.

In addition, the term alluding to Christ's kingly *rule* can also be traced back to the composite statue of Nebuchadnezzar's dream where it denotes a succession of historical empires. Specifically, the aforesaid term is used in reference to the major kingdoms "which will *rule* over all the earth" (Dan. 2:38-39, emphasis added). We have also established that the symbol of *iron* signifies the *empire of the Greeks*. The obvious conclusion drawn from the aforecited prophecy concerning one who *will rule . . . [the nations] with a rod of iron* (Rev. 19:15) is that Jesus "will rule over all the earth" (Dan. 2:39) with the rod of Greece, denoting the "iron" Byzantine Empire! (Dan. 2:40-42). As it turns out, these cryptic symbols of Greece are attributed to the apocalyptic end-time *Messiah* for the purpose of revealing the mystery of his origin:

> *And she [Mary] gave birth to a son, a male child, who is to rule all the nations with a rod of iron; and her child was caught up [taken] to God and to His throne [royal court].*

> *(Rev. 12:5)*

We will present further evidence to show that the oracle about Christ "rul[ing] all the nations with a rod of iron" refers to the succeeding empires of the Danielic text as represented in the vision of the composite statue. In recounting these successive empires, the book of Daniel tells us that the last empire of *iron* will be so powerful that it will effectively demolish all the previous kingdoms that preceded it:

> *Inasmuch as iron crushes and shatters all things, so, like iron that breaks in pieces, it [the fourth empire] will crush and break all these [prior empires] in pieces.*

> *(Dan. 2:40)*

As far as this divided Roman Empire is concerned, which is described as being *"partly of potter's clay and partly of iron"* (Dan. 2:41), we are told that its two parts *"will not adhere [or become unified] to one another, even as iron does not combine with pottery"* (2:43). Let us now try to ascertain exactly how the NT exploits these OT phrases in the service of apocalyptic prophecy.

Notice that the foregoing verses from the book of Daniel contain several symbols that are now attributed to Jesus Christ:

> AND HE [CHRIST] SHALL RULE THEM WITH A ROD OF IRON, AS THE VESSELS OF THE POTTER ARE BROKEN TO PIECES.

> (Rev. 2:27)

Consider the aforesaid phrase, "BROKEN TO PIECES," and its relation to Daniel's *iron empire* that will "break all these [prior empires] in pieces" (Dan. 2:40 f.). The terms being used are almost identical. Both passages are referring to the image of *pottery*, which mainly represents Rome, as if it is "*broken to pieces*" (Dan. 2:40-41, Rev. 2:27). In like manner, scripture reveals the connection of the messianic symbols to the book of Daniel by attributing these specific images to Christ himself who will "*rule*" the world "*with a rod of iron*" (Dan. 2:39, 41); his divine might thereby causing "*THE VESSELS OF THE POTTER*" to be "*BROKEN TO PIECES.*" In the book of Psalms, we find a similar reference to the Messiah which bears out our position:

> Thou [Messiah] shalt break [rule] them with a rod of iron, thou shalt shatter them like earthenware [pottery].

> (Ps. 2:9)

An analogous type of prophecy can be found in the book of Daniel. It is directly related to the preceding thematic material wherein Christ is depicted in metaphorical imagery that characteristically describes the Greeks. A symbol of Christ's death is conveyed through a vision of a tree being cut down. Then, "*An angelic watcher, a holy one, descended from heaven*" and proclaimed the oracle, "*Yet leave the stump with its roots in the ground, . . . with a band of iron and bronze around it . . . and let seven periods of time [seven Sabbaths] pass over him*" (4:14-16). Isaiah further elucidates what is meant by this elaborate imagery: "*Like a terebinth or an oak whose stump remains when it is felled; the holy seed [Christ] is its stump*" (6:13). This constitutes additional proof that Jesus—whose death is said to occur during the seventh Sabbath—is described through various symbols pertaining to the Greeks, namely, the "*iron and bronze*" (Dan. 2:39-41). Curiously, it seems that the "*angelic watcher . . . [who] descended from heaven*" to articulate the prophecy is himself representative of the Messiah. The language used to introduce this angel—namely, that he "descended from heaven"—is identical to the one that describes Christ: "For the Lord Himself will descend from heaven" (1 Thess. 4:16). Jesus, in referring to himself, says, "*And no one has ascended into heaven, but [except] He who descended from heaven, even [that is] the Son of Man*" (John 3:13).

On these grounds, the symbolic messianic connections to the book of Daniel are unmistakable. Therefore, it seems relatively unquestionable that the *"rod of iron"* with which Christ *"rules"* denotes the *iron* Greeks, who also appear to be the Gentile heirs to the OT promises. This notion is also articulated by Isaiah who declares that during Judgment day, Christ "will strike the earth with the rod of His mouth" (11:4). Here, the *"rod of iron"* that smashes the earth has become *the rod of His mouth.* Since Jesus is considered to be the *Logos* (means "Word" in Greek) or "the Word of God" (Rev. 19:13), *the rod of His mouth* signifies his divine *Word.* Not surprisingly, the NT reveals Christ's mysterious identity by using exclusively Greek *words* that represent the divine Name of God; that is, the divine "I AM" (cf. Exod. 3:14, John 8:58):

> I am the Alpha and the Omega.

> *(Rev. 1:8)*

Evidently, there is immense value in follow-up studies of terms, phrases and symbols that are found consistently throughout the Bible. Phrases like the *Lord's Day* or the *last days,* as well as other conceptual symbols—such as those indicating the images of *bronze, iron,* and the like—appear to reveal the mysteries that are concealed under the veil of the biblical descriptive process. These images in and of themselves are veritable repositories of knowledge whose prophetic import is indisputable. The result of this type of investigation is not based on speculation since the essential *meaning* of the symbol in question has been extracted and confirmed through a meticulous cross-referential analysis. The subsequent invariability of *meaning* of a particular symbol across different contexts will provide the overall evidence, proving the result. It follows that we are talking about a certain kind of biblical methodology, the equivalent of a scientific type of inquiry, where repeated observations and results yield authentic and reproducible data.

The most trustworthy approach in comprehending the Bible is when we allow scripture to interpret itself. This methodology renders the conclusion as nonnegotiable since the result is derived directly from the text per se. Our task, as interpreters, is simply to organize the descriptive material and to allocate it to the appropriate places as scriptural dictates demand. Maintaining the transparency of the text is of paramount importance. And that is precisely what we have done in our query.

TIMOTHY AND THE MACEDONIAN FACTOR
IN PAUL'S VISIONS

And a vision appeared to Paul in the night: a certain man of Macedonia was standing and appealing to him, and saying, "Come over to Macedonia and help us."

—Acts 16:9

Paul's vision is inexplicably intertwined with, and runs parallel to a similar vision encountered by Daniel. The latter also envisions "a certain man" (a celestial entity) who has an altercation with the prince of Persia and on whose behalf "Michael, one of the chief princes, came to help" fight the Persians (Dan. 10:5, 13). Then the heavenly figure alludes to the association between Michael and Alexander the Great. He says to Daniel,

But I shall now return to fight against the prince of Persia; so I am going forth, and behold, the prince of Greece is about to come. . . . Yet there is no one who stands firmly with me against these forces except Michael your prince.

(Dan. 10:20-21)

Ultimately, one is left with the unshakable impression that Michael represents the prince of Greece: Alexander the Great. And so he who "came to help" fight the Persians, in the book of Daniel, turns out to be a *Macedonian*. By comparison, "a certain man" (an angel) appears to Paul in a vision and pleads, "Come over to Macedonia and help us." This verse employs the same essential message and idiomatic phrasing of the Danielic text. It resonates with the cryptic meaning that the world will be saved by a Macedonian. Thus the underpinning of both texts intimates the coming of a Greek Prince!

But Paul's deeper revelations of Jesus do not end there. In the interests of disclosing Christ's identity, Paul addresses his directive to a certain man whom he unexpectedly equates with the anticipated Messiah. His letter explicitly refers to a mysterious male figure identified only as *Timothy*. In his recommendation, he says,

> *This command I entrust to you, Timothy, my son, in accordance with*
> *the prophecies previously made concerning you, that by them you may fight*
> *the good fight.*

> *(1 Tim. 1:18)*

Paul tells Timothy that he ascribes to him all "the prophecies previously made concerning you"! Astoundingly, the apostle does not only contend that this statement obviously alludes to Jesus, but also that the NT scriptures represent "the prophecies previously made concerning" him. According to the preceding verse, the only legitimate conclusion that can be reached is that Christ's future incarnation is prophesied by scripture and written in advance.

But who is this enigmatic Timothy? Surprisingly, we learn that he is "the son of a Jewish woman," whose "father was a Greek" (Acts 16:1, cf. 18:5-6). Besides being an allegory of the Jewish and Greek Testaments, the clear implication is that the prophesied child is the progeny of Greece. Being a *male*, he assumes his father's name:

> *Christ Jesus, . . . promised beforehand through His prophets in the holy*
> *Scriptures, . . . to bring about the obedience of faith among all the Gentiles,*
> *for His name's sake.*

> *(Rom. 1:1-5)*

The above quote references God's incarnation and emphasizes that it was already prophesied "beforehand" that he would be found "among . . . the Gentiles, for His name's sake." And as we have previously noted, God's name is *Yahvah*, a transliteration of *Yavan*, meaning Greece (Ps. 68:4, Isa. 12:2, 26:4, 38:11, *New King James*).

All these clues remind us of the last chapter of Paul's Epistle to the Romans where he pays tribute to certain famed Greek legends. It seems exceedingly strange that Paul would send greetings in homage to what appear to be Hellenic personages from the time of antiquity: a commingling of Greek gods and mythic heroes. These biblical characters suggest that the ancient oracles of the Delphic temples as well as the prophecies inherent in Ionic mythology have always pointed to the coming of a Greek demigod. Paul openly calls some of these figures "my kinsmen" (Rom. 16:21). He documents a long list of names that are substantially taken from Greek mythology: Apollo, Narcissus, Perseus, Hermes, Nereus, Jason, and Olympus (Rom. 16). As a matter of fact, all of them share a common trait with the Messiah; they are all depicted as half-human and half-divine. Olympus, of course, represents heaven, the transcendent abode of the gods (cf. Ezek. 28:14). The sheer size of this list is unprecedented. It is highly unlikely that these names belonged to actual human figures and more than probable that they served as hidden imprints of the God man, Jesus Christ. Bear in mind that this is no ordinary letter. It is part of the biblical canon and, as such, it is imbued with profound symbolic and prophetic import. Therefore the accumulation of our evidence has reached such proportions that it can no longer be ignored.

ANTIPAS AND THE LINEAGE OF
THE SEVEN HEADED DRAGON

The little horn arrives in *the last hour* (1 John 2:18). In order to do so, he must await the completion of the preceding empires where each one is exponentially worse than the last. For he is known as the preeminent leader of *a great red dragon having seven heads and ten horns* (Rev. 12:1-5):

> *Here is the mind which has wisdom. The seven heads are seven mountains [or kingdoms], . . . and they are seven kings; five have fallen, one is, the other has not yet come; and when he comes, he must remain a little while. And the beast [antichrist] . . . is himself also an eighth, and is one of the seven, and he goes to destruction. And the ten horns which you saw are ten kings, who have not yet received a kingdom, but they receive authority as kings with the beast for one hour [1 century].*

> *(Rev. 17:9-12)*

The sentence, *"Here is the mind which has wisdom,"* draws the reader out of a literal context as the author supplies the term *"wisdom"* to argue for a different type of interpretation. The kingdom cited as the *"one [that] is"* should not be associated with the actual time period in which John wrote the book of Revelation. This historical connection does not appear to be the author's intention. How, then, do we arrive at the apocalyptic period that he implies? John claims to be a *partaker in the [great] tribulation . . . on the island called Patmos* (Rev. 1:9). Aside from the revelation which he announces, why would he himself be in tribulation? Could it be a result of the Roman occupation? The text does not support this conclusion as John is neither in Jerusalem, at the time of Jesus, nor is there any allusion to any Roman conquests. On the contrary, he happens to be on a Greek island, and his message is primarily intended for those living under heavy persecution in Asia Minor: *the seven churches* (Rev. 1:11).

The conventional argument that the empire which exists at this time is the Roman completely neglects the overall context and character of prophetic literature. If the intent of this type of literature is to reveal, then the message to the seven churches in Asia Minor is itself such a prophecy. And yet, the purpose in sending these letters to the seven churches that are located in modern-day Turkey remains inexplicable. This connection has eluded the experts. The prospect for answers is to be found in the clue that all these churches are located in Asia. In reality, this happens to be the same location of Lysimachus's earlier empire through which the antichrist's kingdom will emerge. Scripture presents another important clue to get this point across: Paul is "forbidden by the Holy Spirit to speak the word [of God] in Asia." In fact, as Paul and his companions tried "to go into Bithynia, . . . the Spirit of Jesus did not permit them" to do so (Acts 16:6-7).

Thus, as the book of Daniel leaves off with the fourth and fifth empires of the Romans, the book of Revelation picks it up from there with the sign of the sixth kingdom, which persecuted the Christian churches of Anatolia. As we read the contents of these letters that John sends to the churches of Asia, we are left with the indelible impression that the latter are under severe persecution and tribulation. We are even told that *Pergamum*, a prosperous city of Anatolian commerce and culture, is the place *"where Satan's [antichrist's] throne is"* (Rev. 2:13) located. What could be the reason for such turmoil in this vicinity? There can only be one: the emergence of another great empire: the *Ottoman Turks*! They expanded out of Bithynia, formerly held by Lysimachus, to reign for over 620 years. In their heyday, they controlled vast areas of land in as many as three continents: Asia, Europe and Africa. Greece, where John penned the book of Revelation, was conquered by the Ottoman Turks for nearly four hundred years (cf. Acts 7:6). But if one thing stands out more than any others, it is that the persecution and tribulation of the seven churches stems from their Anatolian neighbors. The number seven, of course, gives us the specific time frame associated with the signs of the apocalypse: seventh Sabbaths of years (cf. Lev. 25:8). This, then, is the setting in which the story of the *Apocalypse* begins.

Daniel's composite statue presents the first four great empires: Babylon, Medo-Persia, Greece, and Rome (Dan. 2). But since the Roman Empire is *a divided kingdom* (Dan. 2:41), it presupposes two similar, yet distinct empires; in that event, Rome is the fourth, while the Byzantines become the fifth. Then through the apocalyptic sign of the seven persecuted churches of Anatolia, the book of Revelation introduces the sixth empire—the *"one [that] is"*—namely, the Ottoman Turks! The essential meaning of the latter's presence in the text is to symbolically reveal the persecution of the church by the last religious empire of the Moon religion, which will also precipitate the coming apocalypse (cf. Rev. 9:13-16, 12:1). Hence, we are treading on the fringes of a religious battle set to take place at the end of time (cf. Rev. 13:7-12, 16:13-14). There is a prophetic timetable which substantiates this biblical exposition:

> *Here is the mind which has wisdom; . . . they are seven kings; five have fallen, one is, the other has not yet come; and when he comes, he must remain a little while.*

> (Rev. 17:9-10)

Historically speaking, the seventh empire that *"must remain a little while"* can only refer to the Soviet Union (USSR), which existed for the short duration of approximately 70 years. By contrast, the Turkish Empire lasted for 620 years, while the Byzantine that preceded it survived for 1,123 years. And so the five empires that exist no more are: Babylon, Medo-Persia, Greece, Rome, and Byzantium. The one that is said to exist "now," in the modern setting of the great tribulation story, is the sixth empire: the Ottoman Turks. The seventh is the short-lived Soviet Empire while the antichrist represents *an eighth* kingdom (the Russian Federation) that arises from *one of the seven* (Rev. 17:11). Insofar as prophecy is concerned, the last great empire, represented by the seven headed dragon, is of the utmost importance in that it is contemporaneous with the incarnation and manifestation of the Messiah (Rev. 12:1-8).

This theme is further expanded in Revelation 2:13 where there is a mysterious allusion to an end-time Christ. In fact, to ensure that Jesus is a contemporary of the final earthly empire, this line is then paired with another verse, which cryptically connotes *"the Nicolaitans,"* the Soviet Empire that, scripturally speaking, bears the name of its founder *Nikolai Lenin* (Rev. 2:15). Within this context, we find references to *"My witness"* and *"My faithful one,"* biblical terms that are used consistently in conjunction with the *Messiah* (cf. Rev. 1:5). Since the book of Revelation is an unveiling of prophetic events, we therefore become privy to the divine secrets concerning the Messiah's identity and future sacrifice:

> *[You] did not deny My faith, even in the days of Antipas, My witness, My faithful one, who was killed among you, where Satan [antichrist] dwells.*

> *(Rev. 2:13)*

Scripture designates the Messiah as *Antipas*, a decidedly Greek name. It is the abridged version of *Antipater* (*Antipatros* in Greek), as in the appellation of Alexander's Macedonian General *Antipater* (c. 398-319 BC). Thus the etymological elements of this name are derived from the Greek language. The contextual meaning of the prefix *anti* is construed as "in place of" while the suffix *patros* is rendered as "father." If we recombine these linguistic components that essentially mean "in place of" the "father," the name Antipas would suggest that the messianic figure of *Revelation* is the Greek representation of God the Father on earth! (cf. Col. 1:15-17). To be sure, this appealing idea flies in the face of our conventional view of Jesus.

CHAPTER 9

THE PROPHECIES OF VIRGIL, NOSTRADAMUS, AND THE DEAD SEA SCROLLS

True, you are immersed . . . in the World of Becoming; worst, you are besieged on all sides by the persistent illusions of sense. But you too are a child of the Absolute.

—*Underhill 42*

*E*usebius of Caesarea (c. AD 263-339), the celebrated biblical scholar, wrote that "as the Supreme God gave oracles to the Hebrews through their prophets, . . . so also He gave them to the other nations through their local oracles. For He was not only the God of the Jews, but of the rest of mankind as well" (Pamphili Book V). *Virgil* is a case in point. We are told that "the Fourth Eclogue in particular, the so-called messianic prophecy, with Virgil in the role of a pagan Isaiah, has been a center of attraction for the allegorizers of every generation" (Maro, x-xi). The renowned Roman poet named Virgil (70-19 BC), otherwise known as *Plebius Vergilius Maro*, is also a great visionary who embraces the ancient Apollonian oracles and gives them a voice through the art of sacred poetry. In his celebrated book called *Eclogues*, he verifies and validates the results of our research by documenting an augury of the end of days:

> *Now is come the last age of the Cumaean prophecy: the great cycle of the periods is born anew. Now returns the Maid, returns the reign of Saturn [the Golden age]: now from high heaven a new generation comes down. . . . At that boy's birth . . . shall this glorious age enter . . . : under thy rule what traces of our guilt yet remain, vanishing shall free earth for ever from alarm. He shall grow in the life of gods, and shall see gods and heroes mingled, and himself be seen by them. . . . But on thee, O boy,*

untilled shall Earth first pour childish gifts: . . . unbidden thy cradle shall
break into wooing blossom. The snake too shall die, and die the treacherous
poison-plant. . . . Then shall a second Tiphys [Greek Argonaut] be, and
a second Argo to sail with chosen heroes: new wars too shall arise, and
again a mighty Achilles be sent to Troy. . . . Run even thus, O ages, said
the harmonious Fates to their spindles, by the steadfast ordinance of doom.
Draw nigh to thy high honours . . . O dear offspring of gods . . . ; behold
how all things rejoice in the age to come. . . . Begin, O little boy: of them
who have not smiled on a parent, never was one honoured at a god's board
or on a goddess' couch

(Maro, 274-275).

Virgil seems to complement the sacred writings of the Israelites and the Greeks—namely, the Old and New Testaments—by pronouncing his own verdict concerning "the last age of the Cumaean prophecy." The Cumaean *Sibyl* was the source of this prophecy. "Sibyl" is derived from an ancient Greek term, *sibylla*, which signifies a female prophet. She was the high priestess who presided over Apollo's Temple at Cumae, the first ancient Greek settlement in mainland Italy. Much to everyone's surprise, Virgil vindicates our position that the end-times Messiah is of Greek descent! He declares that the Sibyl's prophecy takes place at "the last age" of human history, while the messianic figure that emerges from this story possesses all the characteristics of a traditional Greek hero; the "little boy," the "offspring of gods" is a "second Tiphys" or "a mighty Achilles." Arguably, the Apollonian oracle finds deep underpinnings in Isaiah's messianic message that "a little boy will lead" (11:6) mankind towards enlightenment. In the *Aeneid*—an epic poem that traces the founding of ancient Rome—Virgil seemingly makes reference to the biblical prophecy concerning *"the accepted sacrifice"* of a Greek Messiah (Rom. 15:16, Heb. 10:10, 14, *New King James*):

With blood of a slain maiden, O Grecians, you appeased the winds
when you first came . . . ; with blood must you seek your return, and an
Argive life [from Argos, Greece] be the accepted sacrifice.

(Maro 26, emphasis added)

But more than that, we will soon come to realize that the prophecy of a Greek Messiah appears to permeate across many distinct spiritual traditions.

THE MESSIANIC ORACLES OF NOSTRADAMUS

Michel de Nostredame is the reputed sixteenth-century augur whom we have come to know under the Latin name *Nostradamus*. His exciting predictions have captured the popular imagination. A plethora of his premonitions have been deemed as accurate adumbrations of past historical figures, places and events (McCann, 6). Among those who were called seers, none surpassed the great Nostradamus. It is with this view in mind that we present a brief portion of his work in which he seems to put forth, on more than one occasion, the auspicious coming of a Greek Messiah. Nostradamus writes,

> *Through the Attic land fountain of wisdom,*
> *At present the rose of the world*

(The Prophecies, *Century 5, Quatrain 31*).

This quatrain is reminiscent of "the Alchemical . . . Rose, birthplace of the 'Filius philosophorum'" (Campbell, 254), otherwise known as the *philosopher's stone*. Given that the vision is issued in the form of an oracle, the seemingly anachronistic phrase "at present" does not refer to Nostradamus's age per se, but to a future age when the content of this augury will materialize. Admittedly, the concept of time becomes ambiguous within the context of prophecy. The visionary's concepts of past, present, and future become blurred in comparison to the *infinite-now* presence of the prophetic moment that may conceivably belong to what *Husserl* calls a "living self-presence" (Frank, 411-412). This is another way of saying "eternity coexisting with the present time."

Attica is the region of Greece which includes Athens, one of the principal and most influential cities of antiquity. Fittingly, Nostradamus suggests that *the rose of the world* is born near the city of Athens, which has long been known as the *fountain of wisdom* (cf. Song of Sol. 2:1). The seer's eloquent use of poetic hyperbole connotes the ethereal and majestic nature of *the rose*. To ensure his audience that *the [divine] rose* represents a coming figure on the world stage, Nostradamus adds,

> *The rose upon the middle of the great world,*
> *For new deeds public shedding of blood:*
> *To speak the truth, one will have a closed mouth,*
> *Then at the time of need the awaited one will come late*

(The Prophecies, *Century 5, Quatrain 96*).

The Attic rose of the previous quatrain has suddenly blossomed, if you will, into a full-grown Messiah: *the awaited one*! He eventually becomes the center of human attention as he is revealed *upon the middle of the great world* stage. Christ's foretold sacrifice is here reiterated as a new deed regarding the awaited one's *public shedding of blood*. By the same token, Nostradamus complements the biblical notion of an end-time Messiah (Heb. 9:26) by stating that *the awaited one will come late*. Next, the seer issues an inspired utterance which upholds the sentiment that the prophetic office of Nostradamus is indeed conferred on him by divine grace; he proclaims, "To speak the truth, one will have a closed mouth." This event is prophetically foreshadowed in the book of Exodus: Moses could not speak so Aaron, his older brother, became his spokesman (Exod. 4:10-16). But it is only during the approaching time of Christ's manifestation that we will fully comprehend why this is considered to be an inspired promulgation (cf. Luke 1:22, 64; Isa. 28:11). All in all, Nostradamus's vision suggests that an eagerly awaited Messiah will emerge from Greece to offer himself as a blood sacrifice; an event that has been prophesied since the time of Abraham, Isaac (Gen. 22:6-8), and Jacob! (Gen. 49:10-11).

A GREEK MESSIAH PREDICTED BY THE DEAD SEA SCROLLS

The extant texts found at *Qumran* in the 1940s and '50s bear further revelations in regard to the coming of a Greek Messiah. As we reexamine these timeless manuscripts, we will focus our attention exclusively on the famous *War Scroll*, also known as *1QM* (*the Dead Sea Scrolls*, 150-171). It contains prophecies about a pivotal episode in human history: the final battle between the forces of light and the forces of darkness. This decisive conflict has been known since the time of the ancient Persian prophet *Zoroaster*. The clear adversary of God is named *Belial* (*War Scroll* 1:1).

The *1QM* text indicates that there will ultimately be an "eternal annihilation for all the forces of Belial" (1:5):

> *And cursed is Belial for his contentious purpose, and accursed for his reprehensible rule. And cursed are all the spirits of his lot for their wicked purpose.*

> *(Column 13, Line 4)*

The *Essenes*, the presumed Jewish sect credited with writing this manuscript, inform us that God "made Belial for the pit, an angel of malevolence, his [dominio] n is in darkne[ss] [sic]" (13:10-11). What is more, God implicates that there is an appointed day for the removal of Belial from authority (15:17, 18:1). As a consequence, Belial emerges in the text as the unequivocal chief antagonist to the Deity.

On the other hand, the conspicuous opponent of Belial is *the king of the Kittim*, one of the professed sons of Greece (cf. Gen. 10:4). In the Old Testament, the coastlands of the Kittim play a pivotal role in afflicting evildoers (Num. 24:24) as well as opposing the coming antichrist:

> *For ships of Kittim will come against him [the antichrist]; therefore*
> *he will be disheartened, and will return and become enraged at the holy*
> *covenant [the Messiah] and take action; so he will come back and show*
> *regard for those who forsake the holy covenant.*

> *(Dan.11:30)*

Once again, scripture highlights Christ's deep identification with the Greeks. The Danielic text helps clarify why the antichrist's wrath against the Greeks is now diverted to Christ who is represented by *"the holy covenant"* (Matt. 26:28).

The New King James version of the Bible suggests that the name *Kittim* refers to *Cyprus* and its neighboring islands; thus it represents *the Greek coastlands* (1115). And who is Belial's greatest rival? Insofar as scripture is concerned, it is none other than Jesus Christ. Paul writes, "What harmony has *Christ* with *Belial*, or what has a believer in common with an unbeliever? Or what agreement has the temple of God with idols?" (2 Cor. 6:15-16, emphasis added).

In a similar vein, we find a surprising inclusion of the Christian concept of the Triune Godhead (*Trinity*) within the War Scroll manuscript: "[m]ighty ones of the gods are girding themselves for battl[e, and] the formation[s of the 3 h[o]ly ones [are rea]dying themselves for a day of [vengeance . . .] [sic]" (15:14-15). All things considered, the War Scroll predicts two eternal foes that square off against each other at the final battle of Armageddon: the forces of *the king of the Kittim* versus the army of *Belial*. So it is not difficult to see how Christ, the foretold Messiah, is denoted as the king of the Kittim. Moreover, there are multiple references in the War Scroll that forecast the death of the king of Greece; this is illustrated with terms such as the *fall* of the Kittim or *the slain of the Kittim*. The same prediction of Christ's death ("falling away") is also established in the New Testament (2 Thess. 2:1-9, *New King James*). Therefore, the stage is set for the ultimate showdown between the sons of light and the sons of darkness at the end of days.

In the book of Daniel, the antichrist "was waging war with the saints and overpowering them until the Ancient of Days came" (7:21-22); this state of affairs is not unlike the description of the *War Scroll* manuscript concerning these end-time events:

> *Then the . . . [priests shall blow on the tr]umpets of the slain. . . . As*
> *the sound goes forth, the infantry shall begin to bring down the slain of*
> *the Kittim, and all the people shall cease the signal, [but the priest]s shall*

continue blowing on the trumpets of the slain and the battle shall prevail against the Kittim [sic].

(Column 16, Lines 7-9)

This column refers to *the slain of the Kittim* as well as to *the trumpets of the slain.* We know that the former phrase signifies the death of a Greek king, but what does the latter idiomatic expression represent? To whom do the trumpets belong? As their name suggests, they belong to *the slain of the Kittim!* In fact, they are *the trumpets of the slain.* Notice that after the death of this Greek king, which is the main implication of column 16:7-9, the people lose heart and consequently halt their signal to advance. Yet even though Belial is prevailing against the forces of Kittim, the devoted priests *continue blowing on the trumpets of the slain* (cf. Rev. 8:2-13). These specific War Scroll symbols may be traced back to "First Thessalonians, [which] is probably the earliest letter of Paul that we have, written in AD 50" (1367, *New Jerusalem Bible*). According to this NT letter, Christ will reappear "with the trumpet of God; and the dead in Christ shall rise first" (4:16; cf. 1 Cor. 15:51-52). This Pauline death and resurrection theme may help explain why we find several references to Christ's atonement, such as "the Offering of God" (4:1) within the 1QM manuscript. Therefore, the War Scroll story seems to portray the redemptive death of a Greek king, whose priests nevertheless continue to call on his name insistently and without respite:

[Then they shall gather]. . . . In the morning they shall come to the p[la]ce of the battle line, [where the mi]ghty men of the Kittim [fell]. . . . When they stand before the s]lain of the Kitt[im, they shall pr]aise there the God [of Israel. And they shall say in response: . . .][. . . [sic] to God most high

(Column 19, Lines 9-14).

The foregoing quote supplies further evidence that the *slain* Greek king of the *Kittim* is associated with the highest divinity. Astoundingly, the faithful stand at his grave and praise him! Other portions of the War Scroll also attest to an incarnate God amongst men during this end-time period. Here is such a line: "And he (Moses) [sic] told us that You are in our midst, a great and awesome God" (10:1). Moreover, the Essenes recount the riveting, messianic resurrection prophecy of the end-times: "the King of Glory is with us. . . . The Hero of Wa[r] [sic] is with our company. . . . Rise up, O Hero, take your captives, O Glorious One" (12:8-10), they exclaim. Equally important are the following lines that concentrate on the same resurrection theme:

Rise up, rise up, O God of gods, and raise Yourself in power, [O King of Kings . . .] let all the Sons of Darkness [scatter from before You] [sic].

(Column 14, Lines 16-17)

The Essenes, who are supposedly responsible for writing this text, quote a verse from Isaiah concerning the fall of Assyria (Isa. 31:8). The reason why the Essenes refer to Isaiah (*War Scroll* 11:12) is for the purpose of bequeathing a *sign*: "Ships shall come from the coast of Kittim, and they shall afflict Asshur" (Num. 24:24). *Asshur* was one of the foremost cities of ancient Assyria. Biblically, this nation symbolizes the great enemy of God (Isa. 10:5-6). But the word *Assyria* is also a cryptic anagram for *Russia*. In the OT, "the arrogant heart of the king of Assyria" (Isa. 10:12) comes to represent the little horn! (cf. Dan. 7:8, 2 Thess. 2:4). For example, observe how God's prophecy concerning the antichrist's death on the mountains of Israel relates to both Assyria and Russia in two OT texts (Isa. 14:25-26, Ezek. 38:2, 21). In quoting Isaiah, the Essenes are thereby asserting and reinforcing the notion that *the Kittim* are on God's side, as they punish Assyria. But since it is God himself who ultimately punishes Assyria (Isa. 14:25), *the Kittim* must therefore be represented by the end-time Christ.

Isaiah describes this apocalyptic battle in the starkest terms as he prophetically envisions God "waging war with the dragon" (Rev. 12:7, cf. Isa. 27:1) in the air. He writes, just "like flying birds, so the Lord of hosts will protect . . . and deliver" (Isa. 31:5) his people. In like manner, the War Scroll manuscript indicates that the "king of; [sic] the Kittim . . . shall go forth with great wrath to do battle against the kings of the north" (1:4). This is reminiscent of Ezekiel's prophecy pertaining to the "prince of Rosh" (the antichrist) who "will come from . . . the remote parts of the north" (38:15-16) to overwhelm the nations, and "whom the Lord will slay with the breath of His mouth" (2 Thess. 2:8). Therefore, the War Scroll reveals that during this ultimate war of the gods, *"the princes of God"* (3:3) will do battle on humanity's behalf:

You appointed the Prince of Light from of old to assist us.

(Column 13, Line 10)

Remarkably, this extrabiblical work also seems to prophesy the age of this messianic Prince (cf. Isa. 9:6):

The congregation's clans, fifty-two. . . . The chiefs . . . from the age of fifty upwards, shall take their stand . . . on their festivals, new moons and Sabbaths.

(War Scroll, Column 2, Lines 1-4)

The War Scroll's frame of reference is attempting to make known that the biblical calculations in relation to the appointed time of the Messiah are actually based on Old Testament festivals and Sabbaths (cf. Lev. 25:8-13). Similar to the consummate determination of the *seven weeks'* oracle of Daniel (Dan. 9:25), the War Scroll arrives at an analogous conclusion. The implication is that the chief Prince shall make a stand *from the age of fifty upwards.* To that extent, both the book of Daniel and the War Scroll denote that the coming of Christ is associated with the fifty-year mark, variously known as the *Pentecost.*

But who are the mysterious *chiefs* that are signified in the previous quote? They are meant to be symbolic representations of the Triune God. You may recall that the book of Daniel references Christ as "Michael, one of the chief princes" (10:13, cf. 12:1) of the Trinity. In the same vein, the Essenes' "banners" reflect the signposts that point to the approaching Messiah: *"Michael"* (*War Scroll* 9:16), "the right hand of God," "the appointed time of God," "the tumult of God," "the slain of God" (*War Scroll* 4:6-7, cf. Dan. 10:6), and the like. To indicate the armor of faith in Christ held by the army of God, the text illustrates that "all of them shall bear shields of bronze" (*War Scroll* 5:4). In this instance, the kingdom of God is likened to the *kingdom of bronze*; namely, the Greeks (cf. Dan. 2:39). As for the assortment of prophetic imagery that is in view—from the "seven priests . . . dressed in fine . . . linen" to the "varicolored design" on their tunics (*War Scroll* 7:9-11)—these evocative symbols enunciate the prefigured Christ (cf. Rev. 19:14, Gen. 37:3) whose manifestation commences at the end of the seventh Sabbath.

It is true that the War Scroll's use of abstract diction makes interpretation all the more difficult. Moreover, some of the original fragments of the text have since been lost. Add to this the problems of translation, and you are left with the task of searching for the proverbial needle in a haystack. This turn of events has baffled certain scholars to such an extent that they are still mystified by the king of the Kittim. Even though Belial is decidedly the quintessential adversary of the Deity, they often falsely impute disproportionate attributes of evil to the king of the Kittim (Rich and Shipley, 40).

How is it that *the Kittim* oppose inexorable villains in the Old Testament, as we have amply shown, but in the War Scroll they are uncharacteristically relegated by some experts to a maleficent status? Something is deeply wrong as this conjecture directly contradicts biblical exegesis. In this respect, it is our contention that we cannot profit by the War Scroll manuscript unless we fully understand its connection to the OT and NT writings. In contradistinction to public opinion, our assiduous detective work shows that *the king of the Kittim* literally represents the *God-Messiah* in one form or another: as *the slain of God* or *the Offering of God.* It is only through this underlying concept that the story of the War Scroll becomes meaningfully intelligible and takes on an air of significance in its own right. Here is such an excerpt depicting the death of an anointed one:

> *On the day when the Kittim fall there shall be a battle and horrible*
> *carnage . . . , for it is a day appointed by Him [God] from ancient times*
> *as a battle of annihilation for the Sons of Darkness.*

> *(Column 1, Lines 9-10)*

This quote appears to reflect the terrible violence that will ensue in the aftermath of Christ's death (cf. Luke 21:22, Dan. 7:21, 25). The scriptures teach that the little horn will unleash apocalyptic horrors of such an unimaginable magnitude the world has never known (Matt. 24:21). Since the antichrist will be infuriated by the manifestation of the Messiah, the intensification of this onslaught against the nations, and especially against all Christians, will be completely overwhelming (cf. Dan. 11:30). That this savage slaughter is not exclusively prophesied in the Bible is indicated by its inclusion in the *1QM:*

> *On the day of their battle against the Kittim, they shall g[o forth for]*
> *[sic] carnage in battle.*

> *(Column 1, Lines 12-13)*

But the War Scroll ought to be understood in a biblical sense as well. For example, the Old Testament makes specific mention of the coming Messiah: "I see him," says *Balaam*, the diviner turned prophet, "but not now" (Num. 24:17). The extended treatment of this messianic figure culminates in an adjacent verse which describes ships coming "from the coast of Kittim" to "afflict" the wicked nations (24:24). These two verses, then, formulate a clear identification between Christ and "the coast of Kittim" (cf. Num. 24:17-24). Knowing this, the War Scroll writers recount this inspiring passage from the book of Numbers (cf. *War Scroll* 11:7) in an effort to cryptically establish the idea of the axiomatic King-Messiah who is derived from the Greek coastlands. As we shall see, this point cannot be so easily dismissed:

> *And cursed is Belial . . . for his reprehensible rule. . . . All the spirits*
> *of his lot—the angels of destruction—walk in accord with the rule of*
> darkness.

> (War Scroll, *Column 13, Lines 4-12, emphasis added*)

The War Scroll identifies the distinguishing traits between the forces of light and those of darkness, but it does so in a subtle manner. Thus, it is our task to weave the disparate elements together, piece by piece, until they coalesce to form a coherent tapestry of meaning. In light of this, the following line explicates the antecedent quote:

They shall carry out all this Rule *[on] that [day] at the place where they stand opposite the camps of the Kittim [sic]*

(War Scroll, *Column 16, Line 3, emphasis added*).

As a result, those who act "in accord with the rule of darkness," and who will implement "this Rule" at the end of the ages, are the same forces that "stand opposite the camps of the Kittim"! That much is clear. The last two quotes, then, distinguish the identifiable hallmark of the Kittim within the War Scroll, namely, that they are those who oppose the so-called "rule of darkness." This fact can be evidenced by the following lines included in the 1QM manuscript:

All those pr[epared] for battle shall set out and camp opposite the king of the Kittim and *all the forces of Belial that are assembled with him for a day [of vengeance] [sic]*

(*Column 15, Lines 2-3, emphasis added*).

Notice that both "Belial" and those who "camp opposite the king of the Kittim" represent the Kittim's conspicuous adversaries. That is to say, the people referred to by the clause, *all those pr[epared] for battle*, are identical to the army of the next phrase concerning *all the forces of Belial.* The keyword, *and*, simply conjoins the two sentential structures to explicate the meaning thereof. Therefore, this brief study aptly demonstrates the chief protagonists in the war of Armageddon: *Belial*, defying his archaic archrival, *the king of the Kittim.* Given that *the Greek coastland prophecies* make reference to the isles of the *Kittim* (Num. 24:24), discussed earlier in this book, and that the Kittim (the people of Cyprus) are the sons of Greece (Gen. 10:4), there is considerable evidence to substantiate the claim that *the king of the Kittim* signifies the incarnation of an end-time King-Messiah who will step onto the world stage as the progeny of Greece!

THE GREEK JESUS: A KEY WHICH UNLOCKS THE MYSTERIES OF THE BIBLE

Only for you, children of doctrine and learning, have we written this work. Examine this book, ponder the meaning we have dispersed in various places and gathered again; what we have concealed in one place we have disclosed in another, that it may be understood by your wisdom.

—*Heinrich Cornelius Agrippa von Nettesheim,*
(De occulta philosophia, 3, 65, qtd. in Eco)

It should be clear by now that the *historical Jesus* approach to the gospels poses more problems than it claims to solve. The apparent thematic inconsistencies and historical contradictions of the gospels can neither be solved, nor adequately explained by this perspective. Due to the problems involved in interpreting seemingly conflicting material, modern scholars have been unable to reach a consensus regarding the historical Christ. *Joel*, an OT seer, addresses some of the perplexing enigmas that we have encountered in the text. As the prophet maintains, the deity has forecasted two momentous end-time events: the return of the Jews to Israel, and the approach of Judgment Day (3:1-2). Then in an effort to unravel the age-old messianic riddle, he prophesies concerning the place where the resurrection will occur:

> *[They] sold the sons of Judah and Jerusalem to the Greeks in order to remove them far from their territory, behold, I am going to arouse [resurrect] them from the place where you have sold them [Greece], and return your recompense on your head.*

> (3:6-7)

This shocking oracle states the unequivocal location from where God will *"arouse"* or resurrect Abraham's spiritual offspring that represent the lineage of Christ (cf. Gal. 3:16). This *"place"* is none other than Greece! (cf. Rom. 9:26). The foregoing quote explicitly announces that the new headquarters of the kingdom of God have moved to a new location, namely, to the kingdom of Greece. And this revelation constitutes "the mystery which has been hidden from past ages and generations" (Col. 1:26). As we have long bemoaned the absence of a satisfactory explanation for the Jesus story, ours is a timely interpretation.

As can be readily seen, the new approach that we are proposing provides a deeply meaningful disclosure of these previously misunderstood and, in some cases, unidentified scriptural materials. Our method affords complete biblical unanimity in that it facilitates the understanding of the "last days" revelation of Jesus (Heb. 1:2) which will occur "at the consummation of the ages"! (Heb. 9:26). Our approach is also capable of aptly organizing and connecting an otherwise obscure, seemingly incoherent, and confusing text. Without this primordial secret of an *end-time Greek Messiah*, any hermeneutical effort to decipher the scriptures must remain forever deficient and incomplete. Our premise is corroborated throughout the text.

Indeed, the roots of this assertion can be traced back to the time of the ancient prophets. For example, why does Isaac bless Jacob instead of his older son *Esau?* (Gen. 27). As it turns out, Esau "sold his birthright to Jacob" (Gen. 25:33). Simply put, his prominence as the firstborn is "taken away" (Gen. 27:35). The story has come full circle and is repeated all over again in the allegorical story of Jacob (Israel) who confounds the *blessing* of Joseph's sons (Gen. 48). Therefore, our argument finds deep underpinnings in the legendary stories of Genesis: enigmatic blessings bequeathed by Isaac and Jacob to the apparent detriment of the Jews (Gen. 27, 48) and local heroes, such as Joseph and Moses, who are displaced in alien nations from where they rise to great heights of power and prestige (Gen. 41:41-44, Exod. 2:10). Accordingly, it is only through our aforesaid proposition that the seemingly conflicting accounts of the Old and New Testaments become intelligible. Otherwise, they remain as unsolved mysteries that are put on the back burner of spiritual thought.

The concept of a *Greek Messiah* is, first and foremost, a unique providential find. Clearly, we have hit upon a major new discovery whose proof inundates the pages of the Bible. It constitutes a different version of history that has been suppressed for thousands of years. Devoid of this *inspired* secret, Christianity's posited Messiah is predicated on a false premise! As a result, we take issue with classical Christianity's characterization of Jesus, especially with regard to their views concerning his origin and advent.

Here is a case in point. It is not without reason or purpose that we encounter a controversial biblical passage concerning a Greek Messiah. The Jews "were saying" (John 7:25),

> *"Look, He [Jesus] is speaking publicly, and they are saying nothing to Him. The [Gentile] rulers do not really know that this is the Christ [the Messiah], do they? However, we know where this man is from; but whenever the Christ may come, no one knows where He is from."* . . . *"When the Christ shall come, He will not perform more signs than those which this man has, will He?"* . . . *Jesus therefore said,* . . . *"You shall seek Me, and shall not find Me."* . . . *The Jews therefore said to one another, "Where does this man intend to go that we shall not find Him? He is not intending to go to the Dispersion among the Greeks, and teach the Greeks, is He?"*

> *(John 7:26-35)*

Notice that everything the Jews say in the above extract is both accurate and true. Even when the sentence ends with a question mark, the statement remains valid as a source of information. Arguably, this contentious quote has decisive prophetic value.

Let us break it down. First, the Jews say, *"the rulers [Roman Gentiles] do not really know that this is the Christ, do they? However, we know where this man is from."* The foregoing remark suggests that the Jews are privy to the secret knowledge that Christ is a Gentile, whereas *"the rulers do not really know."* This is precisely why the Jews oppose him by replying, *"Look, He [Jesus] is speaking publicly, and they are [not contradicting him] saying nothing to Him."* Second, the Jews mention that *"no one [really] knows where he is from."* This constitutes another admission of scriptural truth.

Apparently, this comment contradicts our previous notions of a Jewish Jesus since *"no one [really] knows"* his true origin. Third, the Jews ask, the coming Messiah *"will not perform more signs [miracles] than those which this man has, will He?"* Again, a true statement is pronounced since there is no other Messiah besides Jesus according to the Bible (John 1:41).

What is most surprising is how the messianic mystery can be revealed within scripture through a series of questions and comments that seem rather trivial and inconsequential. Shocked by Jesus's remark, the Jews reply in astonishment,

> *"Where does this man intend to go that we shall not find Him? He is not intending to go . . . among the Greeks, and teach the Greeks [instead], is He?"*

> *(7:35)*

Given that all of the preceding observations by the Jews were accurate, it follows that this statement is no exception. The prophetic implication is that *"no one [really] knows where He is from"* except scripture itself, and the latter ultimately reveals where the Messiah intends to appear, namely, *"among the Greeks."* Therefore, it seems indefensible to continue to preach from the pulpits of ignorance about a public figure that is, by definition, unknown!

And he [the angel] said, "Go your way, Daniel, for these words are concealed and sealed up until the end-time."

(Dan. 12:9)

PART III
The Signs of the Times

CHAPTER 10

JUDAISM AND THE SIGN OF RESURRECTION

[God says,] "This is My covenant, which you shall keep, between Me and you and your descendants after you: every male among you shall be circumcised. And you shall be circumcised in the flesh of your foreskin; and it shall be the sign of the covenant between Me and you. And every male among you who is eight days old shall be circumcised throughout your generations."

—Genesis 17:10-12

*J*udaism holds that this passage is the inscribed foundation of God's covenant with the Jewish people. This is the alleged sign of the covenant between "God Almighty" and Abraham, "the father of a multitude of nations" (Gen. 17:1-5). But what does it mean? Traditionally, the Jews have interpreted this sign in the literal sense of the word. As stated in Acts 15:1, Judaism maintains that, "unless you are circumcised according to the custom of Moses, you cannot be saved" (cf. Gen. 17:14). Yet to claim that the circumcised will be saved as opposed to the uncircumcised is to entertain an indeterminate idea which is tantamount to saying that redemption is based solely on a physical ritual. It is downright erroneous, if not utterly preposterous. Circumcision is certainly not contingent on a person's salvation. The true meaning of God's covenant is anything but that. One passage, clearly dealing with the issue of circumcision, reads,

The Lord your God will circumcise your heart [spirit] and the heart of your descendants, to love the Lord your God with all your heart and with all your soul, in order that you may live.

(Deut. 30:6)

Despite what Judaism says to the contrary, the foregoing quote yields compelling evidence that the deity is interested in one thing and one thing only: the *circumcision* of the heart! (cf. Rom. 2:28-29). God appends the following mandate: do this "in order that you may live," which is another way of saying that this is the way to attain salvation. Clearly, the concept of circumcision is a symbol that represents the *"day of atonement"* for the remission of humanity's collective sins (Lev. 23:26-28, Heb. 10:16-17). As Paul asserts, we cannot save ourselves through good deeds, no matter how lofty they may be, but only through faith in Christ's sacrifice (Eph. 2:7-9, Rom. 8:1-4, Gal. 2:16, 21). For "we are not [any longer] under [the Mosaic] law but under grace" (Rom. 6:14-15), which represents "the free gift of God" (Rom. 6:23). Let us now explore the concept of *circumcision* in more detail. Daniel delivers a timely prophecy:

> *Then after the sixty-two weeks the Messiah will be cut off.*

> *(9:26)*

The aforesaid quote refers to the death of a coming Messiah. To denote this predicament, scripture uses the words *"cut off."* But these are precisely the same words for which the term circumcision would be used. That this phrase refers to death is illustrated once again in Genesis 9:11 wherein God says to Noah, "And all flesh shall never again be cut off by the water of the flood" (cf. 1 Sam. 20:15). Accordingly, a close reading of the OT texts suggests that the "covenant of circumcision" is an apt metaphor for *the death of Christ*, the anointed Messiah. Therefore, the Messiah's atonement is certainly worthy of being called a *covenant* or a *sign* between God and man (cf. Isa. 53:5, Exod. 30:10).

In effect, Jesus's disciples must undergo a similar spiritual procedure in order to contact the divine realities. In fact, Jesus claims that if you wish to receive the spirit of God, *"you must be born again"* (John 3:3-8). Spiritual rebirth (Rom. 8:9-14) is akin to what philosophers call an *existential* death. As such, the concept of *rebirth* is germane to the theme under consideration (cf. Col. 2:11). It constitutes the same message proclaimed by the deity to all the inhabitants of the earth, articulated through the metaphorical language of *circumcision*:

> *Circumcise yourselves to the LORD and remove the foreskins of your heart.*

> *(Jer. 4:4)*

The concepts that have been brought into this discussion have aroused an intriguing question: why does the deity ascribe the eighth day to the symbolic sign of circumcision? (Gen. 17:12). If the covenant of circumcision signifies the *Day of*

Atonement (Lev. 23:28) or the remission of one's sins through the sacrificial death of the Messiah, then what does the eighth day signify? The answer is as fascinating as the question. To put it bluntly, because the "Passion" of Christ (John 10:17-18) is tied to and cannot be understood apart from his victory over death, the eighth day of circumcision mainly represents Jesus's awe-inspiring *resurrection*! This marvelous event, then, is deemed to be the ultimate *sign* of the covenant, so much so that God commands the Jews to transmit this sign to their posterity (Gen. 17:9). And this is the crucial point where the Christian and Jewish writings converge.

It has been said that the *Sabbath* is intimately associated with the death of Jesus. The Sabbath is the seventh day, as when God wrought the universe and then "rested on the seventh day" (Gen. 2:2), denoting that Christ himself will rest or pass away on the seventh Sabbath. This is why the number seven is repeated over and over again from Genesis to Revelation. During a discussion of the approaching Judgment, the prophet Hosea asks us, what will you do "on the day of the appointed festival," "on the day of the feast of the Lord?" (9:5). Besides referring to *the Feast of Tabernacles* (Lev. 23:39, Zech. 14:16), which is the seventh feast of the Lord, he is also alluding to the Jubilee year (Lev. 25:10) that is represented by the number *seven*: seven Sabbaths of years.

If you recall, God told Noah that the flood will come "after seven more days" (Gen. 7:4). In like manner, Isaiah informs us that the prophetic *"Sabbath"* is *"the holy day of the Lord"* (58:13-14), *"the favorable year"* or the appointed time set for the appearance of the Messiah (Luke 4:16-21). The seven Sabbaths are also represented by the mythical story of Jacob who serves Laban, his father-in-law, for seven years followed by an additional seven years (Gen. 29). For this reason the number 7 holds the key to the mysteries of the apocalypse:

> The walls of Jericho fell down, after they had been encircled for seven
> days.

> (Heb. 11:30)

Correspondingly, we are told that the Messiah will emerge on the world stage after "seven weeks" (Dan. 9:25). This particular time frame is imputed to the seven Sabbaths posterior to his birth. And this is the comparable meaning of "the day of Pentecost" when the promise of God finally arrives on earth (Acts 2:1). As we stated earlier, the concept of the *Pentecost* means "fifty" in Greek. We can see, then, how all these stories relate to the Lord's sacrifice on the *Sabbath* day!

No wonder God is known as the "LORD OF SABAOTH" (Rom. 9:29). Although most scholars translate the word *Sabaoth* from the Hebrew to mean "armies," a few critics suggest that the cryptic meaning of *Sabaoth* may be derived from a transliteration of the Hebrew term *Shabbat*, meaning "Sabbath." Hence, the aforesaid phrase becomes *"Lord of the Sabbath"* (Luke 6:5). As a matter of fact, Jesus

began "on the Sabbath, and stood up to read" in the presence of the faithful so as
"TO PROCLAIM THE FAVORABLE YEAR OF THE LORD" (Luke 4:16-21). In the
gospel of Matthew, Jesus's discourse indicates that the end of the world begins "on
a Sabbath" (24:20). By comparison, the well-noted *Pentecost* of the seven Sabbaths
transpires "IN THE LAST DAYS" (Acts 2:1-4, 17-21):

> *I gave them My sabbaths to be a sign between Me and them, that they*
> *might know that I am the LORD who sanctifies them.*

> *(Ezek. 20:12)*

To illustrate this point, consider the number *40*, a number that is constantly
alluded to by scripture. An angel mystically feeds the prophet *Elijah* who "went in
the strength of that food" for "forty days" (1 Kings 19:8). According to the *day-year
principle*, days are translated as years (Ezek. 4:5-6). Therefore, Elijah's *"forty days"*
should be translated as forty years. By comparison, Israel spent forty years in the
wilderness (Acts 13:18). Most people are unaware that Moses was over forty years
of age when he first encountered the vision of God in the form of a burning bush
(Acts 7:20-30):

> *And after forty years had passed, AN ANGEL APPEARED TO HIM*
> *[Moses] IN THE WILDERNESS OF MOUNT Sinai, IN THE FLAME*
> *OF A BURNING THORN BUSH.*

> *(Acts 7:30)*

Likewise, Jesus "had fasted [from sin for] forty days" before "the tempter came"
to test him (Matt. 4:2-3). Again, in employing the *day-year principle*, the text suggests
years, not days. Like Moses, Jesus is apparently over forty years of age during this
harrowing ordeal. In Luke's gospel, Christ may have been roughly thirty years old
(3:23) when he first came into contact with God, but he did not become a public
figure until much later than that. There is considerable biblical evidence that, for
some reason not specified, he was forced into hiding for a long time (John 7:2-5). If
you think we are exaggerating, ponder what the Jews once said to Jesus:

> *You are not yet fifty years old, and have You seen Abraham?*

> *(John 8:57)*

Strangely enough, not only is Jesus over forty years old, but scripture indicates that he is approaching the age of *fifty*! This can also be seen from the cryptic Bible verse which states that Jesus was "alive, . . . appearing to them [mankind] over a period of forty days [years are implied]" (Acts 1:3). The background to this story can be found in the book of Genesis wherein we are told that "Sarah conceived and bore a son to Abraham in his *old age*, at the appointed time of which God had spoken to him" (21:2, emphasis added). Paul then decodes this story and affirms that God's promise "to Abraham and to his seed [offspring] . . . is Christ" himself (Gal. 3:16). Therefore, all these connotations denote the aforementioned *Pentecost* of the seventh Sabbath.

Irenaeus, an erudite theologian, wrote a famous multivolume work called *Against Heresies*, which first achieved print in the second century of the Common Era. In book 2 chapter 22 of this polemical treatise against various heretical views, he disputes the interpretations of conventional Christianity while asserting that the biblical descriptions of Christ's death would imply that the savior is approaching fifty years of age! God's earthly visitation may also be deduced from the prophetic legend of *Beowulf*, an Old English epic poem of late antiquity. In his third and final battle, Beowulf fights against a great dragon and defeats him, even though he dies in the end. The text, however, emphasizes that this confrontation took place fifty years after Beowulf's initial appearance.

THE EIGHTH-DAY SIGN OF THE JEWISH COVENANT

Let us now proceed to explain the hidden meaning behind the reputed *eighth-day* sign of the Abrahamic covenant. Mind you, if the Sabbath is the seventh day, then the eighth day must portend a day after the Sabbath. Indeed, that is precisely what it forecasts. As stated earlier, the sign of the eighth day connotes the day of *resurrection*. This point should be well taken as the Bible is imbued with frequent intimations to that effect:

> *Now after the Sabbath, as it began to dawn toward the first day of the week [the eighth day], Mary Magdalene and the other Mary came to look at the grave.*

> *(Matt. 28:1)*

Consider the scriptural portrayal of Mary Magdalene arriving at the tomb of Jesus on the day "after the Sabbath." Insofar as the eighth-day sign of the covenant is concerned, Jesus's resurrection stands out as the principal focus of attention. In an effort to facilitate this point, Mark's gospel describes a similar theme:

> *And when the Sabbath [the seventh day] was over, Mary Magdalene,*
> *and Mary the mother of James, and Salome, brought spices, that they might*
> *come and anoint Him [Jesus]. And very early on the first day of the week*
> *[the eighth day], they came to the tomb when the sun had risen.*

> *(16:1-2)*

Try to discern the pun in Mark's language when he likens Jesus's resurrection to the time of day "when the sun had risen" (Nah. 3:17, Mal. 4:2, Rev. 10:1). On account of this repeated portrayal, it is evident that Christ's resurrection bursts forth on the world scene during the mysterious and figurative *eighth day.*

The gospel of Luke recounts virtually the same story:

> *And on the Sabbath they rested according to the commandment. But*
> *on the first day of the week [after the Sabbath], at early dawn, they came to*
> *the tomb, bringing the spices which they had prepared. And they found the*
> *stone rolled away from the tomb, but when they entered, they did not find*
> *the body of the Lord Jesus.*

> *(23:56-24:3)*

At this point it should be abundantly clear that the extensive references to Jesus's resurrection bespeak the sign of the eighth day. Of primary importance to the indelible eighth-day prophecy is the recognition that all four gospels depict it as "the first day" after the Sabbath. The gospel of John completes the quartet ensemble of predictions:

> *Now on the first day of the week [the eighth day] Mary Magdalene*
> *came early to the tomb, while it was still dark, and saw the stone already*
> *taken away from the tomb.*

> *(20:1)*

In an effort to adumbrate this resurrection, *John*, a harbinger of the divine oracles, reinforces the reiterated insight concerning the eighth-day premonition. As if to shun further uncertainty about the time frame of Christ's resurrection, he writes,

> *And* after eight days *again His disciples were inside, and Thomas*
> *was with them. Jesus came, the doors having been shut, and stood in their*
> *midst, and said, "Peace be with you."*

> *(John 20:26, emphasis added)*

John transcribes how *Jesus came* back from Hades (cf. 2 Pet. 2:4) "after eight days," transformed and transfigured, following his glorious resurrection from the world of the dead! (cf. 1 Pet. 3:18-20).

However, the gospels' repetition of and constant recourse to the phrase, *on the first day of the week,* has an alternative meaning; besides referring to the symbolic eighth day of Christ's resurrection, it also reflects the *salvation* of humankind (Heb. 9:28). In fact, there can be no redemption unless there is a resurrection effected by Christ (1 Cor. 15:14, 17). And this event is said to occur at a time which succeeds the transitional period commonly known as the "great tribulation" (Matt. 24:29-30). As this seven-year tribulation—represented by the seventh Sabbath—draws to a close, the new day of *redemption,* signified by the eighth Sabbath, will commence. But in the meantime, unthinkable calamities will befall the earth the likes of which the world has never known. The troubling array of predictions terminating in an unparalleled seven-year period of cataclysmic proportions is largely derived from a passage found in the book of Daniel. We read,

> *And he [antichrist] shall confirm the covenant [treaty] with many for one week [seven years]: and in the midst of the week [after three and a half years] he shall cause the sacrifice and the oblation [Holy Communion] to cease, and for the overspreading of abominations he shall make it desolate, even until the consummation, and that determined shall be poured upon the desolate.*

> *(9:27, King James)*

The above quote describes an absolutely terrifying time in human history when a series of preternatural events will defy the natural order and plunge the world into an infernal abyss, forcing mankind to pause and contemplate its fate (cf. 1 Thess. 5:3). The Bible affirms that "there were giants on the earth in those days"! (Gen. 6:4, *New King James*). These figures, which are beyond human description, represent the gods that have come down upon the earth in the form of *Christ* and *antichrist,* to whom scripture devotes a brief but noteworthy depiction: "the mighty men who were of old, men of renown" (Gen 6:4). The text is suggesting the approaching battle of Armageddon, the most devastating war in world history. Hence, the eighth day of circumcision that is associated with the Jewish covenant represents Christ's *resurrection* (salvation), which will occur during the eighth Sabbath: the last age of mankind. As far as this event is concerned, it is not a question of "if" but "when."

From our observations of scripture we can even deduce the actual time period that will elapse between the death and resurrection of Jesus. Scripture itself indicates the duration of this interim which allows us to infer that it is approximately a three-year period:

> Jesus answered and said to them, "Destroy this temple, and in three
> days [years] I will raise it up."

> (John 2:19)

As with other time periods recorded in the Bible, the phrase "three days" is a figure of speech; it does not literally refer to seventy-two hours (cf. Rev. 8:1, 17:12). In keeping with the day-year principle, the days must be translated as years (cf. Rev. 11:3, 11). Thus the three days that traditionally denote the extent of Christ's time among the dead are now rendered as three solar years. Given that this period of time comes after the seven symbolic days (seven Sabbaths) since the birth of Jesus, the resurrection is prophetically conveyed as the eighth day. The reason for this is quite obvious: the eighth day represents the beginning of the eighth Sabbath. For if seven days represent seven Sabbaths, then eight days must, by definition, represent eight Sabbaths.

THE FALLACIES OF MILLENNIALISM

Millennialism is the premise that the Messiah will return to earth at the end of the world to reign for one thousand years. Certain Christian "churches" of various persuasions put forth this assertion which is primarily extracted from the twentieth chapter of the book of Revelation. This position holds that Satan will be rereleased at the end of the thousand-year period for his second and final battle with Christ. As evidence of this, they point to their literal interpretations of the following passage:

> And I saw an angel coming down from heaven, having the key of the
> abyss and a great chain in his hand. And he laid hold of the dragon, the
> serpent of old, who is the devil and Satan, and bound him for a thousand
> years, and threw him into the abyss, and shut it and sealed it over him, so
> that he should not deceive the nations any longer, until the thousand years
> were completed; after these things he must be released for a short time.

> (Rev. 20:1-3)

Having taken stock of the foregoing material, they have devised a whole theoretical framework of end-time events which supports their claims. Nowadays, millennialism is considered to be the mainstream view of Christian eschatology.

The advocates of millennialism believe in the idea of two general resurrections and two great apocalyptic events that will usher in the ultimate end. But caution is advised here because the Bible does not allow for such a vague and amorphous view; it neither develops the notion of two great world endings, nor does it support the concept of a second, collective resurrection. Scripture only speaks of one all-inclusive resurrection, which will be preceded by Christ's personal resurrection from the dead: and "then comes the end, when He [Christ] delivers up the kingdom to the God and Father, when He has abolished all rule and all authority and power" (1 Cor. 15:22-24). If the thousand years were to follow the chronological period just mentioned, then this idea would contradict scripture since the latter just stated what "the end" of time consists of. Another passage declares that the risen dead will ascend to heaven together with those "who are alive," and that the great multitude of believers "shall be always with the Lord" (1 Thess. 4:15-17). This passage does not indicate that they will be with Christ for only an intermittent time interval, but forever. The Bible does refer to a *second death*, but this concept clearly represents an incorporeal, not a physical death:

> And death and Hades were thrown into the lake of fire. This is the second death, the lake of fire.
>
> *(Rev. 20:14)*

According to scripture, when the Messiah comes to reign on earth it is for the purpose of introducing "everlasting righteousness" (Dan. 9:24). In other words, Christ will then rule forever, not simply for one thousand years. Thus the thousand-year reign and the two universal resurrections clearly contradict the sacred text. It is said that after Christ defeats his end-time adversaries, these will then be cast into the abyss (Rev. 19:20). And that is the end of the story. The Satanic figure that is loosed in Revelation chapter 20 is the same antichrist that died in the previous chapter; but, here, the story is described in more detail.

Millennialists are befuddled by this matter. For instance, Revelation 20:2 presents the devil chained for one thousand years, after which he is released. This is the big picture, as it were. Then various details are furnished concerning all that he will accomplish (Rev. 20:7-9). In fact, there is a biblical equation, which provides clarity to an otherwise ambiguous passage. The Bible establishes that *the first resurrection* is clearly associated with the idiom of "the thousand years completed," during which the dead will come to life (Rev. 20:5). Notice, however, that Satan would also be unleashed when "the thousand years were completed" (Rev. 20:3). Thus the aforesaid idiom equates "the first resurrection" with the specific time period in which the devil will be released from prison.

Keep in mind that those who "came to life" (Rev. 20:4) were not resurrected within the thousand-year time span during which the devil was bound, but upon his release (Rev. 20:6). But here comes the catch; while still referring to "these" folk who have "a part in the first resurrection," scripture then says that "they . . . will reign with Him [Christ] for a thousand years" (Rev. 20:6). How could the same people who would not be resurrected "until the thousand years were completed" (Rev. 20:5) simultaneously reign with Christ for a millennium? They cannot be both dead and alive. As you can see, a literal explanation leads to an absurd anachronism!

In other words, Revelation 20:5 clearly defines "the first resurrection" as an event that takes place only after the completion of the one thousand-year period (1000 years elapse and then comes "the first resurrection"). So how can the "blessed" take part in "the first resurrection" and yet "reign with" Christ "for a thousand years"? (Rev. 20:6). It would seem to be a contradiction in terms.

How, then, can we reconcile this pair of contradictory idioms? By pointing out that the aforesaid phrases bear equivalent terms! In other words, the idiomatic expression "reigned with Christ for a thousand years" (Rev. 20:4) is interchangeable with its counterpart: "until the thousand years were completed" (Rev. 20:5). Hence, the thousand-year reign is equal (=) to the one thousand years completed; that is to say, both idioms represent the sign of the times when the dead will come to life and begin to reign with Christ (cf. Rev. 5:10, 20:6) at the *end* of the millennium. This emphasis on the "end" of the millennium, rather than on its duration, also helps explain the commencement of Armageddon due to the concurrent appearance of the antichrist: "And when the thousand years are completed, Satan will be released from his prison, and will come out to deceive the nations . . . , to gather them together for the war" (Rev. 20:7-8, cf. 9:1-2, 11).

But there is also a literal sense that can be attributed to the one thousand year reign: it represents the inception and ascendancy of Christ at the end of the twentieth century. In the book of Daniel, "Michael, one of the chief princes," was delayed in coming to the world "for twenty-one days" (Dan. 10:13). The epistle of Peter reveals a scriptural formula that a day can symbolize a thousand years (2 Pet. 3:8), or an extended period of time. This means that twenty-one days could actually represent twenty-one centuries, which may also help clarify the twenty-one judgments in the book of Revelation. According to this scheme, the completion of the one thousand year period has already ushered in the twenty-first century: the temporal sign representing the beginning of the apocalypse.

But as for the thousand-year reign, what does it actually mean? Simply put, the one thousand years represent the rise and domination of the Moon religion (cf. Gal. 4:29). For instance, the *Fatimid Caliphate* took control of Palestine in 969 AD, and in the year 1009, it destroyed the *Church of the Holy Sepulchre* in Jerusalem. Then in 1071, the *Seljuk Turks* captured Jerusalem, and thus began the persecution of Christians and the desecration of churches in Palestine that would set the stage for the onset of the crusades around 1095 AD. Therefore the millennial reign of the Moon religion helps explain why the Messiah would be born of a woman who had "the moon under her feet"! (Rev. 12:1).

On the whole, most of the hermeneutical confusion stems from the rather vague and sketchy details put forth in the text. Given that there are "those who had been beheaded" for not worshipping the beast (Rev. 20:4) and those who are called "the rest of the dead" (Rev. 20:5), we assume that there are two collective resurrections. But as stated earlier, this unique physical resurrection is not limited to a certain few because all who have died will be raised together (cf. Ezek. 37:10; John 5:28-29,

6:39-40; 1 Cor. 15:22-24, 51-52). What the Bible is telling us is that the former group represents the tribulation saints (believers) who died recently while the latter group signifies those who have been dead for many centuries. Both groups, however, will constitute the masses who will take part in the general resurrection of the dead (cf. Ezek. 37:7-10, Dan. 12:1-2, Matt. 27:52-53, 1 Thess. 4:15-17).

Clearly, there has never been another resurrection before it, nor will there be one after it. The truth of the matter is that the reference to *the first resurrection* (Rev. 20:5) ever encountered in human history represents yet another sign of the future incarnation of Jesus because without him, there can be no resurrection of the dead. In other words, the last event is itself a clue that the Messiah's incarnation is concurrent with the coming of Satan when the thousand years are completed (Rev. 20:3, 5). Therefore it is more consistent with scripture to view the millennial reign of Christ as simply another way of referring to *the day of the Lord*. At which point, several contemporaneous occurrences will transpire: Christ's resurrection, which will energize the general resurrection of the dead, Satan's last stand, followed by the transformation of the universe. All these signs denote that when the thousand years are completed, the final end will come. But the argument does not end there.

After the completion of the millennium, the book of Revelation tells us that the devil "must be released for a short time" (20:3). Scripture uses this specific terminology to help the reader determine Satan's human origin. If we compare it to another excerpt, we will understand the implied associations:

> *Here is the mind which has wisdom. The seven heads are seven mountains . . . and they are seven kings; five have fallen, one is, the other has not yet come; and when he comes, he must remain* a little while
>
> *(Rev. 17:9-10, emphasis added).*

The origin of the seventh and final king cannot be known apart from what is revealed elsewhere in scripture. For this reason, the text correlates the two aforesaid idioms by using similar phraseology: "for a short time" (Rev. 20:3), and for *"a little while"* (Rev. 17:10). Given that the USSR is implicated in the latter verse—namely, he who "must remain a little while"—we come to realize that the former verse contains an equivalence that is intended to convey the same unique theme: Satan's incarnation and military involvement in modern-day Russia.

Next, *Revelation* furnishes a second clue about the devil's whereabouts: he will be released from the abyss to incite "Gog and Magog, to gather them together for the war" (20:8). If we compare this verse to Ezekiel 38:2-9, we will notice that the exact same war is being described in both texts. In fact, the location of "Gog and Magog" further verifies the biblical intimations that trace the antichrist's descent through a Russian bloodline (cf. Ezek. 38:2, 15-16; Rev. 20:3, 17:10). Moreover, Ezekiel's prophecy signifies that fire will come down from heaven and consume the

Russian coalition (38:22, 39:6), similar to what *Revelation* predicts will happen to this satanic figure and his horde (20:9). Thus the matching scriptural clues are evidence enough for our conclusion that there is only one apocalypse, not two!

There is a third clue which supports our premise. In a so-called millennial context, the book of Revelation states that the devil's armies will surround "the beloved city," which is a biblical name for Jerusalem (20:9). Now compare what Jesus says in the gospel of Luke:

> *But when you see Jerusalem surrounded by armies, then recognize that*
> *her desolation is at hand.*

> *(21:20)*

The term *desolation* connotes the time of the apocalypse (cf. Mark 13:14-19). As you can see, this final war is couched in biblical jargon and presented in two parallel accounts, namely, the above references to the armies that "surround" Jerusalem (Rev. 20:9, Luke 21:20). This is in fact a recurrent biblical theme that serves as an illustration of a *single* event that will take place in prophetic history! (cf. Ezek. 38:8-9, 15-16; Dan. 11:41; Zech. 14:2).

Therefore, our brief inquiry suggests that the doctrine of millennialism concerning two great wars, two world endings, and two general resurrections is scripturally inaccurate and unfounded. Moreover, the alleged "thousand-year reign of Christ on earth" appears nowhere in the Bible. Only two verses make mention of those who "reigned with Christ for a thousand years" (Rev. 20:4, 6). However, due to reasons outlined earlier, these fragments are not meant to be taken literally but rather understood as a sign concerning the time of Jesus's coming. Anything else simply contradicts the sacred writings.

CHAPTER 11

THE TWO FICTIONAL
COMINGS OF JESUS

Thus declares the LORD . . . , "Behold, . . . when the siege is against Jerusalem, . . . and all the nations of the earth will be gathered against [her], . . . in that [future] day the LORD will defend the inhabitants of Jerusalem, . . . and it will come about in that [latter] day that I will set about to destroy all the nations that come against Jerusalem. . . . They will look on Me whom they have pierced [shot]; and they will mourn for Him [Christ], as one mourns for an only son. . . . In that [last] day there will be great mourning.

(Zech. 12:1-11)

Scripture has been widely studied but poorly understood through the lens of biblical scholarship. Researchers have made no convincing attempt to systematically combine and incorporate the various passages therein, thus being unable to piece the biblical puzzle together. Their unmistakable nescience, at once unnerving and amusing, reduces prophetic utterances to unspeakable misconceptions. A prime example is their vague and ambiguous theory that within the first and second coming of Jesus lies a period of a few millennia in between. Despite this ghastly teaching, we can still rely on the veritable and authoritative words of Jesus:

A little while, and you will no longer behold Me; and again a little while, and you will see Me.

(John 16:16)

Here, Jesus is clearly prophesying about his *death* (cf. John 16:17-22), yet he adds, "But I will see you again, and your heart will rejoice, . . . and in that day you will ask Me no question" (John 16:22-23). Why is it that all questions will cease when we see him again? Because following Jesus's resurrection at *"the end of the age,"* the secrets of God will ultimately be revealed (Matt. 28:20, cf. Rev. 10:7). Clearly, this gap between Jesus's two appearances is very short; in fact, it is described as *"a little while."* To think anything but that is a far cry from the truth. How can twenty centuries be reconciled with a time period that is akin to *"a little while"*? They cannot! In contradistinction, Jesus is painting a picture of his proximate three-year absence (John 2:19) that is revealed to us through the sign of Jonah (Matt. 12:39-40).

Accordingly, scripture suggests the notion that certain figures who have beheld Jesus would not pass away:

> *This saying [rumor] therefore went out among the brethren [believers] that that disciple would not die; yet Jesus did not say to him that he would not die, but only, "If I want him to remain until I come, what is that to you?"*

> *(John 21:23)*

Jesus says that a certain disciple will "remain [continue to live] until I come." This constitutes further proof of the short time span between the two appearances because the same disciple who will be a witness to Christ's death will ultimately see him again. A variation on this theme concerns a prophet named *Simeon*:

> *And it had been revealed to him [Simeon] by the Holy Spirit that he would not see death before he had seen the Lord's [God's] Christ.*

> *(Luke 2:25-32)*

Since the aforesaid figures behold Christ prior to their death, it stands to reason that they must be contemporary witnesses of Jesus's visitation during *the end of the age* (Matt. 13:39, 40, 49). They are part of the last generation of mankind (Ps. 24:6, Mark 13:30). But when does this generation begin?

To briefly recap, the final generation commences when the Jews return to Israel (cf. Dan. 9:24-27). Yet we know that this event has already occurred. This means that the last *generation* is the one associated with the time period of Israel's restoration (cf. Ezek. 37:21). It is this generation that will inevitably witness the short duration between the two manifestations of Jesus: one from below (earth) and one from above (heavens). In contradistinction to current opinion, Christ's reply concludes in the following rebuttal:

> *Truly I say to you, this generation will not pass away until all things take place.*

> *(Luke 21:32)*

The fact of the matter is that there never were, nor will there ever be *two comings* in connection with Christ. We have already furnished compelling evidence to call into question his formerly reputed Advent. This event did not occur two thousand years ago; rather, it is predestined for the foreseeable future. How do we know this? Because the sacred writings seek to educate us on this point by enunciating the prophecy: "But now once in the end of the world hath he [Jesus] appeared to put away sin by the sacrifice [death] of himself" (Heb. 9:26, *King James*). That's quite an admission!

This is graphic language that depicts Christ's one and only coming in such vivid detail that it would be ludicrous to assume otherwise. More especially when there is no definitive scriptural evidence to suggest that Jesus will take part in two widely separated and independent comings. Thus the phrase "second coming" is a misnomer. The sole reference to Jesus who "will appear a second time, apart from sin, for salvation" (Heb. 9:28, *New King James*) does not indicate a second coming, as this would obviously contradict what the text just cited two verses earlier, namely, that the Messiah appears "once and for all" (Heb. 9:26, *New Jerusalem Bible*). Quite the contrary, it means that Christ will appear a second time, from above, following his glorious resurrection! Specifically, he will return from the dead on account of the rapture: "I will come again, and receive you to Myself; that where I am, there you may be also. And you know the *way* where I am going" (John 14:3-4, emphasis added). Here lies the clue to Jesus's so-called second coming. He says, "And you know the way where I am going." Indeed, we do: he is going to his death! In this *"way"* we, too, must follow Christ's example (Rom. 6:3) and await the rapture: "For to this end Christ died and lived again" (Rom. 14:9). This is why the Messiah says, and it bears repeating:

> A little while, and you will no longer behold Me; and again a little while, and you will see Me.

> *(John 16:16)*

As one biblical writer put it, "No Old Testament passage indicates that Messiah will come twice" (McCallum, 38). And this is by far the most plausible conclusion. These points cannot be easily dismissed as they argue against a literal interpretation which ignores the profound symbolism found in scripture's nomenclature. It is only through the superlative notion of the *last days* that the prophetic material remains intact (Heb. 1:1-2). In fact, *"this [last] generation"* evokes a final doomsday scenario, which implicates the initial appearance of the Messiah (Luke 11:30, 32, 50-51). What then is the "first coming of Jesus" but that which might have been?

Traditionally, Christianity separates Christ's *coming* from Christ's *reign*. It views them as two distinct historical events: the first and second coming of Jesus. However, scripture itself does not make that distinction. On the contrary, each time Christ's coming is mentioned, it is almost always followed or preceded by some kind of reference to *judgment*, which signifies the commencement of his *reign* on earth (cf. Heb. 9:26-27). Zechariah 9 is a perfect example. Christ appears as a mounted horseman (9:9)—an image that depicts his humanity (cf. Mark 11:1-7)—while keeping a close watch on the end-time armies that surround Jerusalem (Zech. 9:8, cf. 14:2-3; Luke 21:20; Rev. 19:11). Then, as he hovers *over them*, the Messiah begins his deadly attack by throwing thunderbolts and lightning (Zech. 9:13-14) in a situation reminiscent of the Olympian Zeus in battle with the Titans (cf. Zech. 14:3).

Again, when the angel Gabriel announced to Mary, the mother of Jesus, the messianic incarnation, he combined Jesus's *birth* and *reign* by mentioning that Christ would be born to "reign over the [spiritual] house of Jacob forever" (Luke 1:30-33). The same goes for Luke's *apocalyptic* chapter 21 where Christ's manifestation is for the purpose of conquering the armies that devastate the earth (21:24-27). Isaiah declares the same message with considerable exactness; he mentions the Messiah's birth and then immediately embellishes it with the line: *the government will rest on His shoulders* (9:6-7). Isaiah then follows it up with a second prophecy which furnishes more details; it depicts Christ proclaiming the under mentioned message to the world:

> *The LORD has anointed me . . . to proclaim the favorable year of the*
> *LORD, and the day of vengeance [judgment] of our God.*

> *(61:1-2)*

This Isaian passage is mentioned in the gospel of Luke (4:17-21), but biblical interpreters often wrongly dissociate it from the *reign* of Christ which it clearly denotes. In Isaiah's writings, "the Day of Judgment" and "the year of salvation" not only appear repeatedly within the same verses, but they also refer to the same exact date! Here is an example. The Messiah declares, *"For the day of vengeance was in My heart, and My year of redemption has come"* (63:4; cf. Isa. 34:8). *Dennis McCallum*, a noted theologian and author, writes,

> *In some cases, predictions about the [OT] suffering servant are*
> *immediately next to prophecies about King Messiah, without any mention*
> *of a more-than-two-thousand-year gap between them (e.g., cross-reference*
> *Isaiah 61:1 ff and Jesus' commentary in Luke 4:21) [sic]*

> *(38).*

Therefore what is essentially one momentous coming—*once and for all* (Heb. 9:26, *New Jerusalem Bible*)—has been conventionally misconstrued as the two distinct comings of Jesus.

THE CORPSE: A MISSING LINK IN BIBLICAL EXEGESIS

Being in the form of God, . . . [Christ] made Himself of no reputation

(*Phil. 2:6-7, New King James*).

The human embodiment of God presents the paradox of power and vulnerability. The only way to comprehend this mystery can be summed up in two words: God's humility (Phil. 2:5-11). As for those who continue to maintain that the future incarnation of Jesus is largely a matter of personal interpretation, we will shortly attempt to answer their objections. Sooner or later we must come to grips with this inevitable prophecy:

> *And as He [Jesus] was sitting on the Mount of Olives, the disciples came to Him privately, saying, "Tell us, when will these things be, and what will be the sign of Your coming, and of the end of the age?"*

(*Matt. 24:3*)

But before we share with you Jesus's answer, we should consider the following question. If Christ already came to earth, then why would the disciples repeatedly ask him about "the coming of the Son of Man [God incarnate]" (Matt. 24:27): *"Tell us, . . . what will be the sign of Your coming?"* Because from the Bible's perspective it was obviously looked on as a future event! The point is, it never happened. With this information in hand, let us now turn to Jesus's discourse. The aforecited verse (Matt. 24:3), along with its subsequent discussion, is on the topic of the coming apocalypse since one of the biblical terms used to refer to the end of the world is *"the end of the age."* Jesus begins to enumerate a series of events that will necessarily precede his arrival (Matt. 24). Most experts read Matthew 24 and stop at the point where Jesus says that "just as the lightning comes from the east, and flashes even to the west, so shall the coming of the Son of Man be" (Matt. 24:27). Scholars claim that this is the indisputable sign given to mankind, and so they deduce that Jesus will mysteriously and inexplicably appear out of nowhere in the heavens to implement his "second coming."

It is a sad state of affairs when pitiful and incoherent explanations such as these capture the popular imagination. According to the acclaimed spiritual writer *C. S. Lewis*, God may be able to transcend the laws that govern natural phenomena, but he never breaks them (59). Even Jesus must enter the physical world of time through a natural birth (Matt. 2:1). There is no other way around it. Yet the current view, provoked by misinformed scholarship, holds that Christ will somehow emerge out of the sky through supernatural agency so as to enforce his divine will on those who are subject to the laws of space and time. Not only is this theory scripturally unsound, it is wholly without theological merit. Apart from its hyperbole and idealism, the belief in a real sky-Jesus phenomenon is erroneous simply because it circumvents the established laws of nature. Ironically, a literal sky-Jesus precept enunciated in however lofty a tone must always run the risk of being seen as a fanciful exaggeration.

Had the scholars read on, they would have grasped the authentic message of Christ's coming. For the next verse reads,

> *Wherever the corpse is, there the vultures will gather.*

> *(Matt. 24:28)*

But what is the purpose of this reference to a *"corpse"*? Before all else, let us read the complete progression of events that culminates in the *"sign of the Son of Man,"* and then we will understand the gist of Christ's message:

> *Wherever the corpse is, there the vultures will gather. But immediately after the tribulation of those days THE SUN WILL BE DARKENED, AND THE MOON WILL NOT GIVE ITS LIGHT, AND THE STARS WILL FALL from the sky, and the powers of the heavens will be shaken, and then the sign of the Son of Man will appear in the sky, and then all the tribes [nations] of the earth will mourn, and they will see the SON OF MAN COMING ON THE CLOUDS OF THE SKY with power and great glory.*

> *(Matt. 24:28-30)*

Notice that *"the sign of the Son of Man [who] will appear in the sky"* is employed only after the sentence which refers to *"the corpse,"* not before. This implies that the passage is elucidating the precise order of events leading up to *"the sign of the Son of Man."* When Jesus mentions that he comes like lightning in the sky (Matt. 24:27), it is as if he is fast-forwarding to give us the conclusion or the grand finale. But then, as directors often do, he rewinds the film, so to speak, by going back to the beginning so as to provide us with a chronological series of events that will climax in *"the sign of the Son of Man."* Hence, it is a case involving the big picture in one scenario and details in another. The experts often confuse this issue.

So what is the precise sequence of events leading to the beatific vision of Christ emerging from behind "THE CLOUDS OF THE SKY"? First, Jesus references a mysterious *corpse* to which the vultures will gather, presumably to tear it apart. Then, natural and cosmic disturbances ensue as *"the powers of the heavens will be shaken."* Finally, Jesus says, *"and then the sign of the Son of Man will appear in the sky."* This means that the eminent *"sign"* of his coming cannot appear until these prior set of circumstances first take precedence.

Initially, someone important dies; more precisely, he is slain, as the *"vultures"* signify that he is torn to pieces. But why does Jesus interrupt his all-important eschatological discourse in order to make way for some seemingly frivolous comment regarding a corpse? Since Jesus's discourse pertains to the deeply significant sign of his coming, it is plain why he introduces the notion of a corpse therein; because it cannot represent anyone else but Christ himself! He then discloses the sequence leading up to the high point of these events: "immediately after the tribulation of those days," cosmic disasters will take place; "and then," and only then, "the sign of the Son of Man will appear in the sky." Jesus is giving us the entire visitation account, save for his personal resurrection from the dead. In fact, the initial sign of his coming is not his appearance from the heavens, but rather his manifestation on earth: as *"the corpse"*! This corpse turns out to be the missing link, the reason why the Messiah is suddenly seen *"COMING ON THE CLOUDS OF THE SKY."* This last event can only be the consequence of a resurrection that is said to be triggered by a great and mighty earthquake (cf. Ezek. 38:19, Matt. 27:51-54, 28:2). And so the corpse becomes a symbol of Christ's incarnation as *"the Son of Man"* (cf. Rev. 12:1-5). It puts the following quote in a whole new perspective:

> *Behold, two men [angels] in white clothing stood . . . and . . . said,*
> *"Men of Galilee, why do you stand looking into the sky? This Jesus . . . will*
> *come in just the same way as you have watched Him go into heaven."*

> *(Acts 1:10-11)*

In other words, if we could reverse the way in which he went to heaven, we would understand how he will come to earth. Now, initially, the crowds saw Jesus standing on the earth. So the implication is that prior to his ascension, Christ will come as a man! *"The corpse,"* then, is the smoking gun that reveals God's future incarnation. Therefore, the public has been misled by religion's surreptitious novels that pass for doctrines of faith. But time is more concerned with endings than beginnings. Despite the church's abiding contradictions, the apocalyptic caveat grows more urgent as time expires.

However, we must challenge the reader to go further. Because if you do not understand the specific timeline of these end-time events, the biblical script will become very confusing. For example, Matthew 24:23 reads, *"If anyone says to you, 'Behold, here is the Christ,' or 'There He is,' do not believe him."* Some argue that this verse exhorts us to distrust any earthly Messiah that might appear in the last days. But this is simply not true. For one thing, Christ himself appears for the first time in the last days! (Heb. 1:2, 9:26; Gal. 4:4; Eph. 1:9-10; Acts 3:20-21; Rev. 12:5). Not to mention that the Jews themselves are still awaiting the Messiah. Furthermore,

Matthew's gospel sets up the context of this exhortation in its proper chronological order. For instance, notice that Matthew first introduces Daniel's prophecy of "the ABOMINATION OF DESOLATION . . . standing in the holy place" (Matt. 24:15) as the backdrop for this exhortation. This event is set to take place when the antichrist will take "his seat in the temple of God, displaying himself as being God" (2 Thess. 2:4).

Next, we are warned that when this event transpires, we should "flee to the mountains; . . . for then there will be a great tribulation, such as has not occurred since the beginning of the world until now, nor ever shall" (Matt. 24:16-21). But we must remember that Christ will most certainly die before the antichrist could reveal himself to the world (Matt. 24:28). Paul writes, "He [Christ] who now restrains will do so until he is taken out of the way. And then that lawless one will be revealed" (2 Thess. 2:7-8). That Christ's arrival precedes that of the antichrist is further demonstrated in John's gospel, Jesus says, "I will not speak much more with you, for the ruler of the world is coming, and he has nothing in Me" (14:30, cf. Dan. 9:26). Hence, "the ABOMINATION OF DESOLATION" serves as the context in which the previous exhortation was made. So during this particular time period, we are rightly urged to distrust any physical being that claims to be the Messiah.

But we are not out of the woods yet. Here, the many-layered biblical script becomes very complicated because it becomes increasingly difficult to identify the differences between Christ and antichrist. Without going into great detail for lack of time, let us briefly review it. The duplication of Moses's miracles by the Pharaoh's sorcerers (Exod. 7:10-12) is a foreshadowing of what will happen at the end of days. Let us not forget that the antichrist's "coming is in accord with the activity of Satan, with all power and signs [miracles] and false wonders" (2 Thess. 2:9). In Ezekiel 28, beginning with the seventh verse, we are told that the antichrist will die a violent death. Likewise, Daniel 11:45 informs us that the antichrist's life will soon come to an end. However, in a surprising turn of events, the little horn will miraculously come back to life! (Rev. 13:3, 12, 14). What better way to duplicate Christ's miracles than to arise from the dead? Thus, the great and wondrous sign of his resurrection will captivate the whole earth (Rev. 13:12-15). And the world will marvel and follow "after the beast" (Rev. 13:3-4, 17:8). But here is the most important spiritual question of our time: in the midst of this messianic impersonation, how would you recognize Christ?

CHAPTER 12

THE SIGN OF THE FIG TREE AND THE CRESCENT MOON

Now learn the parable from the fig tree: when its branch has already become tender, and puts forth its leaves, you know that summer is near; even so you too, when you see all these things, recognize that He [Christ] is near, right at the door. Truly I say to you, this generation will not pass away until all these things take place.

—*Matt. 24:32-34*

The majority of biblical scholars adhere to the specious theory that the aforementioned portion of Jesus's discourse pertains to the state of Israel. The parable of the fig tree has fueled their imagination in this respect. They make inferences based on the notion that Israel is the key to God's prophetic timetable concerning end-time events (Dan. 9:25). Although this point remains true, their leap of interpretation is really the result of a false premise, namely, that the idiomatic fig tree image represents the modern Jewish state. This notion is so well entrenched in Christian circles as to seem a solid prophecy. Still, an intellectual assent to this idea would be such a breach of the principles of scriptural interpretation as nothing would justify. But can we prove this? Actually, yes!

After the *fall* of Adam and Eve in the Garden of Eden, we read the following account:

Then the eyes of both of them were opened, and they knew that they were naked; and they sewed fig leaves together and made themselves loin coverings.

(Gen. 3:7)

In this verse, the *fig leaves* come to be associated with transgression and sin. During New Testament times, we find a similar theme interspersed throughout the text. For example, Jesus cursed a fig tree and immediately it withered (Matt. 21:18-20). How can Jesus use the fig tree image to signify God's beloved Israel in one passage and yet curse it at the same time in another? It does not make any scriptural sense. Elsewhere, Jesus proclaims an allegory that associates the concept of the fig tree with unbelievers who fail to bring forth any righteous fruit; in keeping with the parable, the fig tree is eventually removed (cf. Luke 13:6-9).

Prior to being initiated into the mysteries of Christ, one of the disciples is appropriately sitting under the dark shade of a fig tree:

> *Nathanael said to Him, "How do You know me?" Jesus answered and said to him, "Before Philip called you, when you were under the fig tree, I saw you."*

> *(John 1:48)*

Here, the fig tree becomes a metaphor for the unenlightened minds that find refuge under the shadow of wickedness. Moreover, there is something to be gained from the gospel of Matthew, which makes it absolutely clear: *"Grapes are not gathered from thorn bushes [images of evil], nor figs from thistles [symbols of good], are they?" (7:16).* By contrast, the olive tree imagery in the Bible—which is oftentimes associated with divine favor—signifies the attributes of the illuminated ones who are guided by the spirit of God (Rev. 11:4). The insightful verse from the subsequent *epistle of James* provides the decisive conclusion:

> *Can a fig tree, my brethren, produce olives, or a vine produce figs? Neither can salt water produce fresh.*

> *(3:12)*

Much to their dismay, the scholars' interpretation of the symbolic fig tree has more shortcomings than they care to admit. Conversely, we propose the diametrically opposite conclusion, which is supported by the biblical record, namely, that the fig tree imagery represents a condition of increasing violence and unrest. The aforesaid parable of Jesus regarding "the fig tree" that "has already become tender, and puts forth its leaves" (Matt. 24:32), is a sign of warning, predicating that the end is near. Thus the budding fig tree does not denote Israel, but rather the widespread escalation of terrorism, which in turn points to the coming Messiah during the *"summer"* months (Matt. 24:32-34). It is as if Jesus was exhorting us that *"the sign of the Son of Man"* (Matt. 24:30) will appear during the heightened expansion of this *struggle* when the world will be on the precipice of nuclear annihilation! (cf. Rev.

6:12-14, Zech. 14:12). To this end, the Bible offers a comparable clue, it seems. In what may be a preemptive nuclear strike from the east, Christ describes a sudden *flash* that will be seen at "the end of the age" (Matt. 24:3):

The lightning comes from the east, and flashes even to the west.

(Matt. 24:27)

The foregoing quote certainly invites comparison with Daniel's striking allegorical description of a fiery furnace, when a nuclear reality sets in and the earth burns "seven times" over (3:19-22; cf. Mal. 4:1).

Many distinct but related biblical passages converge on the theme of this *struggle* that transpires under the banner of the *crescent moon*. For example, their allied campaign during the last days (Ezek. 38:5-6), those beheaded during the great tribulation (Rev. 20:4, Luke 9:9), men prostrating to the east who are responsible for great violence (Ezek. 8:16-17), the religion of *Korah* that assembled at the door of the Jewish temple (Num. 16:19), the end-time armies which are released from the river Euphrates (Rev. 9:13-16); "the kings of Persia" who oppose God's messengers (Dan. 10:13, 20), *the idol of jealousy* which stands on the temple mount in Jerusalem (Ezek. 8:3, 5), the reason why Paul is "forbidden by the Holy Spirit to" preach in Asia (Acts 16:6-7, cf. 2 Tim. 1:15), the religion of "Artemis . . . whom all of Asia and the world worship" (Acts 19:27-28), "the star . . . called Wormwood," which is defined as *Artemisia* and whose preeminent symbol is the *crescent moon* (cf. Rev. 8:11, Deut. 29:17-18, Jer. 23:15-16), the green horseman of the Apocalypse (Rev. 6:8, *Holman Christian Standard*), the seven persecuted churches of Anatolia (Rev. 2, 3), the great military coalition of the end-times whose leaders say, *"Come, and let us wipe them [Israel] out as a nation"* (Ps. 83:2-8); the false prophet (Rev. 16:13, 20:10; Jer. 23:32; 2 Pet. 2:1-3; 1 John 2:22), and so on and so forth. Whereas the Ottoman hordes failed to convert the west to the rule of *submission*, their offspring will succeed (Rev. 13:11-16, 16:13-18). These scriptural sections synthesize the uniform exposition of the divine edict which culminates in "a great sign" of the times: "a woman clothed with the sun and the moon under her feet" (Rev. 12:1). This portent suggests that the birth of the Messiah will represent the ultimate victory over the armies of *submission* (cf. Rev. 11:1-2, Ezek. 30:5, 38:5). In fact, the embodiment of this cryptic message can be traced back to the early Christian symbol of the *anchor*!

Therefore do not go on passing judgment before the time, but wait until the Lord comes who will . . . bring to light the things hidden in the darkness.

(1 Cor. 4:5)

CONCLUSION

Ancient man had a very, very sophisticated mindset. And I think it represents an inconsistency on our part to embrace his rationalism, his historiography, his engineering—to embrace all these things and yet to make no room whatsoever for ancient man's interest in prophecy and oracles.

—*Mitch Horowitz,*
Editor in Chief, Tarcher/Penguin

The Bible offers a contemporary message to mankind. As time speeds incessantly on its way to doomsday, the world should brace itself for the final countdown to the year of apocalypse. We are experiencing all the visible signs of *Revelation* as they are manifested with each successive passage of time: immense inundations, extraordinary and violent earthquakes, global economic collapse and widespread terrorism. Incapable of hearing the foreboding whispers of its coming, we disregard the end-of-the-world story as a thoroughly unscientific and even absurd invention of the human mind. But are we asking the right questions? The answer matters.

A more fruitful approach might be to ask whether man is capable of hearing divine utterances at all. Do these communications merely represent the psychological effects of an unsound mind? Or are they really the cosmic portals of a reality which lies beyond normal perception? Unless we come to terms with this paradox, its mystery will never be seen as anything more than the product of a fanciful imagination. Of course, the biblical answer to the question of whether or not these divine auditions exist is a resounding yes! The NT writers attest to the truth of these divine communications since they claim to have heard them through the spirit (2 Pet. 1:16-18, Heb. 2:2-4). *Edmund Husserl*, the esteemed German philosopher and founder of *phenomenology*, contends that this type of pure *gnosis* is far greater than any knowledge derived from the empirical world of the senses. He calls spiritual knowledge "authentic intuition," denoting its capacity to grasp the essence of being (Frank, 411-412).

But what do these strange prophecies mean for us? And what can we do? These events will ultimately force us to reevaluate and reexamine our very existence. At the heart of the matter lies an invitation to salvation. The prerequisite condition for participating in the *rapture* (1 Thess. 4:14-17) which will occur in the aftermath of Christ's resurrection (1 Cor. 15:22-26), is the indwelling spirit of God (Rom. 8:9).

And now would be as good a time as any to seek out this spirit. The choice is ours. But one thing is clear from the outset. Our previous scientific attitude will merge with a new and more exciting supernatural world view (Acts 2:17-21, Rev. 10:7). In his work on *The Incarnation*, the renowned theologian *Athanasius of Alexandria* (c. 297-373) once said that "God became man so that man might become a god." This is quite true. Scripture adds, "For . . . He [Christ] has granted to us His precious and magnificent promises, in order that by them you might become partakers of the divine nature" (2 Peter 1:4). Keeping this promise alive in an otherwise bleak and meaningless existence constitutes the *apotheosis* (deification) of the faithful. It is a remarkable statement. Thus we will become, dare we say, the gods of the universe!

The upshot of all this means that there is not a shred of conclusive historical evidence to support the notion that we were ever visited by Jesus, whether in antiquity or otherwise. In fact, some scholars have suggested that the NT accounts of Jesus are intrinsically mythological, not only because they lack any independent historical corroboration, but also because the events which they describe could not have been witnessed by the gospel writers themselves (Wells, *The Jesus Myth*). On the basis of archaeological remains, no solid argument for the existence of Jesus has ever been put forth to the contrary. Yet this belief in Christ's formerly reputed advent has taken such a firm hold of our minds that it is obstinately held despite, rather than due to considerable biblical evidence. The gospels have long been regarded as historiographical accounts, when in fact they are mythical oracles. Therefore, the more we interpret the Bible as history, the farther we are from the truth! How can any serious student of the Bible fail to acknowledge this point?

And what is so special about the age of antiquity that God would designate it as the single most important time period of his coming? Answer: nothing at all. On the other hand, "the end of the age" (Matt. 28:20) makes Christ's advent much more pressing than it would otherwise be considering the extraordinarily horrific circumstances that will engulf the earth. Better still, don't you find it odd that a supposed contemporary Jew who rose from the dead made less impact on the Jews than Moses the Egyptian who died and was buried more than a thousand years earlier? Have you ever stopped to wonder why the Jews never accepted Jesus as their Messiah? Could it be because he never really existed? Think about it.

The current religious disposition is by no means sympathetic to an earthly Messiah. Many, if not most religious authorities and scholars misinterpret such a person as the coming antichrist. As you can imagine, the worldwide response to this figure will follow suit and give rise to a catastrophic outcome. In fact, this *apostasy* (a departure from the faith) has already been prophesied to occur (1 Tim. 4:1, 2 Pet. 2:1, 2 Thess. 2:1-3). Christ will most certainly appear, only to find that he will soon be rejected by his own people (Ps. 118:22, John 5:43):

He [Christ] was in the world, and the world was made through Him,
and the world did not know Him.

(John 1:10)

His contemporaries will reject him and ultimately put him to death. And it is at this precise moment that Christ will finally become the quintessential savior of the world by fulfilling the gospel narratives that have been read for thousands of years!

Christ promises to arrive at a time when we least expect him (Matt. 24:44). The overall climate surrounding this event presupposes an awful period in the history of mankind. But it can equally turn out to be a propitious circumstance that could be translated as the possibility to participate in the final transformation of the universe as no other human has ever done before. We may well be the final generation upon the earth to witness these coming events. Jesus speaks to this effect:

Truly I say to you, this [last] generation will not pass away until all
these things take place.

(Matt. 24:34)

He warns us of the cataclysmic events that will soon occur during the *winter* of the great Sabbath (Matt. 24:20). That is when the heavenly signs will begin and all hell will break loose on earth:

For nation will rise against nation, and kingdom against kingdom,
and in various places there will be famines and earthquakes. But all these
things are merely the beginning of [the] birth pangs.

(Matt. 24:7-8)

According to Dr. Fruchtenbaum, a noted Bible scholar, this passage suggests "a world-wide conflict" such as "World War I" and "World War II" (63-64). Enter World War III (cf. Ezek. 38:4-9, 15-17; Rev. 6:4, 8, 9:14-19, 20:8). This dire war will inevitably trigger the last great battle between Christ and antichrist known as Armageddon (Rev. 16:16, 19:11-15). This is essentially the end-time road map:

And this gospel of the kingdom shall be preached in the whole world
for a witness to all the nations, and then the end shall come.

(Matt. 24:14)

This study has established a thematic synthesis that encompasses a wide range of spiritual texts, which are as varied as the authors who wrote them. A few famous French quatrains written by no less than the preeminent seer of the sixteenth-century *Michel de Nostredame* seemingly predict the life and death of a future Greek Messiah. The same can be said about the *War Scroll* (1QM) manuscript, comprising fragments found among the Dead Sea Scrolls. It is only when we integrate these nonbiblical sources with the dizzying array of scriptural signs that we begin to perceive the bigger prophetic picture. Moreover, given that the New Testament is written exclusively in Greek, it is a sign of the milieu in which "the revelation of Jesus Christ" (Rev. 1:1) is set forth. Curiously enough, these various and distinct spiritual traditions seem to point to one and the same conclusion: the appearance of a Greek Messiah!

This work has exposed pervasive distortions in modern conceptions and beliefs about the origin and advent of Jesus. To be sure, we have completely redefined the central tenets of Christianity! The prevailing views regarding both Christ and eschatological events display, for lack of a better term, an eccentric doctrine. Unfortunately, the wider public has been indoctrinated to believe in unscriptural religious principles and creeds. But there is a good reason for that.

The shortcomings of biblical interpretation must be offset with a certain amount of spiritual knowledge. Both forms of knowledge are considered essential for understanding Scripture. However, an imbalance in either direction can lead to disastrous results. For example, without any spiritual *inspiration* whatsoever, biblical scholarship becomes insipidly blind guessing work. On the other hand, seeing visions without the ability to test and verify them through scriptural means may lead to false doctrines and beliefs, if not to psychosis. We have had our share of false sects in the nineteenth and twentieth centuries: the *Last-Days Holy Ones, Yahweh's Watchers,* and the like. These religious movements continue to hold certain Christian views that are based on tenuous evidence with very little biblical grounding. But when one has a firm understanding of the Bible, the *spiritual knowledge* he or she receives is then harnessed appropriately. You suddenly find a key that unlocks most, if not all of the mysteries of scripture! On the other hand, without the aid of any clues to its interpretation, the scriptural overview becomes fairly tedious, and the Bible is easily dismissed as a sheer waste of time.

Of all the famous teachers throughout history—Moses, Confucius, Buddha, and Muhammad—no one has ever made any claims of being divine. All these men admit to being either founders of a particular way of "being in the world" or messengers of God. Only Christ makes mention of his preexisting divinity, which echoes the theophany of God's name in Exodus 3.14: "Truly, truly, I say to you, before Abraham was born, I am" (John 8:58). Moreover, Jesus says, "I am the way, and the truth, and the life; no one comes to the Father, but through Me" (John 14:6). In *the Revelation to John*, Christ emphatically says, "I am the Alpha and the Omega, . . . who is and who was and who is to come, the Almighty"! (Rev. 1:8, cf. 1:1). In the final analysis, either Christ is who he claims to be, or he is the greatest hypocrite the world has ever known. You decide.

Ever since man first peered at the obscure pages of the Bible, he has oftentimes wondered whether there are other worlds lying somewhere between us and the furthest reaches of the universe. The Jesus of Paul has not only answered this question definitively, but he has opened up a whole new world to you hitherto unknown. The Christ of the NT is not simply an abstract literary idea, but rather a universal prophecy of God-incarnate which is as old as time itself. The Messiah appears under various names in many prophetic religious traditions. All the more reason why we must "give heed and note the footsteps of the Messiah" (Bereshit Rabbah XLII: 4, qtd. in Fruchtenbaum). Most people expect him to come from the sky. The truth is, he will come from the earth:

> *Then He opened their minds to understand the Scriptures.*

> *(Luke 24:45)*

And when He [Christ] approached, He saw the city and wept over it, saying, "If you had known in this day, even you, the things which make for peace! But now they have been hidden from your eyes; . . . because you did not recognize the time of your visitation."

(Luke 19:41-44)

NOTES

PREFACE

1. *Logical Positivists* represent an analytic philosophy that views metaphysical questions with skepticism, not because the *truth value* in them is false, but because we have no means to observe and verify these conclusions.
2. *Christianity* is defined as the overall religious organization known as the *Church* comprising many distinct denominations which nevertheless share common doctrines and creeds. This is not to be confused with the biblical "Church," a term which specifically represents the saved people of God, also known as the "body of Christ" (Rom. 12:5; 1 Cor. 10:17, 12:27; Eph. 4:12; Col. 1:24).
3. *Apocalyptic* is a term which does not necessarily signify what has come to be called *apocalyptic literature*, the literary genre of early Judaism and Christianity, but more often than not it refers to specific end-time events as they are *revealed* on earth (Rev. 1:1) and, this sense, best captures our current treatment of the word.
4. *Copernicus* was not the inventor of the *Heliocentric Astronomical Model* which states that the planets revolve around the sun. The credit actually belongs to the Greek astronomer *Aristarchus of Samos* (310—ca. 230 BC) who first proposed the idea.

A GENERAL INTRODUCTION TO THE EXCLUSIVELY PROPHETIC BIBLICAL TEXT

1. *Biblical Concordance* is an alphabetical index comprising most of the key words used by scripture, including the various passages in which they occur.
2. The notion that Gentiles have superseded Jews as heirs of the OT promises is based on the Christian theological view called *Supersessionism*, which is also known as "replacement theology." According to this position, not only does the New Covenant (NT) replace the Mosaic Covenant (OT), but Gentile Christianity itself becomes the fulfillment of Biblical Judaism (cf. Jer. 31:31-34, Heb. 8:7-13).

PART I: THE FUTURE INCARNATION OF CHRIST

CHAPTER 1

1. The *Great Tribulation* is a term that denotes a specific time period of seven years during the last age of mankind, the most intense of which are the last three and a half years (Dan. 9:27; Rev. 11:2; Rev. 12:6, 14; Rev. 13:5) when the earth will experience unsurpassed turmoil and upheaval (Matt. 24:21, Rev. 2:22, 7:14).

CHAPTER 2

1 The *One* is a term used by Plotinus to refer to the absolute and transcendent entity which is beyond all concepts and categories of being and nonbeing. For an insightful analysis See Plotinus, *The Six Enneads*, trans. S. Mackenna and B.S. Page (eBooks @ Adelaide 2010) V, 1 [10].

PART II: THE GREEK JESUS

CHAPTER 6

1. In Greek, the word *Iones* is the plural form of Ionas.

CHAPTER 7

1. The word *Shekinah* is the English transliteration of a Hebrew term that denotes *dwelling* or *habitation* and is used invariably by scripture to represent the concept of the divine presence or "the glory of the LORD" that once dwelled within the various sanctuaries of the Hebrew people (Exod. 40:34).
2. The term *hardening* is a translation of the Hebrew word *Hazak,* which means stubbornness; but the scriptural context suggests a kind of resentful stubbornness proportional to blind ignorance (Rom. 11:25, cf. Rev. 16:11, *King James*).

CHAPTER 8

1. The heavenly *host* is a term that denotes the armies of the invisible God which comprise angelic beings (Luke 2:13, Rev. 19:14).
2. In the Bible, the word *beast* is a technical term used to denote a king (Dan. 7:17) or a kingdom (Dan. 7:23).

3. According to Christian Eschatology, the *antichrist* represents the incarnation of Satan in the final days (2 Thess. 2:3-4, 9; 1 John 2:18; Rev. 13:8, 18, 20:7-8). He is best known as the contemptible "little horn" from the end-times stories in the book of Daniel (Dan. 7:8, 8:9, 11:21).

WORKS CITED

Ashwin-Siejkowski, Piotr. *Clement of Alexandria on Trial: The Evidence of "Heresy" from Photius' Bibliotheca.* (Leiden: Brill, 2010)

Augustinus, Aurelius. *The Confessions of St. Augustine.* Trans. Edward B. Pusey. (Grand Rapids: Baker, 1991)

Barclay, William. *The Letter to the Romans.* The Daily Study Bible Series. Rev. ed. (Philadelphia: Westminster, 1975)

Borg, Marcus J. *Meeting Jesus Again for the First Time: The Historical Jesus and the Heart of Contemporary Faith.* (New York: HarperCollins, 1994)

Campbell, Joseph. *The Mythic Image.* Bollingen Series C. (Princeton: Princeton UP, 1982)

—, and Bill Moyers. *The Power of Myth.* Ed. Betty Sue Flowers. (New York: Anchor, 1991)

Cheetham, Erika, ed. and trans. *The Prophecies of Nostradamus: The Man who Saw Tomorrow.* (New York: Berkley, 1981)

Derrida, Jacques. *Dissemination.* Trans. Barbara Johnson. (Chicago: U of Chicago P, 1981)

Eco, Umberto. *Foucault's Pendulum.* Trans. William Weaver. (New York: Harcourt, 1989)

Foucault, Michel. *Madness and Civilization: A History of Insanity in the Age of Reason.* Trans. Richard Howard. (New York: Vintage, 1973)

Frank, Manfred. *What is Neostructuralism?* Trans. Sabine Wilke and Richard Gray. (Minneapolis: U of Minnesota P, 1989)

Fruchtenbaum, Arnold G. *The Footsteps of the Messiah: A study of the Sequence of Prophetic Events.* (Tustin: Ariel, 1990)

Haffert, John M. *Deadline: The Third Secret of Fatima.* (Asbury: 101 Foundation, 2002)

Harrington, Wilfrid J. *Record of the Promise: The Old Testament.* Key to the Bible. Vol. 2. (New York: Alba, 1974)

John of the Cross. *Ascent of Mount Carmel.* Trans. E. Allison Peers. (Liguori: Triumph, 1991)

Josephus, Titus Flavius. *The New Complete Works of Josephus.* Trans. William Whiston. (Grand Rapids: Kregel, 1999)

Jung, C.G. *Memories, Dreams, Reflections.* Ed. Aniela Jaffe. Trans. Richard and Clara Winston. Rev. ed. (New York: Vintage, 1965)

Larue, Gerald A. *Old Testament Life and Literature*. (Boston: Allyn and Bacon, 1968)

Lewis, C.S. *Miracles: A Preliminary Study*. (New York: Collier, 1960)

Maro, Publius Vergilius. *Virgil's Works: The Aeneid, Eclogues, Georgics*. The Modern Library. Trans. J.W. Mackail. (New York: Random, 1934)

McCallum, Dennis. *Satan and His Kingdom: What the Bible Says and How It Matters to You*. (Bloomington: Bethany, 2009)

McCann, Lee. *Nostradamus: The Man Who Saw Through Time*. (New York: Farrar, Straus and Giroux, 1991)

Milton, John. *Paradise Lost and Paradise Regained*. Ed. Christopher Ricks. (New York: New American Library, 1982)

Morris, Leon. *Revelation*. Tyndale New Testament Commentaries. Rev. ed. (Grand Rapids: Eerdmans, 1990)

Mounce, Robert H. *The Book of Revelation*. New International Commentary on the New Testament. Rev. ed. (Grand Rapids: Eerdmans, 1997)

New American Standard Bible. Text ed. (Nashville: Nelson, 1977)

Newton, Isaac. *Portsmouth Papers*. The Jewish Ntl. and U. Library, Jerusalem. Auc. Unpub. Docs. (London: Sotheby's, 1936)

Nostredame, Michel De. *The Prophecies of Nostradamus*. Comp. John Bruno Hare. *Internet Sacred Text Archive*. Web. 1 Nov. 2011. <http://sacred-texts.com/nos/index.htm>.

Pamphili, Eusebius. *Greek Texts: The Proof of the Gospel Being the Demonstratio Evangelica of Eusebius of Caesarea*. Translations of Christian Literature. Series 1. Vol. 1. Trans. W.J. Ferrar. (New York: Macmillan, 1920)

Pascal, Blaise. *Pensees*. Trans. A.J. Krailsheimer. (London: Penguin, 1966)

Pindar. *Odes*. Ed. and trans. Diane Arnson Svarlien. *Perseus Digital Library*. Eic. Gregory R. Crane. Tufts U, 1990. Web. 2 Nov. 2011. <http://www.perseus.tufts.edu/hopper/>.

Plotinus. *The Six Enneads*. Trans. Stephen Mackenna and B.S. Page. *eBooks@Adelaide*. U of Adelaide, 2010. Web. 29 Oct. 2011.

Rich, John, and Graham Shipley, eds. *War and Society in the Greek World*. (New York: Routledge, 1993)

Schweitzer, Albert. *The Quest of the Historical Jesus*. Ed. John Bowden. Trans. W. Montgomery et al. (Minneapolis: Fortress, 2001)

Singh, Sirdar Attar, trans. *Sakhee Book: Or, The Description of Gooroo Gobind Singh's Religion and Doctrines*. (Benares: E.J. Lazarus, 1873)

The Dead Sea Scrolls: A New Translation. Trans. Michael Wise, Martin Abegg Jr. and Edward Cook. (New York: Harper San Francisco, 1996)

The Holy Bible. Authorized King James Version. (Nashville: Holman, 1979)

The Holy Bible. New King James Version. (Nashville: Nelson, 1987)

The New Jerusalem Bible. Nihil obstat. Anton Cowan. Imp. John Crowley. Reader's ed. (New York: Doubleday, 1990)

The Philokalia: The Complete Text; Compiled by St. Nikodimos of the Holy Mountain and St. Makarios of Corinth. Trans. G.E.H. Palmer, Philip Sherrard and Kallistos Ware. Vol. 2. (London: Faber, 1990)

Underhill, Evelyn. *Mysticism: The Preeminent Study in the Nature and Development of Spiritual Consciousness.* (New York: Doubleday, 1990)

Ward, Charles A. *Oracles of Nostradamus.* (Sioux Falls: NuVision, 2007)

Ware, Timothy. *The Orthodox Church.* New ed. (London: Penguin, 1993)

Wells, G.A. *The Jesus Myth.* (Peru: Open Court, 1999)

Wikipedia: The Free Encyclopedia. Wikimedia Foundation. Web. 11 Dec. 2012. <http://en.wikipedia.org/wiki/yona/>.

Wojcik, Jan, and Raymond-Jean Frontain, eds. *Poetic Prophecy in Western Literature.* (Cranbury: Associated UP, 1984)

Wordsworth, William. *The Prelude: 1799, 1805, 1850.* Eds. Jonathan Wordsworth, M.H. Abrams and Stephen Gill. Critical ed. (New York: Norton, 1979)

INDEX

Edwards Brothers Malloy
Oxnard, CA USA
December 18, 2013